LEAVING CERTIFICATE

CHEMISTRY

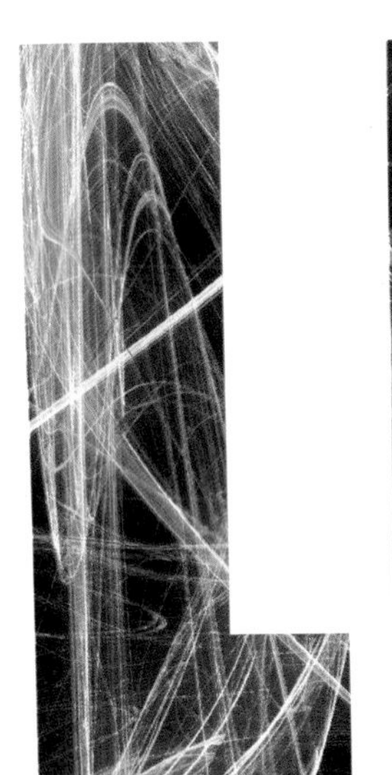
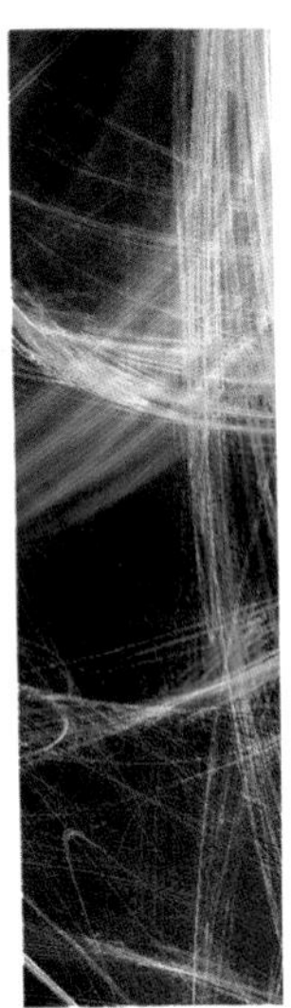
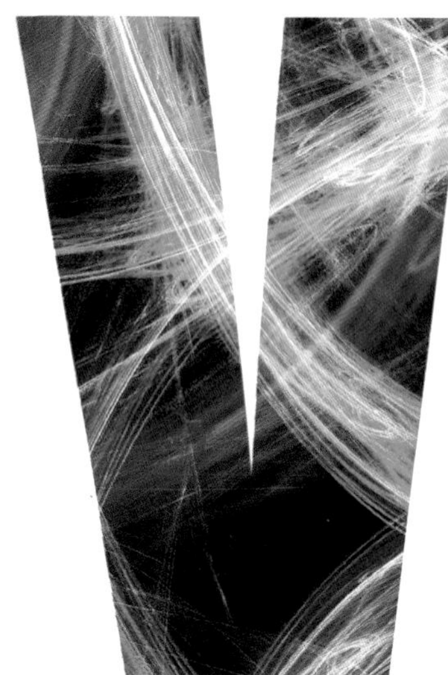
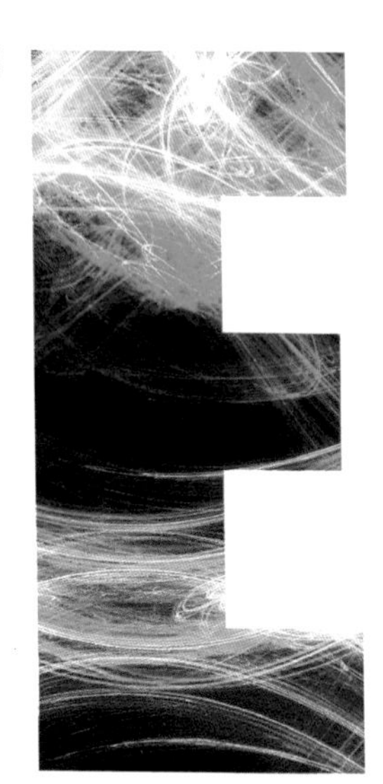
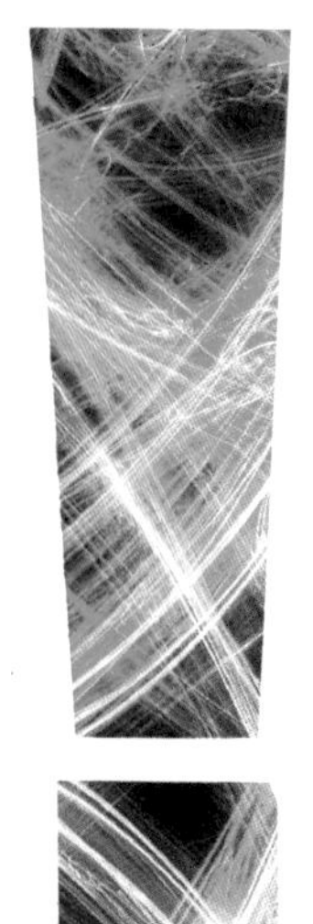

WORKBOOK

INCLUDING OPTION 1 AND OPTION 2

DECLAN KENNEDY MSc, MEd, PhD HDE, FICI

Editor
Dr Sarah Ryan

Cover Design
Suzanne Gannon

Design & Layout
Suzanne Gannon, Rebecca Dobson

Illustrations
Michael Phillips

ISBN 978-1-78090-434-4

Folens Publishers, Hibernian Industrial Estate, Greenhills Road, Tallaght, Dublin 24.

Photo Acknowledgements

The publisher would like to acknowledge the following for permission:

Yara: p. 78 BL, p. 82 BR, p. 83 BL; RHI: p. 85 CR BL; Science Photo Library: p. 90, p. 92 TL BR, p. 108 TR BR, p. 111 TL CL, p. 112 TL CL BR, p. 114, p. 116 CR, p. 122 TR BR, p. 123, p. 126 CR; IStockPhoto: p. 113 TL; RUSAL: p. 127 TL; John Sexton Photography.

Contents

2	The Atom	1
3	Arrangement of Electrons in the Atom	2
4	The Periodic Table	4
5	Chemical Bonding: Chemical Formulas	7
6	Chemical Equations: Tests for Anions	11
7	Trends in the Periodic Table	13
8	Radioactivity	17
9	The Mole Concept	19
10	Properties of Gases	22
11	Stoichiometry I	25
12	Acids and Bases	28
13	Volumetric Analysis: Acid-Base	30
14	Oxidation and Reduction	33
15	Volumetric Analysis: Oxidation–Reduction	37
16	Rates of Reactions	41
17	Chemical Equilibrium	47
18	pH and Indicators	52
19	Enviromental Chemistry – Water	55
20	Electrochemistry I	58
21	Fuels and Heats of Reaction	61
22	Some Families of Organic Compounds	68
23	Types of Reactions in Organic Chemistry	70
24	Stoichiometry II	75

Contents

Option 1

25 Industrial Chemistry: Case Studies 77
25.1 Introduction 77
25.2 General Principles of Industrial Chemistry 77
25.3 The Manufacture of Ammonia and Urea by IFI at Cobh 80
25.4 The Manufacture of Nitric Acid by IFI at Arklow 82
25.5 The Manufacture of Magnesium Oxide by Premier Periclase at Drogheda 85

26 Atmospheric Chemistry 90
26.1 Introduction 90
26.2 Oxygen – The Reactive Gas 90
26.3 Nitrogen – The Unreactive Gas 91
26.4 Inorganic Carbon Compounds 93
26.5 The Carbon Cycle 95
26.6 The Greenhouse Effect 96
26.7 Atmospheric Pollution 98
26.8 The Ozone Layer 100
26.9 CFCs 102
26.10 CFC Substitutes 103

Option 2

27 Materials: Crystals, Metals and Addition Polymers 108
27.1 Introduction 108
27.2 Crystals 108
27.3 Metals and Non-Metals 113
27.4 Addition Polymers 114

28 Electrochemistry II: Extraction of Metals 122
28.1 Introduction 122
28.2 The Electrochemical Series: Corrosion 122
28.3 Electrolysis of Molten Salts 124
28.4 Extraction of Sodium from Molten Sodium Chloride 125
28.5 Extraction of Aluminium from Bauxite 126
28.6 Manufacture of Iron and Steel 128

Answers to Numerical Questions 138

Index 140

02 The Atom

W2.1 (a) Write down two of the ideas expressed in Dalton's Atomic Theory.

(i) Ní féidir adamh a cruthú nó a loit

(ii) Gach cineál damhna déanta as cáithníní beaga nach briste

(b) The electrode connected to the positive end of a battery is called the Anóid

(c) What are cathode rays? bhíogam léas leictreon

(d) Cathode rays are invisible but when they strike glass they cause it to an scath

(e) The man credited with the discovery of the electron is William Crookes

(f) The ratio of charge to mass of the electron is often represented as e/m

(g) Millikan Oil Drop experiment measured the size of the lucht on the leictreon

(h) Alpha particles are Dearfach charged particles.

(i) When Chadwick bombarded a sample of α cáithníní with beirilium particles, he found that a neutral particle called the neodrón was emitted.

(j) Fill in the blanks in Table W2.1.

	Relative Charge	Relative Mass	Location
Proton	1 m.a.a	+	núicléas
Neutron	1 m.a.a	0	núicléas
Electron	1/1850 m.a.a	−	Fithis timpeall núicléas

Table W2.1

W2.2 Outline briefly the experiments performed by William Crookes that led to the discovery of the electron.

W2.3 Give a brief outline of the experiment carried out by J.J. Thomson to investigate if cathode rays consist of charged particles. Summarise the information that J.J. Thomson obtained from his experiment.

By means of a diagram, describe briefly the model of atomic structure proposed by J.J. Thomson in 1898. What is the common name given to this model?

W2.4 The neutron was the last of the three main sub-atomic particles to be discovered. Why do you think it was so difficult to detect? If necessary, look up reference books to find out more details of how Chadwick discovered the neutron.

03 Arrangement of Electrons in the Atom

Fluorescent light strips and lasers make use of electron transitions. Fluorescent light strips contain mercury vapour at low pressure. The electrons in the mercury vapour are excited to higher energy levels by the electric current. As these electrons fall back to lower energy levels, ultraviolet light is emitted. The invisible ultraviolet light causes the fluorescent coating inside the surface of the tube to glow.

A laser works on a similar principle. If you have a laser in your school, it probably contains a mixture of helium gas and neon gas. Bright flashlamps inside the laser excite some of the atoms of these gases. Their electrons are raised to a higher energy level and as they fall back down, light of a particular wavelength is emitted (Fig. 3.12 on page 17 in textbook). This emission of light is called stimulated emission because it was stimulated by the light from the flashlamps. In fact, the word LASER comes from Light Amplification by Stimulated Emission of Radiation. The light emitted by the atoms bounces back and forth off mirrors inside the laser. This causes more atoms to be stimulated and emit light. This results in an intense flash of light emerging from the laser.

W3.1 (a) The spectrum obtained from a discharge tube filled with hydrogen is not a continuous spectrum but a Lineach spectrum.

(b) A sample of a barium salt is burned. What colour is observed? ______________________

(c) An unknown salt when burned gave off a blue-green colour. What metal is present in the salt? __________

(d) In manufacturing fireworks, red colours are obtained using salts of ______________________

(e) Explain the meaning of the phrase 'spectroscopic evidence for the existence of energy levels'. Leiriann Speictream Solas go minioniocht seasfuita

(f) When an atom absorbs energy, electrons jump from a __________ energy level to a __________ energy level.

(g) Energy levels are represented by the letter N

(h) Write down the equation relating energy and frequency. e=hf

(i) What do the letters in the word LASER represent? Light amplication Stimulated emissi radiation

(j) Fig. W3.1 shows an emission spectrum of the element lithium. Draw a diagram to indicate what the absorption spectrum would look like.

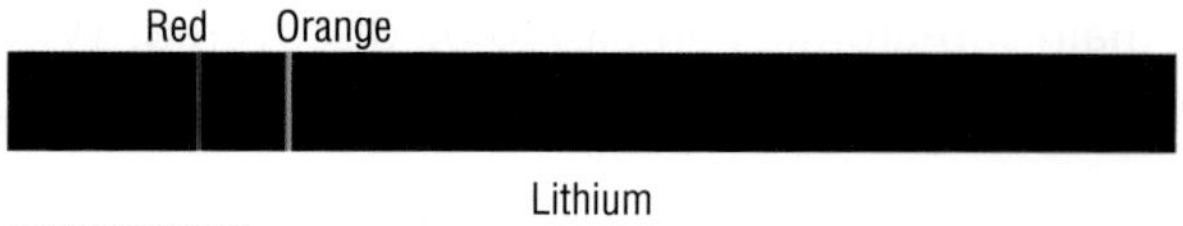

Red Orange

Lithium

Fig W3.1

W3.2 Explain the meaning of the term *atomic absorption spectrometry* and give a brief account of how such a spectrum arises.

If you were given unlabelled photographs of an emission spectrum of hydrogen and an absorption spectrum of hydrogen, how would you distinguish between them?

Give one use for atomic absorption spectrometry.

W3.3 With regard to the electronic structure of atoms, state what you understand by energy levels, sublevels and orbitals.

Show how the idea of energy levels in atoms results from a study of the emission spectrum of hydrogen. [LCH]

W3.4 Give a brief account of the electronic structure of atoms under the following headings:

(i) the spectroscopic evidence for the existence of energy levels.

(ii) s and p orbitals. [LCH]

W3.5 (a) The four letters S, P, f and D are used to indicate sublevels.

(b) The idea that all moving particles have a wave motion associated with them was suggested by a French scientist called de Broglie

(c) An orbital is defined as Réigiún mórthimpeall an núicléas le dóchúlacht is fearr leictreon a fháil ann

(d) Give one piece of evidence which suggested to scientists that sublevels existed. Speictreascóip

(e) State Heisenberg's Uncertainty Principle. Ní féidir luas agus suíomh a thomhas ag an am gceanna

(f) An Austrian physicist called Schrodinger used mathematical equations to work out the probability of finding a particular electron in an atom.

(g) Why are p orbitals labelled p_x, p_y and p_z? Tá siad aiseanna éagsúla

(h) The p orbitals are at an angle of 45° to each other.

(i) Draw the shape of an s and the three p orbitals on the axes shown in Fig. W3.2.

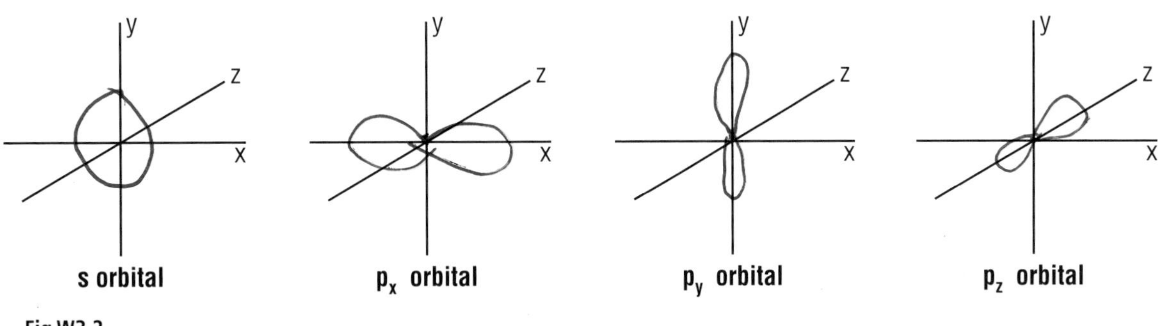

Fig W3.2

04 The Periodic Table

W4.1 (a) An Irish chemist called ________________ was the first scientist to give a proper definition of the term 'element'.

(b) What is a triad in Dobereiner's classification of the elements? ________________

____

(c) Write down one example of Dobereiner's triads. ________________

(d) State briefly the contribution of Newlands to the classification of the elements. ________

____

(e) Mendeleev predicted the discovery of a number of elements. Name any one of these elements. ________________

(f) Define

(i) atomic number ________________

____

(ii) mass number ________________

____

(g) State two differences between Mendeleev's form of the Periodic Table and the modern form of the Periodic Table. ________________

____

(h) How many (i) neutrons, (ii) electrons are there in the ion $^{65}_{30}Zn^{2+}$? ________________

(i) The modern name for atomic weight is ________________

(j) Name the scientist who built the first mass spectrometer. ________________

(k) Give two important items of information about an element that can be obtained using a mass spectrometer. ________________

____

(l) There are five stages involved in the operation of a mass spectrometer. Name them. ________

____

____

W4.2 (a) Discuss briefly the contributions of Dobereiner, Newlands and Mendeleev to the development of the Periodic Table.

State two differences between Mendeleev's form and the modern form of the Periodic Table. [LCH]

(b) What do you understand by (i) atomic number, (ii) mass number, (iii) isotopes, (iv) relative atomic mass, of an element?

Explain why the relative atomic masses of the naturally-occurring elements are not whole numbers.

Using a mass spectrometer, it was found that boron consisted of 81% $^{11}_{5}B$ and 19% $^{10}_{5}B$. Estimate the relative atomic mass of boron. [LCH]

W4.3 Fig. W4.1 represents the main parts of a mass spectrometer. Fill in the labels A–H as shown on the diagram.

Give a brief description of the function of each part.

Using a mass spectrometer, it was found that neon consists of 90% $^{20}_{10}Ne$ and 10% $^{22}_{10}Ne$. Calculate the relative atomic mass of neon.

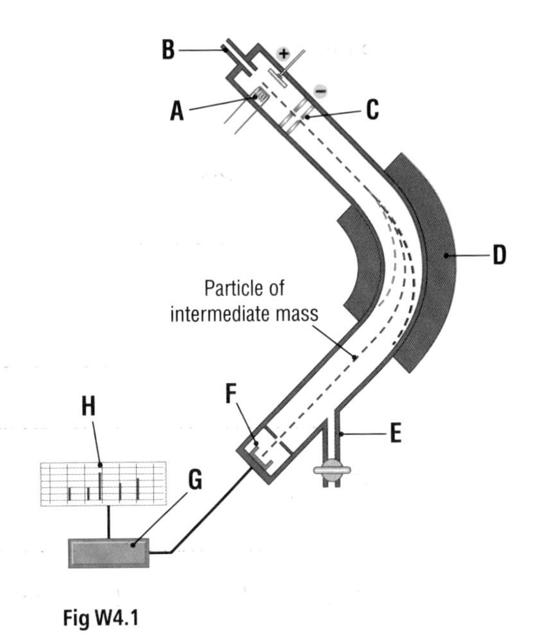

Fig W4.1

W4.4 Distinguish between the terms *triad* and *octave* in the history of the classification of the elements. Name the scientists associated with the introduction of these terms into chemistry.

When the term *octave* was introduced, it was found to apply to only about the first 16 elements known at that time. Could the term be correctly used for the 16 elements from lithium to argon in the modern Periodic Table? Give a reason for your answer.

[Hint: The noble gases had not been discovered when the Law of Octaves was put forward.]

W4.5 (a) State the Aufbau Principle. ______________________

____

(b) Write down the s, p configuration of chlorine and indicate briefly how the two isotopes of chlorine differ. ______________________

____

(c) Write down the s, p, d configuration for (i) iron and (ii) copper. ______________________

____

(d) Write the s, p configuration of the Ca^{2+} ion. Which neutral atom has the same configuration?

____

(e) Identify the species represented by each of the following electronic configurations:

(i) $[1s^2, 2s^2, 2p^6, 3s^2, 3p^6]^{2-}$ ______________________________

(ii) $1s^2, 2s^2, 2p^6, 3s^2, 3p^6, 4s^2, 3d^3$ ______________________________

(f) What have the ions K^+, Ca^{2+}, Cl^- and S^{2-} in common? ______________________________

____

(g) State Pauli's Exclusion Principle. ______________________________

____

(h) By means of an 'arrows-in-boxes' diagram indicate how the electrons are distributed among the p orbitals in an atom of sulfur.

W4.6 Identify the species $[1s^2]^-$.

Show by means of a diagram, how the electrons are distributed in the 4p sublevel of arsenic.

State Hund's rule and show how it is illustrated by the s, p configurations of aluminium, silicon, phosphorus and sulfur.

Using a mass spectrometer, it was found that nickel consisted of 70% of $^{58}_{28}Ni$, 26% of $^{60}_{28}Ni$ and 4% of $^{62}_{28}Ni$. Calculate the relative atomic mass of nickel based on the given figures. [LCH]

05 Chemical Bonding: Chemical Formulas

W5.1 (a) Give one example of an element that does not usually obey the Octet Rule. ____________

(b) What is an ion? ____________

(c) The arrangement of ions in a crystal is called a crystal ____________

(d) The formula of aluminium sulfate is ____________

(e) $Na_2Cr_2O_7$ is called ____________

(f) Give two characteristic properties of transition metals. ____________

(g) Which one of the following elements would you expect to show variable valency: K, Mg, Ne, Al, Mn? ____________

(h) Write down the formula of copper(II) oxide. ____________

W5.2 (a) State the Octet Rule and list two examples of exceptions to this rule. With the aid of electron dot-and-cross diagrams, explain how the bonding in magnesium chloride is formed.

With reference to sodium chloride, explain the terms crystal lattice and unit cell.

Draw the unit cell of sodium chloride.

(b) Define the term *transition metal*. State three properties of transition metals.

Explain why scandium and zinc are not considered to be transition metals.

Write down the formula of (i) potassium permanganate [potassium manganate(VII)] and (ii) sodium dichromate [sodium dichromate(VI)].

W5.3 (a) Explain the term *valency*. Give an example of an element that has a valency of 3.

Distinguish between a sigma bond and a pi bond. With the aid of diagrams explain the formation of sigma and pi bonds in (a) a molecule of O_2 and (b) a molecule of N_2.

Write a note on the strengths of pi bonds compared with sigma bonds.

(b) Explain why ionic compounds do not conduct electricity in the solid state. Describe how you would test a sample of water to see if ions are present in it.

Explain how the VSEPR theory may be used to determine the shape of molecules of (i) ammonia and (ii) water.

W5.4 (a) Explain the term *molecule*. Why is this term normally used to describe covalent compounds rather than ionic compounds?

Use dot-and-cross diagrams to explain the bonding in (i) chlorine (ii) oxygen and (iii) carbon dioxide.

(b) Compare the properties of ionic and covalent compounds in terms of (i) hardness and (ii) melting points. Explain the difference between the observed properties of these two types of compound.

(c) Which one of the following molecules is not polar?

HCl, CO_2, NH_3, CH_3Cl, H_2O

(d) An electronegativity difference greater than ________ indicates ionic bonding.

(e) What term is used (i) for a bond in which the bonding electrons are not equally shared ________

(ii) for a bond in which there is a complete transfer of electrons? ________

(f) What type of bond exists (i) between the atoms in a molecule of hydrogen chloride ________

(ii) between molecules of hydrogen chloride? ________

(g) When liquid air is allowed to warm up, nitrogen boils off at –196 °C but oxygen does not boil off until –183 °C. Suggest a reason for this. ________

____

(h) At room temperature, chloroform, $CHCl_3$, is a liquid but methane, CH_4, is a gas. Suggest a reason for this. ________

W5.5 (a) Distinguish between *intramolecular bonding* and *intermolecular forces*. ________

____

(b) What are van der Waals forces?________

____

(c) Give an example of a compound that has polar bonds but is not a polar molecule.________

(d) Give an example of a molecule in which permanent dipole–dipole forces exist. ________

(e) Hydrogen bonding is observed in compounds in which hydrogen is bonded to one of three elements. Name these elements. ________

(f) Name the type of attractive forces that exist between molecules of bromine. ________

(g) What type of binding forces (i) hold water molecules together in a crystal of ice ________

(ii) hold carbon dioxide molecules together in a crystal of dry ice? ________

(h) Hydrogen bonding exists in HF but not in HCl. Explain. ________

(i) Carbon dioxide has two polar bonds but it is a non-polar molecule. Explain. ________

W5.6 (a) (i) Explain what is meant by an ionic bond, taking potassium chloride as an example. List the general properties of ionic compounds.

(ii) Write down the formula of an oxide of copper that is ionic.

(b) Gallium is a metallic element in Group 3 of the Periodic Table. It is normally trivalent in its compounds.

(i) Write the formula for (a) gallium chloride, (b) gallium oxide.

(ii) What type of bonding is most likely in gallium chloride? Give a reason for your answer. [LCH]

W5.7 Define the term *electronegativity*. With reference to the Table of Electronegativity values on page 59 of your textbook, predict the type of bonding in (a) carbon monoxide, (b) boron trichloride, (c) potassium chloride.

W5.8 A chemistry data book gave the following boiling points for the noble gases.

Name	Helium	Neon	Argon	Krypton	Xenon
Boiling Point (°C)	–269	–246	–186	–152	–108

(a) Name the type of forces that exist between the atoms.

(b) Suggest a reason for the increase in boiling points.

W5.9 (a) Name (i) a non-metal that exists as single atoms, (ii) a non-metal that exists as a liquid at ordinary temperatures.

(b) Which two of the first thirty-six elements would you expect to form the bond with the greatest ionic character? Write the electronic configurations (s, p) for the ions involved.

(c) Write the formula for the compound usually formed when the elements of atomic numbers 6 and 16 combine together.

(d) Explain why ionic substances do not conduct electricity in the solid state but do conduct in the molten state or in solution.

(e) Write the formula of the simplest chloride you would expect the element of atomic number 33 to form. Draw a diagram showing the bonding present in this chloride. State the shape of this chloride molecule.

(f) What type of bond is formed between chlorine and the element of atomic number 19? Show the formation of the bond by means of a suitable diagram. Explain why this chloride is a high melting point solid.

(g) Name the bond responsible for the forces of attraction between water molecules and comment briefly on its effects on the properties of water. [LCH]

W5.10 Which one of each of the following pairs of substances would you expect to have the higher boiling point? Give a reason for your choice in each case.

(a) H_2O and H_2S, (b) HCl and H_2, (c) HCl and HF.

W5.11 The variation of boiling points of the inert gases is shown in the following table:

Element	Boiling Point (°C)
Helium (He)	–269
Neon (Ne)	–246
Argon (Ar)	–186
Krypton (Kr)	–152
Xenon (Xe)	–108
Radon (Rn)	–61

Table W5.1

Explain the trend observed in the above data.

06 Chemical Equations: Tests For Anions

W6.1 Balance each of the following equations.

(a) $Mg + H_2O \longrightarrow Mg(OH)_2 + H_2$

(b) $Fe + H_2O \longrightarrow Fe_3O_4 + H_2$

(c) $SO_2 + O_2 \longrightarrow SO_3$

(d) $HCl + Ca(OH)_2 \longrightarrow CaCl_2 + H_2O$

(e) $H_2 + N_2 \longrightarrow NH_3$

(f) $C + H_2O \longrightarrow CO + H_2$

(g) $CaCO_3 + HCl \longrightarrow CaCl_2 + H_2O + CO_2$

(h) $NaOH + CO_2 \longrightarrow Na_2CO_3 + H_2O$

(i) $Na_2SO_3 + H_2SO_4 \longrightarrow Na_2SO_4 + H_2O + SO_2$

(j) $CO_2 + H_2O \longrightarrow C_6H_{12}O_6 + O_2$

(k) $Pb(NO_3)_2 + H_2SO_4 \longrightarrow PbSO_4 + HNO_3$

(l) $KClO_3 \longrightarrow KCl + O_2$

(m) $FeCl_3 + NaOH \longrightarrow Fe(OH)_3 + NaCl$

W6.2 (a) The Law of Conservation of Mass is also known as ______________________________

____

(b) A balanced equation is one in which ______________________________

(c) The formula for the hydrogencarbonate ion is ________________. The old name for the hydrogencarbonate ion is the ________________ ion.

(d) ________________ ions are used to precipitate chloride ions out of solution.

(e) Barium sulfate is ________________ in dilute hydrochloric acid but barium sulfite is ________________ in dilute hydrochloric acid.

(f) When a dilute acid is added to sodium carbonate, the gas ______________ is given off.

(g) Write down the formula of limewater. ______________________________

(h) If carbon dioxide continues to be bubbled into limewater, the limewater goes clear. Explain this observation. ______________________________

(i) A solution of magnesium hydrogencarbonate is heated for a few minutes. What would you expect to observe? ______

(j) What name is given to the test used to detect the presence of nitrate ions in solution?

______

(k) Name the two reagents used to test for the presence of the phosphate ion.

______

(l) Concentrated sulfuric acid is used in the test for the presence of the ______ ion and concentrated nitric acid is used in the test for the presence of the ______ ion.

(m) Name one chloride salt which is insoluble in water. ______

(n) How would you distinguish between carbonate and hydrogencarbonate ions in aqueous solution?

______

______ [LCH]

(o) Give the equation for a reaction that can be used as a test for the sulfate ion.

______ [LCH]

(p) When dilute hydrochloric acid was added to a sodium salt, a gas was evolved which turned limewater milky. A solution of the salt formed a precipitate with magnesium sulfate solution. Which of the following could represent the formula of the salt?

$NaCl$, $NaHCO_3$, $NaNO_3$, Na_2CO_3, Na_2SO_4? ______ [LCH]

W6.3 A sodium salt, which was either a sulfate or a sulfite, was given to a student for identification. When barium chloride was added to a solution of the salt, a white precipitate was observed. The precipitate dissolved when dilute hydrochloric acid was added.

(i) Identify the salt. ______

(ii) Give the name of the white precipitate. ______

(iii) Write balanced equations for the two reactions that took place.

______

______

(iv) How would you confirm that the salt contained sodium?

______ [LCH]

W6.4 You are given solutions labelled (a) sodium sulfate and (b) sodium sulfite. Describe the effect (if any), at each stage, of adding to each of these solutions a few drops of barium chloride solution followed by an excess of dilute hydrochloric acid. Explain by means of equations what is happening.

______ [LCH]

07 Trends in the Periodic Table

W7.1 (a) Explain why it is not possible for chemists to determine where exactly the electron cloud of an atom ends. ______

______

(b) Define the term *atomic radius*. ______

______

(c) Atomic radii are often measured in nanometres. What is a nanometre? ______

______

(d) State, giving reasons, how you would expect atomic radius to change across a period. ______

______ [LCH]

(e) The 'screening effect' ______ down the groups.

(f) There is no increase in screening effect across any one period in the Periodic Table. Explain.

______

W7.2 (a) Define *first ionisation energy*. ______ [LCH]

(b) For which of the following processes is the energy change known as the first ionisation energy of an element X? [LCH]

$X^+ + e^- \longrightarrow X$, $X + e^- \longrightarrow X^-$, $X \longrightarrow X^+ + e^-$, $X^- \longrightarrow X + e^-$ ______

(c) Account for the decrease in first ionisation energy (i) from nitrogen to phosphorus, (ii) from phosphorus to sulfur. [LCH]

(i) ______

(ii) ______

(d) Why is there a decrease (i) in the atomic radius, (ii) in the first ionisation energy, in going from the element of atomic number 12 to the element of atomic number 13? [LCH]

(i) ______

(ii) ______

(e) Why is the value of the second ionisation energy of an element always greater than that of the first ionisation energy? ______

(f) Explain why the value of the first ionisation energy of oxygen is lower than that of fluorine and is also lower than that of nitrogen. [LCH]

____

____

(g) Which one of the following represents the energy change known as the second ionisation energy of element X? [LCH]

$X^{2+} \longrightarrow X^{3+} + e^-$, $X \longrightarrow X^+ + e^-$, $X^+ \longrightarrow X^{2+} + e^-$ ______________________

W7.3 Fig W7.1 shows a graph of ionisation energy versus atomic number for the elements hydrogen to sodium. Study this graph and answer the following questions.

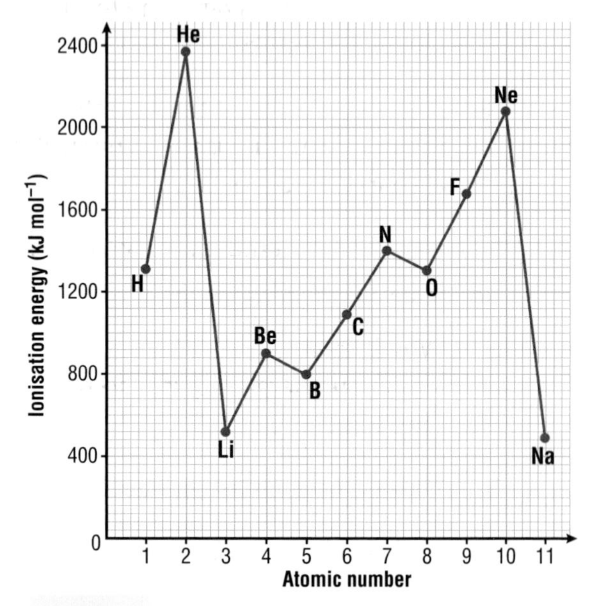

Fig W7.1

(a) Which element in the graph has the highest ionisation energy value?

____

(b) Which element in the graph has the lowest ionisation energy value?

____

(c) Why do the ionisation energy values increase from lithium to neon?

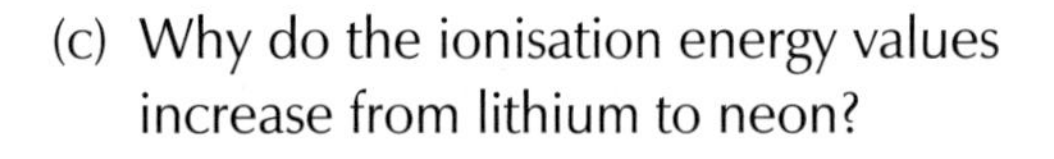

____

(d) Explain why beryllium and nitrogen do not follow the general trend.

____

____

(e) Why is the ionisation energy of sodium lower than that of lithium?

____

(f) Why is there a sudden drop in ionisation energy after neon?

____

W7.4 (a) What do you mean by the 'first ionisation energy' of an element? Suggest reasons for the general increase in first ionisation energies across a period. Why is the increase not uniform?

If the twelve successive ionisation energies of magnesium were known, what evidence for the existence of energy levels would you expect to find? [LCH]

W7.5 Define the *first ionisation energy* of an element.

Discuss the factors that account for the general increase in first ionisation energies across a typical period, e.g. Na to Ar.

Explain why the general trend is reversed on passing from magnesium to aluminium and from phosphorus to sulfur.

How do you account for the decrease in first ionisation energies down a group, e.g. Li to Cs?

W7.6 All of the 12 electrons were removed from a certain element and a plot was drawn of the log of the successive ionisation energies vs. the number of electrons removed as shown in Fig. W7.2.

(a) Explain the meaning of the term 'ionisation energy'.

(b) Why was the log of the ionisation energy rather than the ionisation energy itself used in the above graph?

(c) Identify the element from which the electrons were removed.

(d) Why is there such a large increase in ionisation energy required to remove the third electron?

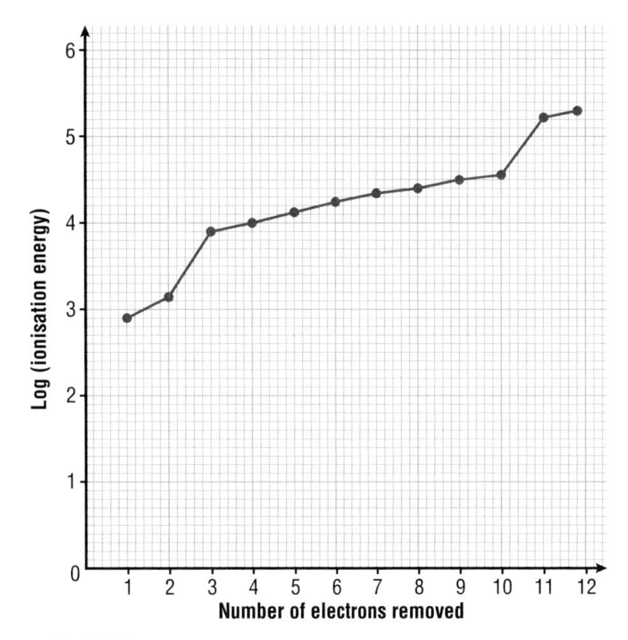

Fig W7.2

(e) Why is there such a gradual increase in ionisation energy for the removal of electrons 3–10?

(f) Explain why there is a sudden increase in the ionisation energy for the 11th electron.

W7.7 (a) Electronegativity values __________ down the groups and __________ across the periods.

(b) Name the two factors that affect the electronegativity values moving down any one group in the Periodic Table. ______________________________

(c) The alkali metals must never be brought in contact with an acid as an __________ would occur.

(d) The elements in group VII are commonly called the ______________________________

(e) The most reactive halogen is ______________________________

(f) Which one of the halogens is a liquid at room temperature? ______________________________

(g) Sodium reacts with water to form ____________________ and ____________________

(h) An alkali metal is added to water and the gas generated burns with a lilac flame. Name the alkali metal. ______________________________

(i) Why would you be unlikely to find fluorine in a school laboratory?

____

W7.8 Answer the following questions with reference to the eight elements (a) to (h) in the part of the Periodic Table shown in Fig. W7.3. (Refer where necessary to Formulae and Tables booklet p. 79 to p. 81.)

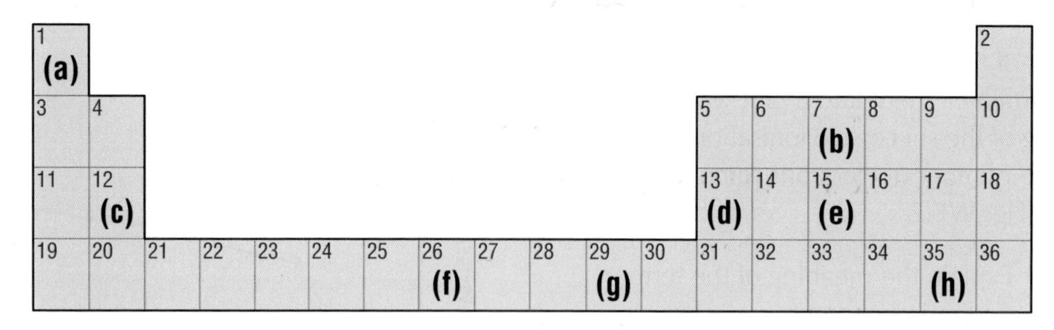

Fig W7.3

(i) Which element exists as a liquid at room temperature? At temperatures below –7.2 °C, this element is a crystalline solid. What binding forces hold the crystal together?

(ii) Write the electronic configurations (s, p) for elements (c) and (d). Explain, in terms of these configurations, why there is a drop in the value of the first ionisation energy from (c) to (d).

(iii) Write the formula for the compound formed between elements (a) and (e) and also for the compound formed between elements (d) and (h). State the shapes of the molecules of these two compounds and account for the difference between them.

(iv) Explain clearly why the compound formed between elements (a) and (b) is much more soluble in water than the compound formed between elements (a) and (e).

(v) Element (e) and two of the other elements commonly exhibit variable valency. Identify the two elements. In the case of either one of them, state two of the valencies exhibited. [LCH]

08 Radioactivity

W8.1 (a) Name the two scientists who discovered polonium and radium. ______

(b) Name the ore from which polonium and radium were extracted. ______

(c) What is the origin of the name polonium? ______

(d) Define the term *radioactivity*. ______

(e) Alpha particles consist of ______

(f) Beta particles consist of ______

(g) The charge on an alpha particle is ______ but that on a beta particle is ______

(h) A Geiger–Müller tube is usually connected to a ______ which measures the rate at which the nuclei are disintegrating.

(i) Why do alpha particles travel more slowly than beta particles? ______

______

(j) Of the three types of radiation (alpha, beta and gamma), which one is the most dangerous? Explain your answer. ______

W8.2 Give one example in each case of radioactive isotopes that emit (a) alpha particles, (b) beta particles and (c) gamma rays.

Explain the meaning of the term 'half-life'.

The results of an experiment to measure the half-life of a radioactive isotope are plotted in Fig. W8.1.

Using this graph, work out the half-life of the isotope.

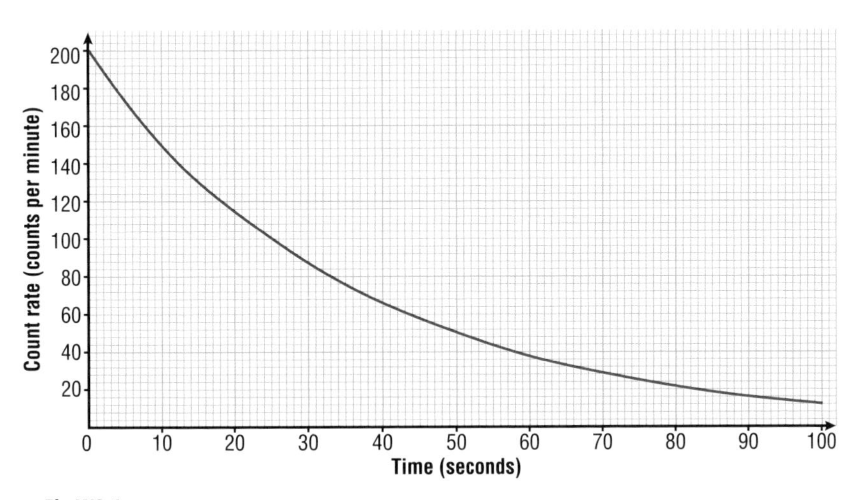

Fig W8.1

W8.3 Complete the following nuclear equations:

(a) ${}^{32}_{15}\text{P} \longrightarrow$ .... + ${}^{0}_{-1}\text{e}$

(b) ${}^{24}_{11}\text{Na} \longrightarrow$ .... + ${}^{0}_{-1}\text{e}$

(c) ${}^{210}_{84}\text{Po} \longrightarrow$ .... + ${}^{4}_{2}\text{He}$

(d) ${}^{66}_{29}\text{Cu} \longrightarrow$ .... + ${}^{0}_{-1}\text{e}$

W8.4 (a) Explain how irradiating food with gamma rays helps to preserve it. Gamma rays are also used in treating patients suffering from cancer. Explain how this treatment works. What is the common source of gamma radiation that is used in this treatment?

(b) Discuss the origin of radioactive radiation in our environment.

Name one precaution that people should take when working with radioactive materials.

09 The Mole Concept

When answering these questions, use the following values of relative atomic masses: H = 1, He = 4, Li = 7, C = 12, N = 14, O =16, F = 19, Na = 23, Mg = 24, Al = 27, Si = 28, P = 31, S = 32, Cl = 35.5, K = 39, Ca = 40, Cr = 52, Fe = 56, Cu = 63.5, Zn = 65, Br = 80, Ag = 108, Sn = 119, I = 127, Pb = 207.

W9.1 What is the mass of one mole of:

(a) lithium atoms ~~10 × 35.5 = 355g~~

(b) sodium atoms ______

(c) calcium atoms ______

(d) iron atoms ______

(e) silver atoms ______

(f) lead atoms? ______

W9.2 What is the mass of:

(a) 10 moles of chlorine atoms 10 × 35.5 = 355g ✓

(b) 0.125 mole of bromine molecules 0.125 × 160 = 20g ✓

(c) 0.25 mole of H_2O 0.25 × (2 + 16) = 4.5g ✓

(d) 0.5 mole of sulfur molecules, S_8 0.5 × (32×8) = 128g ✓

(e) 0.5 mole of HNO_3 0.5 × (1+14+48) = 31.5g ✓

(f) 0.5 mole of SO_4^{2-} ions 0.5 × (32+64) = 48g ✓

(g) 0.05 mole of oxygen molecules? 0.05 × 16×2 = 32 = 1.6g ✓

W9.3 Calculate the mass of:

(a) 4 moles NaOH 4 × (23+16+1) = 160g ✓

(b) 0.5 mole $CaCl_2$ 0.5 (40 + 71) = 55.5g ✓

(c) 2 moles Cl_2 2 × 71 = 142g ✓

(d) 0.05 mole MgO 0.05 × (24+16) 40 = 2g ✓

(e) 3 moles Fe_2O_3 3 × (56×2+16×3 = 480g ✓

(f) 0.1 mole C_2H_6 0.1(24+6) = 3g ✓

(g) 0.6 mole $CaCO_3$ 0.6(40+12+48 = 60g ✓

(h) 0.3 mole NaCl 0.3(23+35.5) = 17.55g ✓

(i) 4 moles H_2O — 4×(2+16) = 72g ✓

(j) 0.075 mole $Ca(NO_3)_2$ — .075(40+28+48) = 124 = 9.3g ✗

(k) 0.02 mole $(NH_4)_2SO_4$ — 0.02(36+32+64) = 132 = 2.64g ✓

(l) 0.25 mole CuO — 0.25(64+16 = 80 = 20g ✓

(m) 0.1 mole SO_3 — 0.1(32+48) = 8g ✓

(n) 0.25 mole Cu_2O — 0.25(64×2=128+16) = 36g ✓

(o) 3 moles $(NH_4)_2CO_3$ — 3(36+12+48) = 288g ✓

(p) 0.25 mole Br_2 — 0.25(160) = 40g ✓

(q) 0.8 mole H_2SO_4 — 0.8(2+32+64) = 78.4g ✓

(r) 4 moles $FeCl_2$ — 4(56+71) 126.9g × 4 = 507.6

(s) 10^{-4} mole $C_{12}H_{26}$ — 10^{-4}(144+26) = 0.017g ✓ (170)

W9.4 Find the number of moles in:

(a) 80 g methane, CH_4 — 80/(12+4) = 80/16 = 5 mol ✓

(b) 288 g sulfur dioxide, SO_2 — 288/(32+32) = 288/64 = 4.5 mol ✓

(c) 0.32 g water, H_2O — 0.32/(2+16) = 0.32/18 = 0.0178 mol ✓

(d) 441 g sulfuric acid, H_2SO_4 — 441/(2+32+64) = 441/98 = 4.5 mol ✓

(e) 10 g ammonium nitrate, NH_4NO_3 — 10/(14+4+14+48) = 10/80 = 0.125 mol ✓

(f) 18 g glucose, $C_6H_{12}O_6$ — 18/(6(12)+12+6(16)) = 18/180 = 0.1 mol ✓

W9.5 Calculate the number of moles in:

(a) 500 g $CaCO_3$ — 500/(40+12+48) = 500/100 = 5 mol ✓

(b) 351 g NaCl — 351/(23+35.5) = 351/58.5 = 6 mol ✓

(c) 4 g NaOH — 4/(23+16+1) = 4/40 = 0.1 mol ✓

(d) 25.25 g KNO_3 — 25.25/(39+14+48) = 25.25/101 = 0.25 mol ✓

(e) 24.95 g $CuSO_4.5H_2O$ — 24.95/(64+32+64+10+16) (90) = 24.95/... = 0.898 m

W9.6 Find how many molecules are present in:

(a) 0.25 mole H_2O ________________

(b) 7.2 moles CH_4 ________________

(c) 8 moles CO_2 ________________

(d) 0.001 mole H_2SO_4 ________________

(e) 5×10^{-3} mole NH_3 ________________

W9.7 Find how many molecules are present in:

(a) 0.4 g O_2 ________________

(b) 142 g Cl_2 ________________

(c) 40 g CO_2 ________________

(d) 50 g CH_4 ________________

W9.8 (a) How many grams of aluminium are present in 2×10^{25} atoms? ________________

(b) How many grams of magnesium are present in 3×10^{21} atoms? ________________

(c) How many grams of silver are present in 1.15×10^{12} atoms? ________________

(d) How many grams of water are present in 1.5×10^{25} molecules of water? ________________

(e) How many grams of carbon dioxide are present in 8×10^{21} molecules of carbon dioxide? ______

Revision Question

W9.9 (a) Define a mole of a substance. [LCH]

(b) How many moles of Al^{3+} are there in 3 moles of $Al_2(SO_4)_3$? [LCH]

(c) How many sulfite ions, SO_3^{2-}, are present in 2.1 g of anhydrous sodium sulfite (Na_2SO_3)? [LCH]

(d) How many atoms are there in 0.36 g of magnesium? [LCH]

(e) What mass of magnesium contains the same number of atoms as 8.0 g of calcium?

(f) How many moles of magnesium atoms are there in 0.2 g of the metal?

(g) What mass of magnesium contains the same number of atoms as 7 g of iron?

(h) How many moles of oxygen atoms are there in 6.3 g of nitric acid, HNO_3?

(i) How many moles of hydrogen atoms are there in 6.4 g of methane, CH_4?

(j) Fig. W9.1 shows a copper bracelet of mass 22 g, an aluminium block of mass 46 g and an iron nail of mass 2.6 g. How many moles of each element are present?

Fig W9.1

(k) What mass of carbon contains the same number of atoms as 39 g of potassium?

(l) How many moles of nitrate ions are there in 2 moles of magnesium nitrate, $Mg(NO_3)_2$?

(m) What mass of water contains the same number of molecules as 22 g of carbon dioxide?

10 Properties of Gases

Given: Standard temperature = 273 K, standard pressure = 100 kPa = 1×10^5 Pa, R = 8.31 J mol^{-1} K^{-1}.
Molar volume at s.t.p. = 22.4 L

W10.1 A sample of carbon dioxide of volume 30 cm^3 is stored in a syringe at 25 °C and 975 kPa. What will be the volume of the gas at s.t.p?

W10.2 A meteorological balloon is filled with helium at atmospheric pressure. What will be the volume of the balloon if it is to hold all the gas from a 2.5 litre gas cylinder at 300 kPa, the temperature being kept constant?

W10.3 A sample of chlorine gas occupies a volume of 1.2 m^3 at a pressure of 101 kPa and at a temperature of 5 °C. Determine the new volume of the gas if its pressure is increased to 108 kPa and the gas is heated to 30 °C.

W10.4 State Avogadro's Law and comment briefly on how this law explained Gay-Lussac's Law of Combining Volumes.

Describe a laboratory experiment to verify Gay-Lussac's Law.

W10.5 Calculate the volume occupied at s.t.p. by:

(a) 10 g oxygen gas

(b) 12 g carbon dioxide

(c) 8 g ammonia

(d) 25 g carbon monoxide

(e) 12 g nitrogen dioxide, NO_2

(f) 13 g hydrogen sulfide, H_2S

W10.6 How many moles of nitrogen gas are present in 100 cm^3 of the gas at 30 °C and a pressure of 200 kPa?

W10.7 1.236 g of a volatile liquid gave 512 cm^3 of vapour at 20 °C and a pressure of 101.325 kPa. Calculate the relative molecular mass of the liquid to the nearest whole number.

W10.8 What is the relative molecular mass of a gas to the nearest whole number if 1.00 g occupies a volume of 200 cm^3 at 25 °C and 101.3 kPa?

W10.9 In order to determine the relative molecular mass of a volatile liquid, a conical flask was filled with the vapour of the liquid. The results of the experiment were summarised as follows:

Mass of empty flask, foil and band = 101.41g

Mass of flask, foil, band and condensed liquid = 102.84 g

Volume of flask = 328 cm^3

Atmospheric pressure = 9.8×10^4 Pa

Temperature of vapour in flask = 100 °C

Calculate the relative molecular mass of the liquid to the nearest whole number. (Take standard pressure as 1×10^5 Pa.)

W10.10 The following results were obtained in an experiment to measure the relative molecular mass of a gas using a gas syringe:

Temperature of furnace = 100 °C

Atmospheric pressure = 1.02×10^5 N m^{-2}

Initial volume of air in gas syringe = 6 cm^3

Final volume of air and vapour in gas syringe = 67 cm^3

Initial mass of hypodermic syringe and liquid = 13.179 g

Final mass of hypodermic syringe and liquid = 12.910 g

Using the above data, calculate the relative molecular mass of the volatile liquid to the nearest whole number.

W10.11 State *Boyle's Law*. Define *relative molecular mass* (M_r).

What is understood by an ideal gas? Give two ways in which real gases depart from ideal behaviour. Under what conditions of temperature and pressure would a real gas depart most from ideal behaviour?

Write down the Equation of State for an Ideal Gas.

A mass of 5.6 grams of a gaseous diatomic element occupies a volume of 4.98×10^{-3} m^3 at 27 °C and a pressure of 1.0×10^5 N m^{-2}. Find the relative molecular mass of the element and give its name.

Outline an experimental procedure used to determine the relative molecular mass of a volatile liquid. [LCH]

W10.12 The Equation of State for an Ideal Gas (Ideal Gas Equation) is given as $pV = nRT$.

(i) What is an ideal gas? What does the quantity n represent in this equation?

(ii) Give two reasons why real gases differ from ideal behaviour. State, giving your reason, which of the gases hydrogen, oxygen, hydrogen chloride or methane you would expect to differ most from ideal behaviour at room temperature.

(iii) 1.1 g of a gas occupied 3.15×10^{-4} m^3 at 300 K and at a pressure of 10^5 N m^{-2}. Use the Ideal Gas equation to calculate the relative molecular mass of the gas. [LCH]

Revision Questions

W10.13 (a) What does *n* represent in the ideal gas equation $pV = nRT$? [LCH]

(b) A gas occupies 500 cm^3 at 273 K and 1.01×10^5 N m^{-2} pressure. What volume will it occupy at 819 K and 2.02×10^5 N m^{-2} pressure? [LCH]

(c) What is the volume at s.t.p. of one gram of nitrogen gas? [LCH]

(d) State two ways in which real gases depart from ideal behaviour. [LCH]

(e) A certain gas has a density of 2.5 g L^{-1} at s.t.p. Calculate the relative molecular mass of the gas. [LCH]

(f) Which of the gases: hydrogen, ammonia, carbon dioxide would you expect to come closest to ideal behaviour? Give a reason for your answer. [LCH]

(g) Draw a simple sketch graph to indicate the relationship between T and V/T for a definite mass of an ideal gas at constant pressure. [LCH]

(h) Draw a simple sketch graph to indicate the relationship between pV and p for a definite amount of an ideal gas at constant temperature. [LCH]

W10.14 The Equation of State for an Ideal Gas (Ideal Gas Equation) is given as $pV = nRT$.

(i) What do you understand by an ideal gas?

(ii) Write equations for two of the gas laws on which the general gas equation is based.

(iii) Explain the meaning of the terms *R* and *n* in the equation.

(iv) Express *n* in terms of actual mass (m) and relative molecular mass (M) of the gas.

(v) Suggest two reasons why real gases differ from ideal behaviour. Under what conditions of temperature and pressure would a real gas come nearest to being ideal?

(vi) 0.3 g of a gas occupied 168 cm^3 at 300 K and a pressure of 1.0×10^5 N m^{-2}. Calculate the relative molecular mass of the gas. ($R = 8.4\ N\ m\ mol^{-1}\ K^{-1}$) [LCH]

Stoichiometry I

When answering these questions, use the following values of relative atomic masses: H = 1, He = 4, Li = 7, C = 12, N = 14, O =16, F = 19, Na = 23, Mg = 24, Al = 27, Si = 28, P = 31, S = 32, Cl = 35.5, K = 39, Ca = 40, Cr = 52, Mn = 55, Fe = 56, Cu = 63.5, Zn = 65, Br = 80, Ag = 108, Sn = 119, I = 127, Pb = 207.

Percentage Composition

W11.1 Calculate the percentage by mass of water of crystallisation in:

(a) washing soda, $Na_2CO_3.10H_2O$

(b) Epsom salts, $MgSO_4.7H_2O$

W11.2 Two of the ores of iron are haematite (Fe_2O_3) and magnetite (Fe_3O_4). Which of these ores contains the higher percentage of iron?

Empirical and Molecular Formulas

W11.3 An alcohol was found on analysis to contain 64.9% carbon, 13.5% hydrogen and 21.6% oxygen by mass. If the relative molecular mass of the alcohol is 74, show that the molecular formula is $C_4H_{10}O$. [LCH]

W11.4 An organic acid isolated from rhubarb contains 26.7% carbon, 2.2% hydrogen and 71.1% oxygen by mass. The relative molecular mass of the compound is 90. Calculate the molecular formula of the acid.

W11.5 Determine the molecular formula of a compound whose composition by mass is carbon 64.8%, hydrogen 13.6% and oxygen 21.6% and whose relative molecular mass is 74.

Gravimetric Analysis

W11.6 When 2.07 g of lead combined with iodine, it was found that 4.61 g of lead iodide were formed. Calculate the empirical formula of lead iodide.

W11.7 When 3.94 g of hydrated copper(II) sulfate crystals were heated, 2.52 g of the anhydrous salt remained. Calculate the formula of the hydrated salt.

W11.8 9.76 g of a metal form 20.9 g of its oxide whose formula is M_2O. Calculate the relative atomic mass of the metal.

Calculations from balanced equations

W11.9 Magnesium reacts with nitrogen to form magnesium nitride according to the equation:

$$3Mg + N_2 \longrightarrow Mg_3N_2$$

What mass of magnesium nitride may be obtained from 33 g of magnesium?

W11.10 In the thermit reaction used to repair railway tracks, aluminium powder reacts with iron(III) oxide to produce iron metal. The equation for the reaction is:

$$2Al + Fe_2O_3 \longrightarrow Al_2O_3 + 2Fe$$

How much iron could be obtained from 30 g of iron(III) oxide?

Volumes of gases

W11.11 Dinitrogen oxide, N_2O, commonly called 'laughing gas', may be made by heating ammonium nitrate. The balanced equation for the reaction is:

$$NH_4NO_3 \longrightarrow N_2O + 2H_2O$$

What mass of ammonium nitrate would have to be heated to make 550 cm^3 of dinitrogen oxide at s.t.p.?

W11.12 Before the invention of the battery-powered bicycle lamp, lamps on bicycles burned the gas ethyne (also called acetylene), C_2H_2. This gas was produced by allowing water to drip on to lumps of calcium carbide and the following reaction took place:

$$CaC_2 + 2H_2O \longrightarrow C_2H_2 + Ca(OH)_2$$

How much calcium carbide would be needed to generate 350 cm^3 of ethyne at s.t.p.?

W11.13 Ammonia may be prepared in the laboratory by heating a mixture of ammonium chloride and calcium hydroxide. The reaction that occurs is:

$$2NH_4Cl + Ca(OH)_2 \longrightarrow 2NH_3 + CaCl_2 + 2H_2O$$

What mass of ammonium chloride is required to produce 800 cm^3 of ammonia at s.t.p.?

W11.14 When potassium chlorate is heated, it decomposes into potassium chloride and oxygen according to the following equation:

$$2KClO_3 \longrightarrow 2KCl + 3O_2$$

What mass of potassium chlorate would be required to prepare 700 cm^3 of oxygen at s.t.p.?

Revision Questions

W11.15 12.7 g of copper react with 3.2 g of sulfur to give a compound X which has a relative molecular mass of 159.

(i) How many moles of copper reacted?

(ii) How many moles of sulfur reacted?

(iii) In what ratio did copper and sulfur combine?

(iv) What is the molecular formula for compound X? Name the compound X. [LCO]

W11.16 The following reaction may be used to reduce emissions of sulfur dioxide in waste gases:

$$2CaCO_3 + 2SO_2 + O_2 \longrightarrow 2CaSO_4 + 2CO_2$$

What volume of sulfur dioxide (measured at s.t.p.) could be removed from the waste gases by this reaction for every kilogram of calcium carbonate used? [LCH]

W11.17 Sulfur dioxide was prepared by heating excess dilute hydrochloric acid with 6.3 g of sodium sulfite according to the equation:

$$Na_2SO_3 + 2HCl \longrightarrow 2NaCl + SO_2 + H_2O$$

(i) How many moles of sodium sulfite were used?

(ii) What was the volume at s.t.p. of sulfur dioxide obtained?

(iii) How many molecules of sulfur dioxide did the volume in (ii) contain?

W11.18 9.6 g of pure iron pyrites were completely oxidised according to the equation:

$$4FeS_2 + 11O_2 \longrightarrow 2Fe_2O_3 + 8SO_2$$

(i) What mass of iron(III) oxide was obtained?

(ii) What volume of sulfur dioxide measured at s.t.p. was obtained?

(iii) How many molecules of sulfur dioxide did this volume contain? [LCH]

W11.19 A chemist analysed the substance used in the antifreeze of a car and found it had the following composition by mass: 38.7% carbon, 9.68% hydrogen and the remainder was oxygen. The relative molecular mass of the compound was measured and found to be 62. Determine (a) the empirical formula and (b) the molecular formula of the compound.

W11.20 In a reaction 4.35 g of manganese dioxide reacted completely with concentrated hydrochloric acid according to the equation:

$$MnO_2 + 4HCl \longrightarrow MnCl_2 + Cl_2 + 2H_2O$$

(i) How many moles of MnO_2 does 4.35 g represent?

(ii) How many moles of HCl are needed to react with this weight of MnO_2?

(iii) What weight of anhydrous $MnCl_2$ could be obtained from this reaction?

(iv) Calculate the volume at s.t.p. of the chlorine obtained.

(v) Calculate the number of molecules of chlorine obtained. [LCH]

12 Acids and Bases

W12.1 (a) A hydrogen atom that has lost an electron is simply a bare proton

(b) A soluble base is called an alkaline

(c) Write down the Arrhenius definition of a base. Sin substaint a dhianscaoileann in uisce chun ian OH^- a thairgeadh

(d) Another name for the hydronium ion is the ______________ ion.

(e) The Brønsted-Lowry definition of an acid is Sin substaint a sholáthraíonn prótón

(f) Give two reasons why the Brønsted-Lowry theory is more satisfactory than the Arrhenius theory. níos simplí, níos cruinn

____

(g) Why are bases such as sodium hydroxide often used in oven cleaners? ______________

____

(h) Distinguish between a weak base as defined by the Arrhenius theory and the Brønsted-Lowry theory. ______________

____

(i) How does the Brønsted-Lowry theory define a strong acid? ______________

(j) An amphoteric substance is ______________

W12.2 Write down the conjugate base of each of the following Brønsted-Lowry acids:

(a) CH_3COOH ______________

(b) HS^- ______________

(c) NH_3 ______________

(d) H_2O ______________

(e) HCO_3^- ______________

(f) NH_4^+ ______________

(g) $H_2NO_3^+$ ______________

(h) OH^- ______________

(i) $CH_3NH_3^+$ ______________

W12.3 Write down the conjugate acid of each of the following Brønsted-Lowry bases:

(a) NH_3 ____________

(b) HSO_4^- ____________

(c) SO_4^{2-} ____________

(d) OH^- ____________

(e) CO_3^{2-} ____________

(f) HCO_3^- ____________

(g) HS^- ____________

(h) HPO_4^{2-} ____________

(i) ClO_4^- ____________

(j) S^{2-} ____________

(k) HF ____________

W12.4 Write down each of the following equations and indicate in each case the acids, bases and conjugate acid–base pairs present.

(a) $HNO_3 + H_2F_2 \rightleftharpoons H_2NO_3^+ + HF_2^-$ [LCH]

(b) $HClO_4 + CH_3COOH \rightleftharpoons CH_3COOH_2^+ + ClO_4^-$ [LCH]

(c) $HNO_3 + OH^- \rightleftharpoons NO_3^- + H_2O$

(d) $CH_3NH_2 + HClO_4 \rightleftharpoons CH_3NH_3^+ + ClO_4^-$ [LCH]

(e) $HBr + HCl \rightleftharpoons Br^- + H_2Cl^+$

(f) $CH_3CONH_2 + NH_2^- \rightleftharpoons CH_3CONH^- + NH_3$ [LCH]

(g) $HSO_3^- + H_2O \rightleftharpoons SO_3^{2-} + H_3O^+$

(h) $H_3PO_4 + NH_3 \rightleftharpoons H_2PO_4^- + NH_4^+$ [LCH]

(i) $NH_4^+ + CO_3^{2-} \rightleftharpoons HCO_3^- + NH_3$ [LCH]

(j) $H_2SO_4 + HNO_3 \rightleftharpoons H_2NO_3^+ + HSO_4^-$

13 Volumetric Analysis: Acid-Base

W13.1 Concentrated hydrochloric acid is a 37.9% w/w solution of HCl in water. What mass of this solution would have to be taken so that it contains 5 g of HCl?

W13.2 Convert the following concentrations to p.p.m.

(a) 0.54 g/L ____________________

(b) 0.18 g/L ____________________

(c) 0.077 g/100 cm^3 ____________________

(d) 0.0009 g/100cm^3 ____________________

W13.3 Calculate the molarity of a solution that contains:

(a) 65 g HCl per litre of solution ____________________

(b) 25 g KOH per 250 cm^3 of solution ____________________

(c) 22 g H_2SO_4 per 100 cm^3 of solution ____________________

(d) 10 g NaOH per 2 litres of solution ____________________

(e) 12.5 g Na_2CO_3 per 200 cm^3 of solution ____________________

W13.4 In Ireland the legal limit for professional, learner and novice drivers for driving with alcohol (ethanol) in their bloodstream is 20 mg alcohol per 100 cm^3 of blood. Calculate the concentration of ethanol, C_2H_5OH, in moles per litre at this level.

W13.5 Calculate the mass of each of the following substances contained in the specified volume of solution:

(a) 20 cm^3 of 0.1 M NaOH ____________________

(b) 25 cm^3 of 0.01 M HNO_3 ____________________

(c) 750 cm^3 of 0.12 M NH_3 ____________________

(d) 2 litres of 2 M HCl ____________________

(e) 20 cm^3 of 0.1 M H_2SO_4 ____________________

W13.6 Magnesium reacts with hydrochloric acid according to the equation:

$$Mg + 2HCl \longrightarrow MgCl_2 + H_2$$

What mass of magnesium is needed to react with 50 cm^3 of 2 M HCl solution?

W13.7 Carbon dioxide may be prepared by reacting marble, $CaCO_3$, with dilute hydrochloric acid. The equation for the reaction is:

$$CaCO_3 + 2HCl \longrightarrow CaCl_2 + H_2O + CO_2$$

A student is given 10 grams of marble chips. What volume of bench dilute hydrochloric acid of concentration 3 M is required to react with all of the marble chips?

W13.8 To what volume must 20 cm^3 of 1 M H_2SO_4 solution be diluted in order to make it exactly 0.01 M H_2SO_4?

W13.9 What volume of concentrated ammonia (16 M) would be required to prepare two litres of 2 M ammonia?

W13.10 A hydrogen peroxide solution is labelled '100 volume'. (This means that a certain volume of hydrogen peroxide will produce 100 times that volume of oxygen.) A student needs 2.5 litres of '20 volume' hydrogen peroxide for an experiment to prepare oxygen. What volume of the concentrated solution ('100 volume') should be diluted to a volume of 2.5 litres?

W13.11 A student is told to make up a standard solution of sodium carbonate. Comment on the effect that each of the following errors would have on the concentration of the sodium carbonate solution.

(a) Some of the sodium carbonate was spilled in transferring it to the beaker.

(b) The student forgot to rinse the glass rod.

(c) Too much water was added to the volumetric flask and the level of the meniscus went above the graduation mark.

(d) The student forgot to invert the volumetric flask a number of times.

W13.12 Limewater is a saturated solution of calcium hydroxide, $Ca(OH)_2$, in water. A student was asked to measure the concentration of limewater and found that 25 cm^3 of limewater was neutralised by 15.2 cm^3 of 0.05 mol/L HCl solution. The balanced equation for the reaction is:

$$Ca(OH)_2 + 2HCl \longrightarrow CaCl_2 + 2H_2O$$

Calculate the concentration of the limewater in (a) mol/L and (b) g/L of calcium hydroxide.

W13.13 Ethanedioic (oxalic) acid, $H_2C_2O_4$, is an acid found in rhubarb and it reacts with sodium hydroxide according to the equation:

$$H_2C_2O_4 + 2NaOH \longrightarrow Na_2C_2O_4 + 2H_2O$$

It was found that 25 cm^3 of 0.12 mol/L NaOH solution was neutralised by 18.7 cm^3 of ethanedioic acid solution. Calculate the concentration of the ethanedioic acid solution in (a) mol/L and (b) g/L.

W13.14 A 50 cm^3 sample of vinegar was diluted to 250 cm^3 in a volumetric flask. This diluted solution was then titrated against 25 cm^3 of 0.15 M NaOH solution. The balanced equation for the reaction is:

$$CH_3COOH + NaOH \longrightarrow CH_3COONa + H_2O$$

The average titration figure was 20.25 cm^3. Calculate the concentration of ethanoic acid in the original vinegar in (a) mol/L, (b) g/L and (c) % w/v.

W13.15 A 25 cm^3 sample of vinegar was diluted to 100 cm^3 in a volumetric flask. This diluted solution was then titrated against 25 cm^3 of 0.12 M NaOH solution. The balanced equation for the reaction is:

$$CH_3COOH + NaOH \longrightarrow CH_3COONa + H_2O$$

The average titration figure was 12.35 cm^3. Calculate the concentration of ethanoic acid in the original vinegar in (a) mol/L, (b) g/L and (c) % w/v.

W13.16 A student was asked to analyse a sample of crystals of hydrated ethanedioic acid (oxalic acid), $H_2C_2O_4.xH_2O$. He dissolved 6.3 g of the crystals in water and made the solution up to one litre in a volumetric flask. 20 cm^3 of this solution were titrated against 0.09 M NaOH solution. The average titration figure was 22.22 cm^3. The balanced equation for the reaction is:

$$H_2C_2O_4 + 2NaOH \longrightarrow Na_2C_2O_4 + 2H_2O$$

Calculate (a) the percentage of water of crystallisation and (b) the value of x in the formula $H_2C_2O_4.xH_2O$.

W13.17 The experiment outlined in question W13.16 was repeated by another student. 5 g of the hydrated crystals of ethanedioic acid (oxalic acid) were dissolved in water and made up to 250 cm^3 in a volumetric flask. 25 cm^3 of this solution were titrated against 0.35 M NaOH solution. The average titration figure was 22.75 cm^3. Calculate the number of molecules of water of crystallisation in the formula $H_2C_2O_4.xH_2O$. Are the results of the two students consistent?

14 Oxidation and Reduction

W 14.1 Write down the oxidation number of each element in the following:

(a) N_2 ______________

(b) PCl_3 ______________

(c) CO ______________

(d) CO_2 ______________

(e) Al ______________

(f) OF_2 ______________

(g) O_2F_2 ______________

(h) $FeCl_3$ ______________

(i) K_2CrO_4 ______________

(j) S^{2-} ______________

(k) PH_3 ______________

(l) KIO_3 ______________

(m) $CoCl_2$ ______________

(n) SO_4^{2-} ______________

(o) SO_3^{2-} ______________

(p) $Cr_2(SO_4)_3$ ______________

(q) NaH ______________

(r) $C_6H_{12}O_6$ ______________

(s) Al_2O_3 ______________

(t) CuS ______________

(u) Cu_2S ______________

(v) $Ca_3(PO_4)_2$ ______________

(w) IF_7 ______________

W14.2 Write down the oxidation number of nitrogen in each of the following:

(a) N_2 ______________

(b) NH_3 ______________

(c) NO ____________

(d) NO_2 ____________

(e) N_2O ____________

(f) N_2O_4 ____________

(g) NO_3^- ____________

(h) NO_2^- ____________

W14.3 Write down the oxidation number of chlorine in each of the following:

(a) HCl ____________

(b) $KClO_3$ ____________

(c) $KClO_4$ ____________

(d) Cl_2 ____________

(e) ClO^- ____________

(f) ClO_2^- ____________

W14.4 What is an oxidation number?

What are the main rules by which oxidation numbers are assigned?

What is the oxidation number of (i) bromine in BrF_3, (ii) chromium in $K_2Cr_2O_7$, (iii) sulfur in $H_2S_2O_7$? [LCH]

W14.5 What is the oxidation number of (a) iron in $K_3[Fe(CN)_6]$, (b) copper in $[CuCl_2]^-$?

(Hint: the cyanide ion has the formula CN^-.) [LCH]

W14.6 What is the oxidation number of (i) nitrogen in NH_4^+, (ii) phosphorus in H_3PO_4, (iii) sulfur in $Na_2S_4O_6$? [LCH]

W14.7 (a) Define *oxidation* in terms of (i) electron transfer, (ii) change in oxidation number.

(b) In the following examples indicate clearly, by showing electron loss or gain, which species is being oxidised and which is being reduced:

(i) $2KI + Cl_2 \longrightarrow 2KCl + I_2$

(ii) $Fe + 2HCl \longrightarrow FeCl_2 + H_2$

(c) State the oxidation number or numbers that apply to:

(i) an atom of a free element

(ii) a simple ion

(iii) oxygen in its compounds

(iv) hydrogen in its compounds

(v) a neutral molecule. [LCH]

W14.8 Write down the oxidation number of oxygen in each of the following species:

(i) O_3 ____________________

(ii) OF_2 ____________________

(iii) Cl_2O ____________________

(iv) O_2^{2-} ____________________

Though (ii) and (iii) above both consist of a halogen combined with oxygen, it is usual to write their formulas with the oxygen first in (ii) and the halogen first in (iii) as shown. Suggest a reason for this. [LCH]

W14.9 In the case of each of the following reactions, use oxidation numbers to show (i) which substances are oxidised and which are reduced, (ii) which substances are oxidising agents and which are reducing agents:

(a) $Fe + S \longrightarrow FeS$

(b) $Fe_2O_3 + 3CO \longrightarrow 2Fe + 3CO_2$

(c) $2Na + Cl_2 \longrightarrow 2NaCl$ [LCH]

W14.10 Use oxidation numbers to determine whether or not each of the following is an oxidation–reduction reaction and, if so, indicate which species is being oxidised and which is being reduced:

(i) $Mg + Cl_2 \longrightarrow MgCl_2$

(ii) $ZnCO_3 \longrightarrow ZnO + CO_2$

W14.11 Use oxidation numbers to show that hydrogen peroxide acts

(i) as an oxidising agent in the reaction:

$H_2O_2 + 2H^+ + 2Fe^{2+} \longrightarrow 2H_2O + 2Fe^{3+}$

(ii) as a reducing agent in the reaction:

$MnO_2 + H_2O_2 + 2H^+ \longrightarrow Mn^{2+} + O_2 + 2H_2O$ [LCH]

W14.12 Use oxidation numbers to determine whether or not each of the following is a redox reaction and, if so, state the species reduced.

$S_2O_3^{2-} + 2HCl \longrightarrow H_2O + SO_2 + S + 2Cl^-$

$BiCl_4^- + H_2O \longrightarrow BiOCl + 2HCl + Cl^-$ [LCH]

W14.13 Using oxidation numbers, investigate if the following reactions are oxidation–reduction reactions:

$Fe^{2+} + H^+ + HNO_3 \longrightarrow Fe^{3+} + NO_2 + H_2O$

$Cu_2O + 2H_3O^+ \longrightarrow Cu^{2+} + Cu + 3H_2O$ [LCH]

W14.14 Using oxidation numbers, balance each of the following equations.

(a) $Cr_2O_7^{2-} + Fe^{2+} + H^+ \longrightarrow Cr^{3+} + Fe^{3+} + H_2O$

(b) $Cl_2 + SO_3^{2-} + H_2O \longrightarrow Cl^- + SO_4^{2-} + H^+$

(c) $Mn^{2+} + BiO_3^- + H^+ \longrightarrow MnO_4^- + Bi^{3+} + H_2O$

(d) $Cu + HNO_3 + H^+ \longrightarrow Cu^{2+} + NO_2 + H_2O$

(e) $H_2O_2 + Fe^{2+} + H^+ \longrightarrow Fe^{3+} + H_2O$

(f) $Fe^{2+} + H^+ + ClO_3^- \longrightarrow Fe^{3+} + Cl^- + H_2O$

(g) $IO_3^- + I^- + H^+ \longrightarrow I_2 + H_2O$

(h) $S_2O_3^{2-} + I_2 \longrightarrow I^- + S_4O_6^{2-}$

(i) $Cr_2O_7^{2-} + SO_2 + H^+ \longrightarrow Cr^{3+} + SO_4^{2-} + H_2O$

15 Volumetric Analysis: Oxidation–Reduction

W15.1 A solution of potassium permanganate is standardised against 0.11 M iron(II) sulfate solution. 25 cm^3 of the iron(II) sulfate solution required 28.5 cm^3 of the permanganate solution. Calculate the concentration of the potassium permanganate solution in (a) moles per litre and (b) grams $KMnO_4$ per litre. The equation for the reaction is

$$MnO_4^- + 8H^+ + 5Fe^{2+} \longrightarrow Mn^{2+} + 5Fe^{3+} + 4H_2O$$

W15.2 22.5 cm^3 of a solution of 0.02 M $KMnO_4$ reacted completely with 25 cm^3 of a solution of ammonium iron(II) sulfate. Calculate the concentration of the ammonium iron(II) sulfate solution in (a) moles per litre and (b) grams of crystalline $(NH_4)_2SO_4.FeSO_4.6H_2O$ per litre. The balanced equation for the reaction is:

$$MnO_4^- + 8H^+ + 5Fe^{2+} \longrightarrow Mn^{2+} + 5Fe^{3+} + 4H_2O$$

W15.3 A chemist analysed a sample of steel in order to determine the percentage of iron in it. He dissolved 1.85 g of the sample in excess dilute sulfuric acid and made the resulting solution up to 250 cm^3 in a volumetric flask. 25 cm^3 of this solution required 23.5 cm^3 of 0.025 M $KMnO_4$ for complete reaction. The equations for the reactions are:

$$Fe + H_2SO_4 \longrightarrow FeSO_4 + H_2$$

$$MnO_4^- + 8H^+ + 5e^- \longrightarrow Mn^{2+} + 4H_2O$$

Calculate (a) the concentration of the iron(II) sulfate solution in moles per litre and (b) grams of iron in 250 cm^3 of the solution. Hence, calculate the percentage of iron in the sample of steel.

W15.4 Some crystals of iron(II) sulfate, $FeSO_4.xH_2O$, which had partly effloresced, were analysed to find out the value of x. A mass of 5.71 g of iron(II) sulfate crystals was dissolved in water and the resulting solution was made up to 250 cm^3 in a volumetric flask. 25 cm^3 of this solution required 19.65 cm^3 of 0.024 M $KMnO_4$ solution.

(a) Explain the meaning of the term *efflorescence*.

(b) Calculate the value of x from the above information.

The balanced equation for the reaction is:

$$MnO_4^- + 8H^+ + 5Fe^{2+} \longrightarrow Mn^{2+} + 5Fe^{3+} + 4H_2O$$

W15.5 What is meant by a standard solution?

A standard solution of ammonium iron(II) sulfate, $(NH_4)_2SO_4.FeSO_4.6H_2O$, was prepared by dissolving 11.76 g of the crystals in dilute sulfuric acid and making up the solution to 250 cm^3 with distilled water.

(i) Why was the salt dissolved in dilute sulfuric acid?

(ii) Calculate the molarity of the solution.

25 cm³ of this solution were taken and further acidified with dilute sulfuric acid. It required 33.3 cm³ of a potassium permanganate solution for complete oxidation according to the equation:

$$MnO_4^- + 5Fe^{2+} + 8H^+ \longrightarrow Mn^{2+} + 5Fe^{3+} + 4H_2O$$

(iii) Why is it necessary to ensure that the solution is strongly acidic?

(iv) Show clearly, using oxidation numbers, where oxidation and reduction occur in this reaction.

(v) Calculate the molarity of the potassium permanganate solution. [LCH]

W15.6 A mass of 8.82 g of ammonium iron(II) sulfate crystals, $(NH_4)_2SO_4.FeSO_4.xH_2O$, was dissolved in deionised water to which some sulfuric acid had been added. The solution was then made up accurately to 250 cm³. A pipette was used to measure 25 cm³ of this solution into a conical flask and a further 10 cm³ of dilute sulfuric acid were added. A burette was filled with a 0.02 M solution of potassium manganate(VII) and a number of titrations were carried out. The mean titration result was 22.5 cm³.

The equation for the titration reaction is:

$$MnO_4^- + 5Fe^{2+} + 8H^+ \longrightarrow 5Fe^{3+} + Mn^{2+} + 4H_2O$$

(i) Why was sulfuric acid added in making up the ammonium iron(II) sulfate solution?

(ii) Outline the correct procedure for diluting the ammonium iron(II) sulfate solution to 250 cm³.

(iii) At what point in the potassium manganate(VII) solution are the burette readings taken? What colour changes would you observe as the solution from the burette flows into the conical flask? How would you identify the end point of the titration?

(iv) During the titration drops of the potassium manganate(VII) solution were noticed high up on the sides of the conical flask. What action would you take to deal with this problem? Why is it possible to take this action without affecting the result of the titration?

(v) What would you observe if insufficient sulfuric acid were present during the titration? Explain clearly the function of the acid in the titration.

(vi) Calculate the concentration of the ammonium iron(II) sulfate solution in (a) moles per litre, (b) grams of $(NH_4)_2SO_4.FeSO_4$ per litre.
Hence, find the percentage water of crystallisation in the ammonium iron(II) sulfate crystals and the value of x in the formula $(NH_4)_2SO_4.FeSO_4.xH_2O$. [LCH]

W15.7 Six tablets of total mass 1.47 g and containing iron(II) sulfate were dissolved in dilute sulfuric acid and the solution was made up to 250 cm³ in a volumetric flask. 20 cm³ portions of the resulting solution were titrated against 0.015 M potassium permanganate. The average titration figure was 5.47 cm³.

(i) Outline the steps taken to dissolve the tablets in dilute sulfuric acid.

(ii) Describe the appearance of the tablet solution.

(iii) Calculate (a) the mass of anhydrous $FeSO_4$ in each tablet, (b) the mass of iron in each tablet and (c) the percentage of $FeSO_4$ in each tablet. The equation for the reaction is:

$$MnO_4^- + 8H^+ + 5Fe^{2+} \longrightarrow Mn^{2+} + 5Fe^{3+} + 4H_2O$$

W15.8 In an analysis of iron tablets to determine the amount of iron sulfate per tablet, five tablets whose total mass was 1.20 g were dissolved in dilute sulfuric acid and the solution was made up to 250 cm³ in a volumetric flask. 25 cm³ portions of the resulting solution, to which a further 20 cm³ of dilute sulfuric acid had been added, were titrated against 0.015 M potassium permanganate. The average titration figure was 5.75 cm³.

(i) The student was warned not to use either hydrochloric acid or nitric acid to acidify the potassium permanganate solution. Why is it not advisable to use these acids?

(ii) What would be observed if the student forgot to add the 20 cm³ of dilute sulfuric acid?

(iii) Calculate (a) the mass of anhydrous $FeSO_4$ in each tablet, (b) the mass of iron in each tablet and (c) the percentage of $FeSO_4$ in each tablet.

The equation for the reaction is:

$$MnO_4^- + 8H^+ + 5Fe^{2+} \longrightarrow Mn^{2+} + 5Fe^{3+} + 4H_2O$$

W15.9 25 cm³ of an iodine solution was titrated against a solution of 0.12 M sodium thiosulfate. The average titration figure was 22.15 cm³. Calculate the concentration of the iodine solution in (a) moles per litre and (b) grams per litre. The reaction between iodine and thiosulfate may be represented as:

$$2S_2O_3^{2-} + I_2 \longrightarrow S_4O_6^{2-} + 2I^-$$

W15.10 25 cm³ of 0.022 M potassium permanganate is pipetted into a conical flask. Some dilute sulfuric acid and excess potassium iodide solution are then added and the liberated iodine is titrated against a solution of sodium thiosulfate of unknown concentration. The average titration figure is 22.45 cm³. Calculate the concentration of the sodium thiosulfate solution in (a) moles per litre and (b) grams per litre of crystalline $Na_2S_2O_3.5H_2O$. The reactions may be represented as:

$$2MnO_4^- + 10I^- + 16H^+ \longrightarrow 2Mn^{2+} + 5I_2 + 8H_2O$$

$$I_2 + 2S_2O_3^{2-} \longrightarrow S_4O_6^{2-} + 2I^-$$

W15.11 A number of groups of students carried out the following experiment to find the percentage purity of a sample of crystalline sodium thiosulfate, $Na_2S_2O_3.5H_2O$. A mass of 10.0 grams of the crystals was dissolved in deionised water and the solution was made up accurately to 500 cm³ in a volumetric flask. A burette was then filled with this solution. A 25.0 cm³ portion of a 0.050 M solution of iodine (previously standardised) was pipetted into a conical flask and the sodium thiosulfate solution was titrated against it. Three titrations were carried out and the titration results were 31.6 cm³, 31.2 cm³ and 31.3 cm³. The equation for the titration reaction is:

$$2S_2O_3^{2-} + I_2 \longrightarrow S_4O_6^{2-} + 2I^-$$

(i) In making up the iodine solution in the experiment, iodine, water and potassium iodide were used.

What was the function of the potassium iodide?

(ii) Which of the three pieces of titration apparatus, the pipette, the burette or the conical flask should **not** be rinsed with the solution it is to contain? Give the reason for your answer.

(iii) Due to a shortage of apparatus, one group used a 500 cm^3 graduated cylinder in place of a volumetric flask and another group used a beaker instead of a conical flask, in carrying out the titration.
Give (a) one reason why a volumetric flask is preferable to a graduated cylinder, (b) one reason why a conical flask is preferable to a beaker.

(iv) What colour change would have been observed in the conical flask as the sodium thiosulfate solution was added from the burette?

(v) Name the indicator usually used in this titration. At what stage in the titration is the indicator added? What is the colour change at the end point in the presence of the indicator?

(vi) Calculate the concentration of the sodium thiosulfate solution in (a) moles per litre, (b) grams per litre of crystalline $Na_2S_2O_3.5H_2O$.

(vii) What was the percentage purity of the sample of crystalline sodium thiosulfate? [LCH]

W15.12 A 50 cm^3 sample of bleach is diluted to 250 cm^3 in a volumetric flask. 25 cm^3 of the diluted solution is added to an excess of acidified potassium iodide solution and titrated against 0.25 M sodium thiosulfate solution. The average titration figure is 19.56 cm^3. Calculate the concentration of the sodium hypochlorite in the bleach in (a) moles per litre, (b) grams per litre and (c) % w/v.

The equations for the reactions are:

$$ClO^- + 2I^- + 2H^+ \longrightarrow Cl^- + I_2 + H_2O$$

$$2S_2O_3^{2-} + I_2 \longrightarrow S_4O_6^{2-} + 2I^-$$

16 Rates of Reactions

W16.1 Thiosulfate ions react in acid solution as follows:

$$S_2O_3^{2-}{}_{(aq)} + 2H^+{}_{(aq)} \longrightarrow S_{(s)} + SO_{2(aq)} + H_2O_{(l)}$$

A series of experiments was carried out in identical flasks at room temperature. The concentration of thiosulfate ions was varied but the concentration of the acid and the total volume of the solution were kept constant. The time taken in each case for a cross marked on paper to be obscured by the suspended sulfur was noted. It can be shown that the initial rate of reaction in each case is inversely proportional to the time taken for the cross to disappear. The volume of standard thiosulfate used is a measure of the concentration of the thiosulfate ions. Results were tabulated as follows:

Vol. of 0.2 M $Na_2S_2O_3$ (cm^3)	Vol. of water added (cm^3)	Vol. of 2 M HCl (cm^3)	Time (t) (secs)	$\frac{1}{t}$ (s^{-1})
60	0	10	40	0.025
50	10	10	48	0.021
40	20	10	62	0.016
30	30	10	80	0.0125
20	40	10	120	0.008
10	50	10	250	0.004

(i) Why is it necessary to use identical flasks?

(ii) Plot on graph paper the volume of thiosulfate solution against $\frac{1}{t}$.

(iii) What conclusion can you draw about the relationship between the rate of the reaction and the concentration of the thiosulfate ions?

(iv) If 24.0 cm^3 of a 0.2 M solution of sodium thiosulfate had been used in one of the above experiments, what time would have elapsed before the cross became obscured? [LCH]

W16.2 When dilute hydrochloric acid is added to a solution of sodium thiosulfate the following reaction occurs:

$$Na_2S_2O_{3(aq)} + 2HCl_{(aq)} \longrightarrow 2NaCl_{(aq)} + SO_{2(aq)} + H_2O_{(l)} + S_{(s)}$$

A student carried out the above reaction between 100 cm^3 of 0.1 M sodium thiosulfate solution and 10 cm^3 of 1.0 M hydrochloric acid at a number of different temperatures. The time (t) taken for a mark on the bottom of the reaction vessel to be obscured by the suspended sulfur was noted for each temperature. The reciprocal ($\frac{1}{t}$) of the time was used as a measure of the initial rate of the reaction in each case. The results are shown in the table on page 42.

Temperature (°C)	Time (t) (s)	Rate $\frac{1}{t}$ (s^{-1})
10	100	0.010
20	59	0.017
30	36	0.028
40	21	0.048
50	12	0.083
60	7	0.143

(i) How would you carry out the above reaction at any one of the given temperatures?

(ii) Plot on graph paper the rate ($\frac{1}{t}$) against temperature.

(iii) If the reaction had been carried out at 35 °C what time would have elapsed before the mark became obscured?

(iv) What change would you expect to see in the graph if 100 cm^3 of 0.5 M sodium thiosulfate had been used? [LCH]

W16.3 (a) Distinguish between the terms 'average rate' and 'instantaneous rate'.

____

____

(b) One gram of manganese dioxide was used to decompose a sample of hydrogen peroxide solution. What mass of catalyst would remain after the hydrogen peroxide had completely decomposed?

____

(c) On 18th October 1982, a flour mill in Metz in France was wrecked by a dust explosion.

Why does dust explode so violently if ignited? ______________________

(d) List the five factors on which the rate of a reaction depends.

____

(e) You have been asked to investigate whether an indigestion tablet or indigestion powder is more effective. You are given a sample of both of these basic materials, containing $Mg(OH)_2$, and some bench dilute hydrochloric acid. Describe briefly how you would carry out the investigation.

____

____

(f) What is an enzyme? ______________________

(g) Distinguish between *heterogeneous catalysis* and *homogeneous catalysis*.

____

____

(h) What is a catalyst poison? ______

(i) Why is it important that catalytic converters start working at as low a temperature as possible? ______

(j) Why do larger potatoes tend to take longer to cook than smaller ones?

______

(k) State the two main assumptions of the Collision Theory.

______

(l) Why does a small increase in temperature often result in a large increase in the rate of a reaction? ______ [LCH]

(m) An energy profile diagram for a reaction is shown in Fig. W16.1. Indicate on this diagram (i) the activation energy for the forward reaction and (ii) the activation energy for the reverse reaction. [LCH]

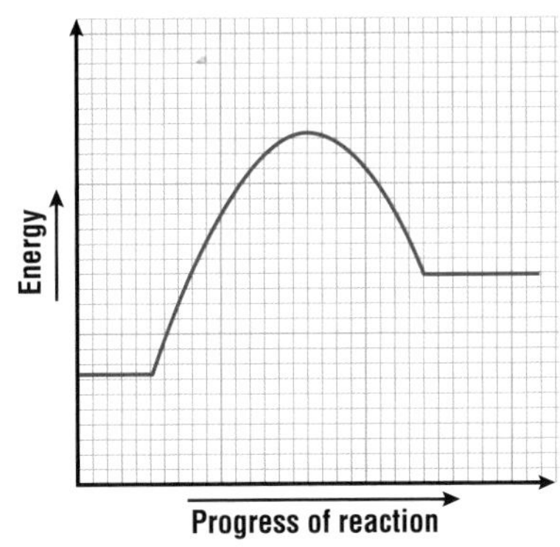

Fig W16.1

(n) Suggest a reason why catalytic converters eventually have to be replaced.

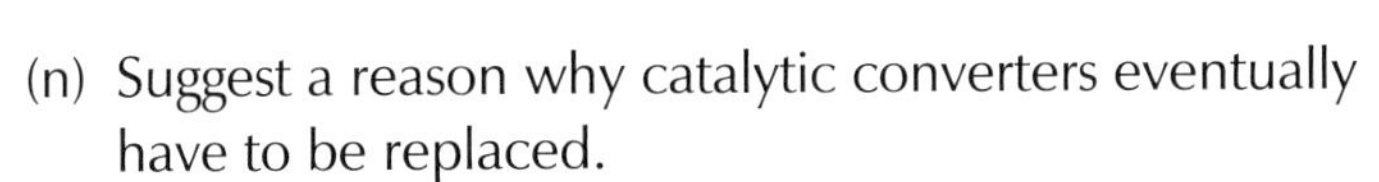

______

(o) Comment on the role played by platinum in the catalysis of the reaction:

$2H_2 + O_2 \longrightarrow 2H_2O$

______

(p) Define the term Activation Energy. ______

______

W16.4 A student carried out three experiments, all at 20 °C, to examine the rate of reaction between marble chips and hydrochloric acid. In each case, he used the same mass of marble chips but the size of the chips differed. He used the same volume of acid in each experiment. The graphs of his results are shown in Fig. W16.2.

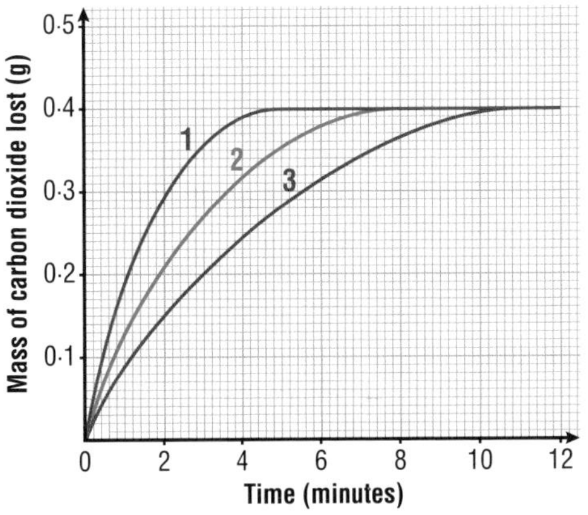

(a) (i) Which experiment gave the fastest reaction?

______

(ii) Give a reason for your answer.

______

Fig W16.2

(b) (i) In which experiment did he use the largest marble chips?

____

(ii) Give a reason for your answer.

____

(c) How much carbon dioxide was lost in Experiment 2 after (i) 2 minutes, (ii) 4.5 minutes?

____

(d) After how many minutes did the reaction in Experiment 1 stop? ________________

(e) What was the total mass of carbon dioxide lost in Experiment 3? ________________

(f) Sketch the curve of the results you would expect if he had carried out Experiment 2 at 50 °C instead of at 20 °C. Sketch this curve on the same graph as the other curves.

W16.5 A mass of 1 g of manganese dioxide was weighed in a small test-tube. 100 cm³ of a hydrogen peroxide solution were measured into a conical flask which was then fitted with a loose plug of cotton wool. The flask was placed on the pan of a direct reading balance, Fig. W16.3, and after adding the manganese dioxide, the mass was recorded at 1 minute intervals.

The results obtained are shown in the following table.

Time (min)	0	1	2	3	4	5	6	7	8
Mass (g)	176.58	176.34	176.22	176.16	176.12	176.11	176.10	176.10	176.10

(i) What was the function of the cotton wool plug?

(ii) How would you find the mass at 0 minutes, i.e. before the reaction had started?

(iii) Using graph paper, plot a graph of **loss in mass** against time.

What difference, if any, would you expect there to be in the graph if 2 g of manganese dioxide had been used? Explain your answer.

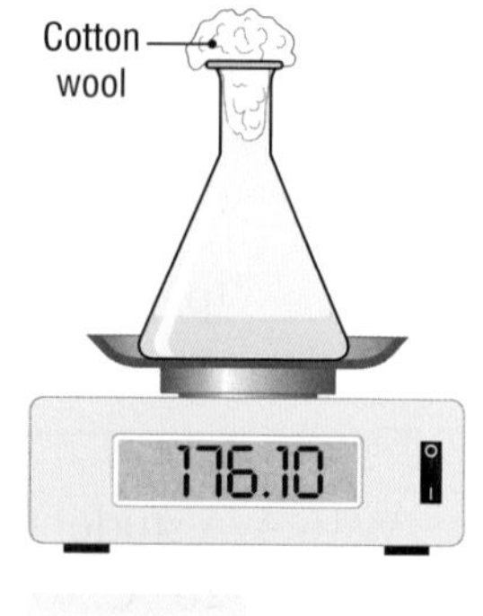

Fig W16.3

(iv) Use the graph to find (a) the time required to liberate 8.75×10^{-3} moles of oxygen, (b) the number of moles of oxygen liberated after 2.5 minutes had elapsed, (c) the instantaneous rate of the reaction at 2 minutes.

(v) The balanced equation for the reaction may be written as

$$2H_2O_2 \longrightarrow 2H_2O + O_2$$

Calculate the total number of moles of oxygen produced and hence find the number of moles of hydrogen peroxide initially present in the 100 cm³ of solution used.

(Hint: Work out the total loss in mass. This is the mass of oxygen produced. Convert this mass of oxygen gas to moles of oxygen gas and, from the balanced equation, work out how many moles of hydrogen peroxide would give this number of moles of oxygen.) [LCH]

W16.6 The energy profile diagram, Fig. W16.4, is for the following uncatalysed reaction.

$$H_{2(g)} + \frac{1}{2}O_{2(g)} \longrightarrow H_2O_{(l)}$$

Platinum, a solid catalyst, may be used to catalyse the reaction.

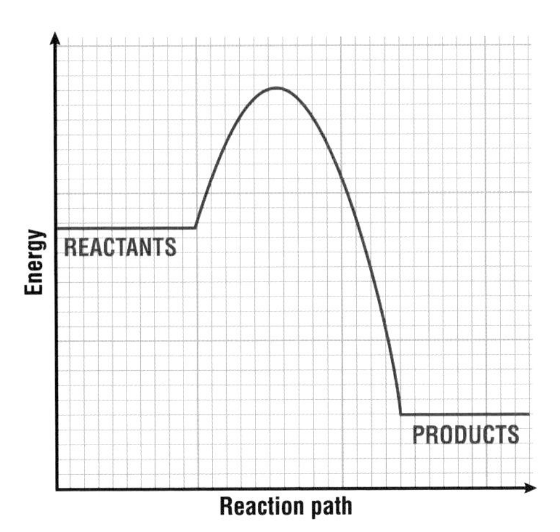

Fig W16.4

(i) Explain the terms *catalyst* and *activation energy*.

(ii) Draw an energy profile diagram similar to the one here, and show on your diagram the probable effect of the catalyst on the activation energy of the reaction.

(iii) Is the catalysed reaction an example of homogeneous or heterogeneous catalysis? Give a reason for your answer.

(iv) Give a brief outline of a theory to explain how the platinum functions as a catalyst in the reaction. [LCH]

W16.7 A solution of hydrogen peroxide will liberate oxygen when a small quantity of granular manganese dioxide (MnO_2) is added. The manganese dioxide is unaffected by the reaction.

The total volume of oxygen liberated from 50 cm^3 of a hydrogen peroxide solution after various intervals of time is shown in the following table:

Time (min)	0	0.5	1.0	1.5	2.0	2.5	3.0	3.5
Volume O_2 (cm^3) (corrected to s.t.p.)	0	28	42	48	53	56	56	56

(i) Draw a diagram of the apparatus you would use in this experiment and show clearly how you would start the reaction at a time which is known precisely.

(ii) 'The manganese dioxide was unaffected by the reaction'. Comment on this fact and refer to the position of manganese in the Periodic Table in your answer.

(iii) Plot a graph of the results.

(iv) How many moles of oxygen were collected after 1.75 minutes?

(v) After what time would 2×10^{-3} moles of oxygen be liberated?

(vi) Using the graph estimate the instantaneous rates of reaction in terms of cm^3 oxygen liberated per second at (a) 0.5 minute and (b) 3.0 minutes. [LCH]

W16.8 Explain as fully as you can the factor or factors affecting the reaction rate in each of the following:

(i) Limestone chips take much longer than the same mass of powdered limestone to dissolve in excess 2 M hydrochloric acid.

(ii) 1 g of magnesium ribbon will dissolve faster in 50 cm^3 of 2 M hydrochloric acid than in 100 cm^3 of 1 M hydrochloric acid.

(iii) Sulfur dioxide on heating with oxygen at 450 °C gives very little sulfur trioxide but in the presence of vanadium pentoxide at this temperature there is a 98% conversion. [LCH]

[Hint: In your answers name the factor that affects the reaction rate and use the collision theory and activation energy in your explanation.]

W16.9 Define (i) reaction rate, (ii) activation energy.

It can be shown from the kinetic theory of gases that a 10 K rise in temperature increases the number of collisions between molecules by only about 2% while the rate of the reaction is doubled or even trebled.

(i) Account for the slight increase in the number of collisions.

(ii) Suggest a reason for the much greater increase in the reaction rate. [LCH]

W16.10 Define *catalyst*.

The following reactions are both carried out at room temperature:

$$2H_{2\,(g)} + O_{2\,(g)} \xrightarrow{Pt} 2H_2O_{\,(l)}$$

$$16H^+_{\,(aq)} + 2MnO_4^-{}_{\,(aq)} + 5C_2O_4^{2-}{}_{\,(aq)} \longrightarrow 10CO_{2\,(g)} + 2Mn^{2+}_{\,(aq)} + 8H_2O_{\,(l)}$$

(i) The first reaction is an example of heterogeneous catalysis. Explain what this means and use the reaction to illustrate the surface adsorption theory of catalysis.

(ii) In the second reaction, the rate increases with addition of permanganate solution. How would you verify this by experiment? Identify the species acting as a catalyst in this reaction and give the term usually used for this type of catalysis. [LCH]

17 Chemical Equilibrium

W17.1 (a) A swimmer swims upstream at the same speed as the water moving in the opposite direction.

Is this a static or dynamic equilibrium? ______________________

(b) What do you mean by saying that a system has reached a state of equilibrium? [LCH]

____

(c) Explain the term dynamic equilibrium.

____

(d) Give one example of a reversible reaction. ______________________

(e) Give one example of an irreversible reaction. ______________________

(f) State Le Chatelier's Principle. ______________________

______________________ [LCH]

(g) Dinitrogen tetroxide, which is a gas at temperatures above 294 K, dissociates according to the equation:

$N_2O_{4(g)} \rightleftharpoons 2NO_{2(g)}$

colourless dark brown

What would you see happening if the temperature of a sample of N_2O_4 were raised from 295 K to 330 K? [LCH]

____

(h) For the equilibrium system:

$2SO_{2(g)} + O_{2(g)} \rightleftharpoons 2SO_{3(g)}$

predict the effect on the equilibrium system of (a) removing SO_3 and (b) adding more O_2.

(a) ______________ (b) ______________

(i) Hydrogen and iodine react together to form hydrogen iodide as follows:

$H_{2(g)} + I_{2(g)} \rightleftharpoons 2HI_{(g)}$

It was found that changing the pressure had no effect on the position of equilibrium. Explain.

____

____

(j) Draw a graph to illustrate the setting up of the equilibrium reaction:

$N_{2(g)} + 3H_{2(g)} \rightleftharpoons 2NH_{3(g)}$

Label the x-axis 'time' and the y-axis 'concentration'.

(k) The production of ammonia from nitrogen and hydrogen is usually carried out at a pressure of around 200 atmospheres and a temperature of about 450 °C. The equation for the reaction is:

$N_{2(g)} + 3H_{2(g)} \rightleftharpoons 2NH_{3(g)}$

Explain why high pressures lead to an increased yield of ammonia. Why are very high pressures (e.g. 1000 atmospheres) not normally used? [LCH]

____

____

(l) What would be the influence of (i) increasing the pressure, (ii) increasing the temperature on the condition of equilibrium in the following exothermic reaction:

$N_2 + 3H_2 \rightleftharpoons 2NH_3$ [LCH]

(i) ______________________________

(ii) ______________________________

(m) $2SO_2 + O_2 \rightleftharpoons 2SO_3$

Comment briefly on the industrial importance of the above reaction and state the conditions under which it is usually carried out. [LCH]

____

____

W17.2 A gas X decomposes to form a mixture of two gases Y and Z. The forward reaction is exothermic. The following equilibrium is set up:

$X \rightleftharpoons Y + 2Z$

How will the yield of Y and Z be affected by (a) an increase in pressure and (b) an increase in temperature?

Explain your answer in each case.

W17.3 In the case of each of the following reactions:

$2NO_{(g)} \rightleftharpoons N_{2(g)} + O_{2(g)}$ $\Delta H = -180$ kJ mol^{-1}

$2NH_{3(g)} \rightleftharpoons N_{2(g)} + 3H_{2(g)}$ $\Delta H = +92$ kJ mol^{-1}

What would be the effect on the dissociation of (a) increasing the pressure and (b) increasing the temperature? [LCH]

W17.4 When iron(III) chloride solution is added to potassium thiocyanate solution the following equilibrium is set up:

$FeCl_3 + CNS^- \rightleftharpoons Fe(CNS)^{2+} + 3Cl^-$

(a) What colour is observed on mixing the two substances?

(b) A student is told to add some dilute HCl to the solution. What colour change is observed on adding the dilute HCl? How would you explain this observation?

(c) A few cm^3 of potassium thiocyanate are then added to the container. What colour change is observed? Explain your observation.

W17.5 'In industry, chemists want a high yield of product. Therefore, they must consider all the factors that shift the equilibrium position to the right. However, they must also consider the rate at which equilibrium is achieved and the cost of shifting the position of equilibrium to the right'.

Discuss the above statement using either the Haber Process or the Contact Process.

Example 17.7

Question

The equilibrium between hydrogen, iodine and hydrogen iodide in the gaseous state was investigated as follows:

560 cm^3 of hydrogen (measured at s.t.p.) was placed in a 1 litre flask together with 6.35 g of solid iodine. The flask was sealed and heated for 30 minutes at 700 K. It was then cooled rapidly and, on analysis, the mass of hydrogen iodide present was found to be 5.12 g.

(i) Write the equilibrium constant expression for the reaction:

$$H_2 + I_2 \rightleftharpoons 2HI$$

(ii) What change does the iodine undergo as the vessel is heated?

(iii) What was the purpose of the rapid cooling?

(iv) Calculate the equilibrium constant (K_c) for this reaction at 700 K.

(v) If the experiment were repeated using the same quantities of hydrogen and iodine in a 500 cm^3 flask, state, giving your reason, whether or not, the value of K_c obtained would have been different.

(vi) For the reaction in (i) K_c has a lower value at 800 K than at 700 K. State and explain what conclusion can be drawn regarding the heat change for the reaction.

(H = 1, I = 127)

Answer

(i) $K_c = \frac{[HI]^2}{[H_2]\,[I_2]}$

(ii) The iodine turns into a vapour (sublimes).

(iii) The purpose of the rapid cooling was to slow down the reaction rate so that the equilibrium will not have time to adjust.

(iv) First convert the quantities given to moles.

Initially,

22,400 cm^3 of H_2 = 1 mole H_2 (at s.t.p)

1 cm^3 of $H_2 = \frac{1}{22\,400}$ mole H_2

560 cm^3 of $H_2 = \frac{560}{22\,400} = 0.025$ mole H_2

i.e. no. of moles of $H_2 = 0.025$

no. of moles of $I_2 = \frac{\text{Mass}}{\text{Rel. molecular mass}}$

$= \frac{6.35}{254} = 0.025$

At equilibrium,
no. of moles of HI $= \frac{\text{Mass}}{\text{Rel. molecular mass}} = \frac{5.12}{128} = 0.04$

	H_2	+ I_2	$\rightleftharpoons$ 2HI
Initially	0.025	0.025	0
At equil.	0.025 – 0.02 = 0.005	0.025 – 0.02 = 0.005	0.04
Conc. at equil. (V = 1L)	[0.005]	[0.005]	[0.04]

$$K_c = \frac{[HI]^2}{[H_2]\,[I_2]} = \frac{(0.04)^2}{(0.005)(0.005)} = 64$$

(v) The value of K_c will be the same since K_c varies only with temperature. Note that the increase in pressure will not shift the equilibrium in either direction since there is the same number of molecules on either side of the equation.

(vi) The lower value of K_c at 800 K means that less HI is being formed. Therefore, the higher temperature favours the backward reaction, i.e. the forward reaction must give out heat (exothermic).

$$H_2 + I_2 \underset{\text{endothermic}}{\overset{\text{exothermic}}{\rightleftharpoons}} 2HI$$

W17.6 Write the expression for K_c for each of the following reactions:

(a) $2NO_{(g)} + O_{2(g)} \rightleftharpoons 2NO_{2(g)}$

(b) $CO_{2(g)} + H_{2(g)} \rightleftharpoons CO_{(g)} + H_2O_{(g)}$

(c) $2N_2O_{5(g)} \rightleftharpoons 4NO_{2(g)} + O_{2(g)}$

(d) $I_{2(g)} \rightleftharpoons 2I_{(g)}$

(e) $2NOCl_{(g)} \rightleftharpoons 2NO_{(g)} + Cl_{2(g)}$

W17.7 The value of K_c for the reaction given below is 4 at 25 °C. Calculate the concentrations of the products if one mole of ethanoic acid and four moles of ethanol reach equilibrium at the same temperature.

$$CH_3COOH + C_2H_5OH \rightleftharpoons CH_3COOC_2H_5 + H_2O$$

W17.8 The following equilibrium was set up at 520 °C:

$$2HI \rightleftharpoons H_2 + I_2$$

0.10 mole of HI was placed in a one litre flask. At equilibrium, the concentration of H_2 was found to be 0.01 mole. What are the equilibrium concentrations of (a) I_2 and (b) HI?

W17.9 Ethanoic acid and ethanol react together as follows:

$$\underset{\text{ethanoic acid}}{CH_3COOH} + \underset{\text{ethanol}}{C_2H_5OH} \rightleftharpoons \underset{\text{ethyl ethanoate}}{CH_3COOC_2H_5} + \underset{\text{water}}{H_2O}$$

A mixture of 27.6 g of ethanol and 36 g of ethanoic acid was allowed to reach equilibrium at a certain temperature. It was found that 12 g of ethanoic acid remained unchanged. Find the equilibrium constant (K_c) for the reaction at this temperature.

Using this value of K_c, calculate the number of moles of ethanol that must be mixed with 60 g of ethanoic acid so that 70.4 g of ethyl ethanoate are present in the equilibrium mixture at the same temperature. [LCH]

W17.10 Write the equilibrium constant expression for the reaction:

$$SO_{2(g)} + NO_{2(g)} \rightleftharpoons SO_{3(g)} + NO_{(g)}$$

When 7.68 g of sulfur dioxide and 4.6 g of nitrogen dioxide were heated together in a closed vessel at a certain high temperature, it was found that at equilibrium 4.8 g of sulfur trioxide were present. Calculate the equilibrium constant K_c for the reaction at that temperature. [LCH]

W17.11 Two moles of hydrogen and one mole of iodine were placed in a one litre vessel at 400 °C and the following equilibrium was set up:

$$2HI \rightleftharpoons H_2 + I_2$$

Given that the value of K_c at this temperature is 0.02, calculate the number of moles of HI, H_2 and I_2 present at equilibrium.

W17.12 At 100 °C the value of K_c for the following reaction is 0.36:

$$N_2O_{4(g)} \rightleftharpoons 2NO_{2(g)}$$

0.10 mole of N_2O_4 is placed in a one litre flask. Calculate the concentrations of N_2O_4 and NO_2 when equilibrium is established.

18 pH and Indicators

W18.1 (a) What is meant by the self-ionisation of water? ______________________________

____

(b) Write down the value of the ionic product of water at 25 °C. ____________________

(c) Write down the concentration in moles per litre of OH^- ions in pure water at 25 °C. ____

(d) A solution contains 10^{-3} mole of H^+ ions per litre. Is it acidic or basic? ____________

(e) What nationality was Sørensen? ______________________________

(f) As the concentration of H^+ ions increases, the pH value ____________________

As the concentration of H^+ ions decreases, the pH value ____________________

(g) Write down the pH of a solution which has 10^{-5} moles of H^+ ions per litre. ________

W18.2 Calculate the pH of the solutions whose hydrogen ion concentrations are as follows:

(a) 10^{-5} mol/L

(b) 8.33×10^{-3} mol/L

(c) 2.25×10^{-1} mol/L

(d) 4.4×10^{-12} mol/L

(e) 3.9×10^{-9} mol/L

W18.3 Calculate the hydrogen ion concentration (in moles per litre) of the solutions whose pH values are as follows:

(a) 1.16

(b) 6.51

(c) 14

(d) 0.21

(e) 10.48

W18.4 Calculate the pH of the following solutions:

(a) 0.1 M H_2SO_4

(b) 0.2 M HCl

(c) 0.05 M HCl

(d) 0.007 g KOH in 500 cm^3 of solution

(e) 0.049 g H_2SO_4 in 200 cm^3 of solution [LCH]

W18.5 Calculate the pH of the following solutions:

(a) 0.33 M NaOH

(b) 0.001 M KOH

(c) 2 g NaOH in 250 cm^3 solution

(d) 5×10^{-5} mole NaOH per litre

(e) 0.008 g KOH in 200 cm^3 solution

W18.6 Find the pH of a 0.05 M solution of ammonia in water given that the dissociation constant (K_b) for ammonia in solution is 1.8×10^{-5}. [LCH]

W18.7 Calculate the pH of a 0.1 M solution of methanoic acid given that K_a is 1.8×10^{-4}.

W18.8 The value of K_w for water at 25 °C is 10^{-14} and at 57 °C the value of K_w is 9.0×10^{-14}.

Calculate the pH of water at these two temperatures. Do your results imply that water is acidic at the higher temperature? Explain your answer.

W18.9 Calculate the pH of a solution containing 8 g of CH_3COOH in 250 cm^3 of solution ($K_a = 1.8 \times 10^{-5}$).

W18.10 Calculate the pH of a solution of ethanoic acid containing 3 g per 250 cm^3 of solution ($K_a = 1.8 \times 10^{-5}$).

W18.11 What concentration of ethanoic acid is needed to give $[H^+] = 1.5 \times 10^{-4}$ mol/L ($K_a = 1.8 \times 10^{-5}$)? Calculate also the pH of the solution.

W18.12 Calculate the pH of a solution of boric acid containing 5.5 g H_3BO_3 per litre of solution.

Assume that all of the acidity is due to the first dissociation ($K_a = 5.8 \times 10^{-10}$).

W18.13 A certain weak acid HX is 3.5% dissociated in a 0.1 M solution. Find the value of the acid dissociation constant, K_a.

W18.14 The first dissociation constant of H_3PO_4 is represented as:

$H_3PO_4 + H_2O \rightleftharpoons H_2PO_4^- + H_3O^+$

Write (i) the equilibrium constant expression for this dissociation.

(ii) the equation for the second dissociation of H_3PO_4.

Given that the acidity of the H_3PO_4 solution is due mostly to its first dissociation and given also that $K_a = 8 \times 10^{-3}$ for this dissociation, calculate the pH of a 0.01 M aqueous solution of H_3PO_4.

[Assume that the concentration of the acid (0.01 M) remains unchanged as a result of the dissociation.]

W18.15 Explain the meaning of the term 'indicator'. Assuming that a certain indicator is a weak acid, explain how it works.

How do indicators assist in finding the end point of a titration?

W18.16 Name a suitable indicator for each of the following acid–base titrations:

(a) Nitric acid and ammonia solution

(b) Ethanoic acid and sodium hydroxide

(c) Hydrochloric acid and sodium hydroxide

(d) Hydrochloric acid and sodium carbonate

W18.17 A certain <u>indicator</u> is a <u>weak</u> acid ($K_a = 2 \times 10^{-5}$ at 25 °C). Its dissociation in water may be represented as follows:

$$HIn_{(aq)} \rightleftharpoons H^+_{(aq)} + In^-_{(aq)}$$

(i) Explain the underlined terms.

(ii) What is the approximate pH of a 0.01 M solution of the indicator at 25 °C?

(iii) The indicator changes colour in the pH range 3.7 – 5.7. State the types of acid-base titration for which it would be suitable and explain why it can be used in these titrations. [LCH]

W18.18 When a solution of ethanoic acid is being titrated against a solution of sodium hydroxide, the pH at the end point changes suddenly from about 6.8 to 9.7. Which one of the following indicators, which change colour in the pH ranges shown, would be most suitable for this titration? Explain your reasoning. [LCH]

Indicator	pH range
Methyl Orange	3.0 – 4.5
Methyl Red	4.2 – 6.4
Bromothymol Blue	6.0 – 7.4
Phenolphthalein	8.2 – 9.8

W18.19 Explain the terms (i) monobasic (monoprotic) acid, (ii) conjugate acid–base pair in the Brønsted–Lowry theory, (iii) acid–base indicator.

Write an equation for the reaction that takes place between a strong monobasic acid (HA) and water. Write also an equation for the reaction that takes place when a weak monobasic acid (HX) accepts a proton from the strong monobasic acid (HA). Identify the conjugate pairs in the reaction between the two acids. [LCH]

W18.20 What concentration of a strong acid (HA) will give an aqueous solution having a pH of 2.7?

A 0.5 M aqueous solution of a weak acid (HX) also has a pH of 2.7. Calculate the value of its acid dissociation constant (K_a).

The weak monobasic acid (HX) can be used as an acid–base indicator with a range of 4 – 6. The molecules (HX) are red and the ions (X^-) are yellow. State what you understand by the range of an indicator and explain briefly how HX acts as an acid–base indicator. For which general classes of acid–base titrations would HX be suitable as an indicator? [LCH]

19 Environmental Chemistry – Water

W19.1 (a) The ions that cause hardness in water are ________________ or ________________

(b) Why is it difficult to form a lather when soap reacts with hard water? ________________

____

(c) Mention, giving the equation, one method by which permanent hardness is removed from water. [LCH]

____

(d) What is the difference, if any, between water that has been distilled and water that has been passed through an efficient deionising resin? Explain the function of the resin. [LCH]

____

____

(e) Bath salts are coloured, perfumed crystals of ________________________

(f) Distinguish between a cation-exchange resin and an anion-exchange resin.

____

____

(g) How does a water deioniser (i) remove positive ions, (ii) remove negative ions from water? [LCH]

(i) ____

(ii) ____

W19.2 A student titrated a 50 cm^3 sample of hard water containing some suitable buffer solution and a suitable indicator against 0.01 M edta solution. It was found that 18 cm^3 of the edta solution were required.

(a) Name a suitable indicator for this titration.

(b) What do the letters *edta* stand for?

(c) What is the purpose of the buffer solution?

(d) What colour change is observed at the end point?

(e) Calculate the hardness of the water in ppm of $CaCO_3$.

W19.3 An experiment was carried out to measure the amount of temporary hardness and permanent hardness in a sample of water. A 50 cm^3 sample of tap water was placed in a conical flask and some buffer solution and Solochrome Black indicator added. On titration with 0.01 M edta solution, the average titration figure was found to be 11.5 cm^3. The water was then boiled for a few minutes and allowed to cool to room temperature. The titration was repeated and the average titration figure was found to be 6.5 cm^3.

(a) What was the purpose of boiling the water?

(b) Why is it necessary to allow the boiled water to cool?

(c) Calculate (i) the total hardness, (ii) the permanent hardness and (iii) the temporary hardness of the sample of water.

(Hint: The value for temporary hardness is calculated by subtracting the value for permanent hardness from the value for total hardness.)

W19.4 A sample of hard water from a dolomite ($MgCO_3.CaCO_3$) district was analysed as follows:

To 50 cm^3 of the sample, 1 cm^3 of a buffer solution of pH = 10 and 5 drops of a solution of Eriochrome Black T (Solochrome Black) indicator were added. The solution required 15.0 cm^3 of a 0.01 M solution of edta for complete complexing of the metal ions. Using H_2Y^{2-} to represent the edta anion, the reaction may be represented as:

$$H_2Y^{2-} + M^{2+} \longrightarrow YM^{2-} + 2H^+$$

(i) State the type of hardness involved and how it could be removed.

(ii) Explain, using equations where necessary, how either Mg^{2+} or Ca^{2+} ions could get into solution from the insoluble dolomite in a quantity sufficient to cause hardness.

(iii) What colour change would indicate the end point in the above titration?

(iv) Calculate the hardness of the water expressed as parts per million (ppm) of calcium carbonate. [LCH]

W19.5 In an experiment to measure the hardness of water, a 50 cm^3 sample of the water was placed in a conical flask with Eriochrome black T indicator and a small quantity of buffer solution. The sample was titrated against 0.01 M edta and an average titration figure of 9.5 cm^3 was obtained.

(i) Name the instrument used to place the sample of water in the conical flask.

(ii) Describe the appearance of (a) the buffer solution and (b) the indicator.

(iii) What precautions are normally taken when storing edta solution?

(iv) Calculate the hardness of the sample of water in (a) grams of Ca^{2+} ions per litre and (b) ppm $CaCO_3$.

W19.6 A student filtered 750 cm^3 of river water and found that the mass of the filter paper after drying had increased by 1.47 g. A volume of 200 cm^3 of the filtered water was then evaporated to dryness in a beaker and it was found that the mass of the beaker had increased by 0.73 g.

Calculate the amount of suspended solids and the amount of dissolved solids in the water expressed as parts per million (ppm).

W19.7 A water sample was analysed for dissolved oxygen content by the Winkler method. The main reactions may be represented:

$$4Mn(OH)_2 + O_2 \longrightarrow 2Mn_2O_3 + 4H_2O$$

$$Mn_2O_3 + 2I^- + 6H^+ \longrightarrow 2Mn^{2+} + I_2 + 3H_2O$$

(i) What initial colour change would you expect in the reaction flask and what deduction would you make if a pure white flocculant precipitate was obtained? Explain your answers.

(ii) Why are the manganese(II) sulfate solution and Winkler's reagent pipetted into the reagent bottle below the surface of the liquid?

(iii) Why would Winkler's method be unsuitable for water which had been chlorinated? [LCH]

W19.8 A sample of polluted water was analysed in order to determine the amount of dissolved oxygen in the water using the Winkler method. The main reactions may be represented as follows:

$$4Mn(OH)_2 + O_2 \longrightarrow 2Mn_2O_3 + 4H_2O$$

$$Mn_2O_3 + 2I^- + 6H^+ \longrightarrow 2Mn^{2+} + I_2 + 3H_2O$$

$$2S_2O_3^{2-} + I_2 \longrightarrow S_4O_6^{2-} + 2I^-$$

A 200 cm^3 sample of the water was diluted to 2 litres with pure, well-oxygenated water. 200 cm^3 of this diluted solution were analysed by the Winkler method and 22.7 cm^3 of 0.01 M sodium thiosulfate were required.

A second 200 cm^3 sample was stored in the dark at 20 °C for five days and then analysed for dissolved oxygen. The liberated iodine required 4.8 cm^3 of 0.01 M sodium thiosulfate.

Calculate the amount of dissolved oxygen in each sample of water. Express your answers in p.p.m. Hence find the B.O.D. of the water.

W19.9 Outline briefly how atomic absorption spectrometry may be used to detect the presence of certain elements in water.

The concentration of nitrates and phosphates may be determined in water using a technique called colorimetry. Give a brief account of the principle of this method.

20 Electrochemistry I

W20.1 (a) Electrolysis is defined as ____

____

(b) In a cell or battery a ____________________ reaction is used to produce an electric current.

(c) In the electrolysis of acidified water, what gas is formed at the negative electrode? __________

(d) When sodium sulfate solution to which a few drops of universal indicator have been added is electrolysed, a ____________________ colour is observed at the positive electrode.

(e) Explain the meaning of the term *electroplating*. ____________________

____

(f) An apparatus to plate a spoon with silver is shown in Fig. W20.1. Re-draw the diagram and show the changes you would have to make if you wanted to plate the spoon with gold instead of silver.

(g) Why are gold-plated objects often chosen in preference to objects made of pure gold?

____

(h) Give two uses of electroplating. ____________________

____

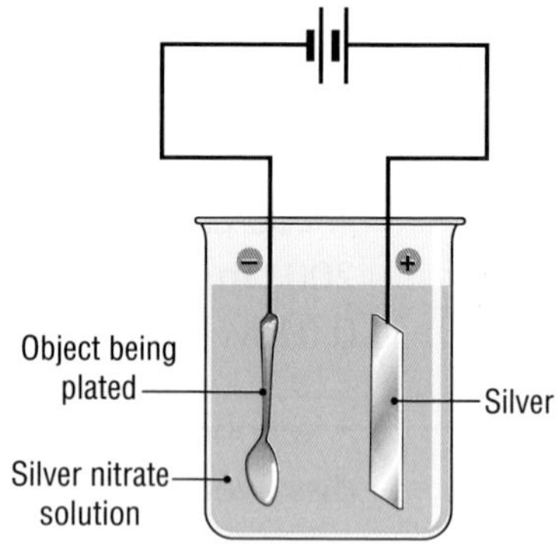

Object being plated

Silver nitrate solution

Silver

Fig W20.1

(i) Copper sulfate is normally used as the electrolyte for electroplating copper on to objects. Why is copper(II) chloride not normally used? ____________________

(j) You are given some crystals of sodium chloride and the apparatus to carry out an electrolysis experiment. Describe two ways that the sodium chloride could be prepared for the electrolysis experiment.

____

(k) Give an example of an active electrode and name the electrolysis reaction in which it is being used. ____________________

____

(l) Some crystals of lead(II) bromide are placed in a crucible as shown in Fig. W20.2. The bulb does not light when the electrodes are dipped into the solid lead bromide. However, the bulb does light when the lead bromide is melted. Explain the reason for this.

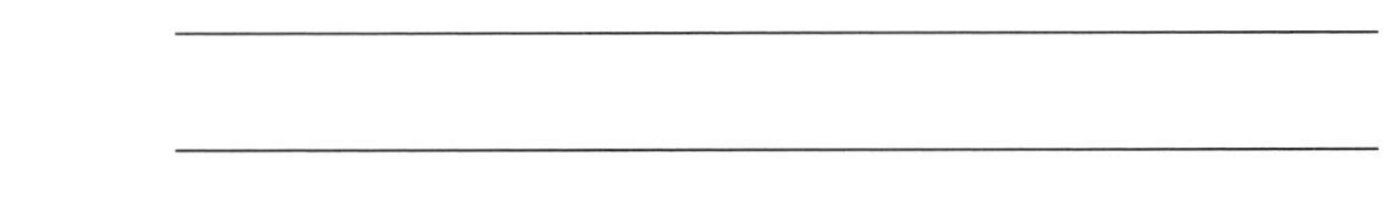

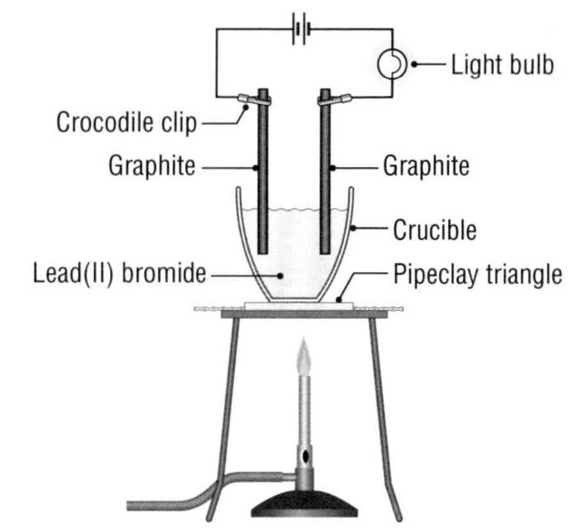

Fig W20.2

W20.2 Some water to which a suitable acid has been added is electrolysed using inert electrodes.

(a) Draw a diagram of the apparatus and circuit used to electrolyse the water.

(b) Name the acid that is commonly used to acidify the water used in this experiment.

(c) Name the gas given off at the positive electrode and the gas given off at the negative electrode.

(d) Name one test in each case to identify the gases named in (c).

(e) Write an equation to describe the reaction happening at each electrode.

W20.3 'Impure copper may be purified by electrolysis'.

(a) Draw a diagram of the apparatus and circuit that could be used to purify a bar of impure copper.

(b) A student was asked to find the mass of each electrode before and after electrolysis had taken place for a suitable time. What would she expect to find?

(c) Write an equation to describe the reaction that takes place at each electrode.

(d) The copper formed after electrolysis has a very high degree of purity. Give one use for this type of copper.

W20.4 (a) Draw a labelled diagram of a galvanic cell containing copper and zinc.

(b) Indicate the approximate voltage which this cell would be expected to produce.

(c) Write down an ionic equation to describe the reaction that takes place at each electrode.

W20.5 A length of magnesium ribbon is placed in a solution containing Cu^{2+} ions.

(a) Describe what you would expect to observe.

(b) Write an ionic equation to describe what is taking place.

(c) Explain your observation in terms of the relative positions of these metals in the electrochemical series.

(d) Draw a diagram of a cell which could be made from magnesium and copper. On your diagram indicate the direction in which electrons would flow.

21 Fuels and Heats of Reaction

W21.1 Draw the full structural formulas and give the systematic names of each of the following compounds:

(a) $CH_3CH(CH_3)CH_2CH_3$

(b) $CH_3C(CH_3)_2CH_2CH(CH_3)CH_3$

(c) $CH_3CH_2CH(C_2H_5)CH(CH_3)CH_3$

(d) $CH_3CH(CH_3)C(CH_3)_2CH_2CH_3$

(e) $CH_3CH(CH_3)CH_2CH_2CH_2CH(CH_3)CH_2CH_3$

W21.2 Draw the structural formula of each of the following compounds:

(a) 2-methylpropane

(b) 2,6-dimethyloctane

(c) 2,2,4-trimethylheptane

(d) 3-methylhexane

(e) 2,4-dimethylpentane

How are compounds (d) and (e) related?

W21.3 Draw the full structural formulas and give the systematic names of each of the following compounds:

(a) $CH_3CH_2CH_2CH_2CH_2CH{=}CH_2$

(b) $CH_3CH_2CH{=}CHCH_2CH_2CH_3$

(c) $CH_3C(CH_3){=}CH_2$

(d) $CH_3CH_2CH{=}C(CH_3)CH_3$

(e) $CH_3CH_2C(C_2H_5){=}CH_2$

W21.4 Draw the structural formula of each of the following compounds:

(a) propene

(b) hept-3-ene

(c) 2-methylpent-2-ene

(c) 2,4-dimethylhex-3-ene

(d) 2-methylbut-1-ene

W21.5 A student prepared a sample of ethyne (acetylene) using the apparatus shown in Fig. W21.1.

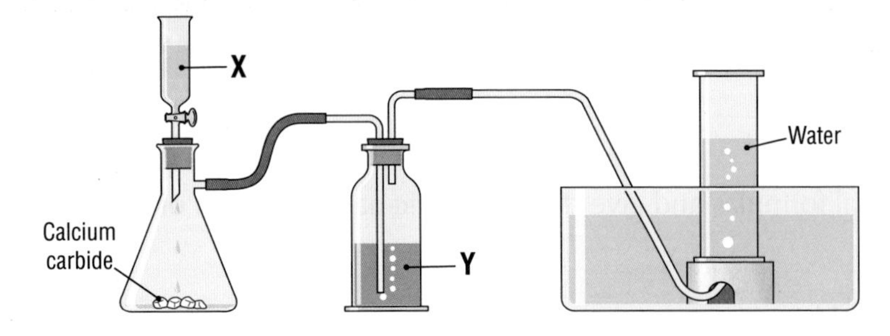

Fig W21.1

Answer the following questions in relation to ethyne.

(i) Describe the physical appearance of calcium carbide.

(ii) Name the substance X. Write a balanced equation for the reaction between substance X and calcium carbide.

(iii) Describe what the student observes in the flask as X is dropped on to the calcium carbide.

(iv) A small quantity of acidified potassium manganate(VII) is added to a gas jar of ethyne and the jar shaken for a short time. State what is observed and what deduction may be made.

(v) Ethyne prepared using the above method normally contains impurities which can be removed by bubbling the gas through solution Y. Name Y and mention any one of the impurities removed. Name one substance in the calcium carbide which could give rise to this impurity. [LCH]

W21.6 A group of students prepared ethene using the apparatus shown in Fig. W21.2.

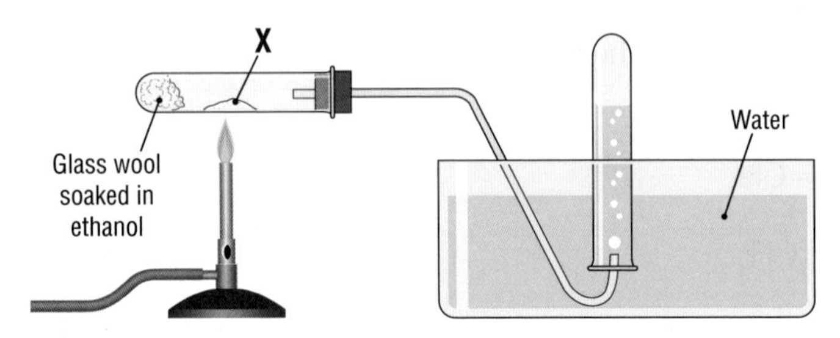

Fig W21.2

The equation for the reaction is

$$C_2H_5OH \longrightarrow C_2H_4 + H_2O$$

(i) Identify X. What term is used to describe its function in the preparation of ethene?

(ii) Describe two tests to show that ethene is an unsaturated compound. [LCH]

W21.7 A group of students prepared and collected ethyne using the apparatus shown in Fig. W21.3. They tested the product for unsaturation (i) using bromine water, (ii) using acidified potassium manganate(VII) solution.

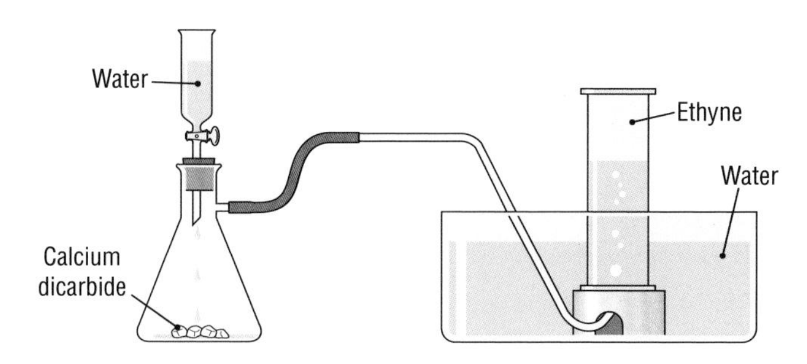

Fig W21.3

(i) Write a balanced equation for the reaction between calcium dicarbide and water.

(ii) What change was observed in the appearance of the calcium dicarbide when the drops of water fell on it? What caused this change in appearance?

(iii) The ethyne obtained by the students was impure. Name one possible impurity other than air or water vapour. What substance present in the calcium dicarbide could have given rise to this impurity? Suggest a method of removing impurities from the ethyne.

(iv) What was observed when the ethyne was tested with the bromine water?

(v) What was observed when the ethyne was tested with the acidified potassium manganate(VII) solution? [LCH]

W21.8 (a) Why is crude oil called a fossil fuel?

(b) What is a fractionating column?

(c) Give one use of (i) naphtha and (ii) bitumen.

(d) What causes 'knocking' in engines?

(e) Define the term *octane number*.

(f) On the scale of octane values, 2,2,4-trimethylpentane is assigned a value of 100. Name the compound that is assigned a value of 0.

(g) How does branching affect the octane number of a hydrocarbon?

(h) Give the name or formula of the lead additive that used to be added to petrol to reduce knocking.

(i) Explain why isomerisation is carried out in oil refineries. Give one example of an isomerisation reaction.

(j) Give two benefits of the cracking of hydrocarbons in the oil refining process. [LCH]

(k) What do the letters MTBE represent?

W21.9 (i) The following table shows a number of alkanes and their octane numbers.

Name of Alkane	Octane Number
Butane	94
Hexane	25
Cyclohexane	83
Pentane	62
3-methylhexane	65
2-methylpentane	73
3-methylpentane	75
2,3-dimethylpentane	91
2-methylbutane	93

(a) Draw the structural formula of each of the above compounds.

(b) Write down the molecular formula of each compound.

(c) Indicate which compounds are isomers of each other.

(d) Use the above data to comment on the factors that affect the octane number of an alkane.

(ii) What do you understand by the term *catalytic cracking?* Why is it carried out in an oil refinery?

An alkane of molecular formula $C_{14}H_{30}$ gave on cracking a branched-chain saturated molecule containing seven carbon atoms, a molecule containing four carbon atoms and one containing three carbon atoms. Show clearly one possible structure in each case for the three molecules formed. [LCH]

W21.10 Oil refining separates crude oil into a number of different fractions. Liquid paraffin is obtained from one of these fractions.

In the laboratory experiment shown in Fig. W21.4, glass wool soaked in liquid paraffin is placed in the test-tube at A and the catalyst consists of steel wool or pieces of porcelain. The catalyst is heated, gently at first and then strongly and, after allowing time for air to escape, several test-tubes of a colourless gas (or mixture of gases) are collected. The gas (or mixture) is found to be flammable and to decolorise bromine water.

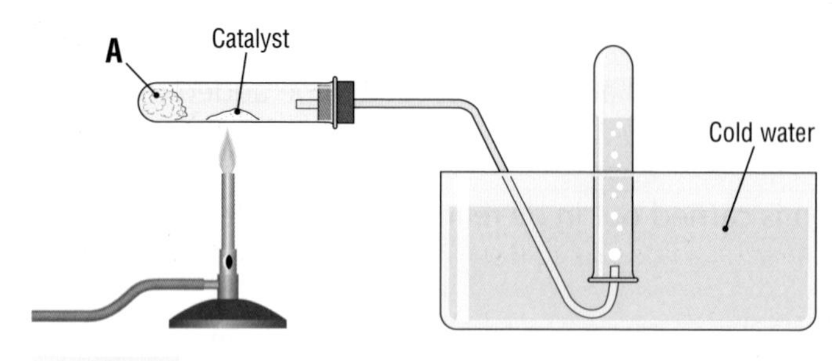

Fig W21.4

(i) What term is used to describe the process illustrated in this experiment? Comment on the industrial importance of this process.

(ii) What is the function of the glass wool? In setting up the apparatus, why is it better to put the liquid paraffin into the test-tube *before* the glass wool?

(iii) When the heat is removed at the end of the experiment, a certain precaution is taken. What is this precaution and why is it necessary?

(iv) Mention another possible hazard in this experiment, stating its cause and the safety precautions that should be taken.

(v) Why would the first test-tube of gas collected contain less unsaturated materials than those test-tubes of gas collected at a later stage?

(vi) Give the name and formula of a gas that could be responsible for the decolorising of the bromine solution. Write an equation for the reaction of this gas with bromine and name the product.

(vii) If one of the straight-chain hydrocarbons in liquid paraffin, of molecular formula $C_{12}H_{26}$, were subjected to the process described in the experiment, suggest three possible products of the reaction giving the name and structural formula in each case. [LCH]

W21.11 The heat of neutralisation of hydrocyanic acid ($HCN_{(aq)}$) is –12 kJ mol^{-1} whereas the heats of neutralisation of hydrochloric, nitric and sulfuric acids are all around –57 kJ mol^{-1}. Explain (i) why the value of the heat of neutralisation is about the same for the three common laboratory acids, (ii) why much less heat is evolved in the neutralisation of hydrocyanic acid.

Describe how the heat of neutralisation of hydrochloric acid by sodium hydroxide may be measured in the laboratory. [LCH]

W21.12 A student carried out an experiment to measure the heat of neutralisation of hydrochloric acid by sodium hydroxide in a container made of plastic of negligible specific heat capacity. He used 50 cm^3 of 1.0 M hydrochloric acid and 50 cm^3 of 1.0 M sodium hydroxide. The initial temperature of the solutions was 14.3 °C and the final temperature of the solution, after mixing, was 21.1 °C.

Given that the specific heat capacity of the solution is 4060 J kg^{-1} K^{-1}, calculate the heat of neutralisation. (Assume that the density of the solution is 1 g cm^{-3}.)

W21.13 When 50 cm^3 of 2.0 M HNO_3 solution were added to 50 cm^3 of 2.0 M KOH solution in a container made of plastic of negligible specific heat capacity, the temperature of the final solution rose by 13 °C. Assuming that the specific heat capacity of the solution is 4200 J kg^{-1} K^{-1} and that the density of the solution is 1 g cm^{-3}, calculate the heat of neutralisation.

What precautions should be taken when carrying out the experiment to ensure an accurate result?

W21.14 Calculate the heat of reaction of the following reaction:

$CH_{4(g)} + 4Cl_{2(g)} \longrightarrow CCl_{4(l)} + 4HCl_{(g)}$ $\Delta H = ?$

given the following heats of formation:

$C_{(s)} + 2H_{2(g)} \longrightarrow CH_{4(g)}$ $\Delta H = -74.9 \text{ kJ mol}^{-1}$

$C_{(s)} + 2Cl_{2(g)} \longrightarrow CCl_{4(l)}$ $\Delta H = -139 \text{ kJ mol}^{-1}$

$\frac{1}{2}H_{2(g)} + \frac{1}{2}Cl_{2(g)} \longrightarrow HCl_{(g)}$ $\Delta H = -92.3 \text{ kJ mol}^{-1}$

W21.15 Methanol burns in oxygen according to the equation:

$CH_3OH_{(l)} + 1\frac{1}{2}O_{2(g)} \longrightarrow CO_{2(g)} + 2H_2O_{(l)}$

Use the following heat of formation data to calculate the heat of combustion of methanol.

$C_{(s)} + O_{2(g)} \longrightarrow CO_{2(g)}$ $\Delta H = -394 \text{ kJ mol}^{-1}$

$H_{2(g)} + \frac{1}{2}O_{2(g)} \longrightarrow H_2O_{(l)}$ $\Delta H = -286 \text{ kJ mol}^{-1}$

$C_{(s)} + 2H_{2(g)} + \frac{1}{2}O_{2(g)} \longrightarrow CH_3OH_{(l)}$ $\Delta H = -250 \text{ kJ mol}^{-1}$ [LCO]

W21.16 Calculate the heat of reaction of the following reaction:

$2CH_{4(g)} + O_{2(g)} \longrightarrow 2CH_3OH_{(g)}$ $\Delta H = ?$

given the following experimental data:

$CH_{4(g)} + H_2O_{(g)} \longrightarrow CO_{(g)} + 3H_{2(g)}$ $\Delta H = +206 \text{ kJ mol}^{-1}$

$2H_{2(g)} + CO_{(g)} \longrightarrow CH_3OH_{(l)}$ $\Delta H = -128 \text{ kJ mol}^{-1}$

$2H_{2(g)} + O_{2(g)} \longrightarrow 2H_2O_{(g)}$ $\Delta H = -434 \text{ kJ mol}^{-1}$

W21.17 Calculate the heat of formation of methane given the following experimental data:

$CH_{4(g)} + 2O_{2(g)} \longrightarrow CO_{2(g)} + 2H_2O_{(g)}$ $\Delta H = -890.4 \text{ kJ mol}^{-1}$

$H_{2(g)} + \frac{1}{2}O_{2(g)} \longrightarrow H_2O_{(l)}$ $\Delta H = -285.8 \text{ kJ mol}^{-1}$

$C_{(s)} + O_{2(g)} \longrightarrow CO_{2(g)}$ $\Delta H = -393.5 \text{ kJ mol}^{-1}$

W21.18 Propane is a gas used as a camping fuel. Its heat of formation may be represented as follows:

$3C_{(s)} + 4H_{2(g)} \longrightarrow C_3H_{8(g)}$ $\Delta H = ?$

Calculate the heat of formation of propane from the following data:

$C_3H_{8(g)} + 5O_{2(g)} \longrightarrow 3CO_{2(g)} + 4H_2O_{(l)}$ $\Delta H = -2220 \text{ kJ mol}^{-1}$

$C_{(s)} + O_{2(g)} \longrightarrow CO_{2(g)}$ $\Delta H = -394 \text{ kJ mol}^{-1}$

$H_{2(g)} + \frac{1}{2}O_{2(g)} \longrightarrow H_2O_{(l)}$ $\Delta H = -286 \text{ kJ mol}^{-1}$

W21.19 Calculate the heat of formation of ethyne (acetylene) from the following experimental data:

$C_2H_{2(g)} + 2\frac{1}{2}\,O_{2(g)} \longrightarrow 2CO_{2(g)} + H_2O_{(l)}$ $\Delta H = -1299$ kJ mol^{-1}

$C_{(s)} + O_{2(g)} \longrightarrow CO_{2(g)}$ $\Delta H = -394$ kJ mol^{-1}

$H_{2(g)} + \frac{1}{2}O_{2(g)} \longrightarrow H_2O_{(l)}$ $\Delta H = -286$ kJ mol^{-1} [LCO]

W21.20 Calculate the heat of formation of ammonia from the following experimental data:

$4NH_{3(g)} + 3O_{2(g)} \longrightarrow 2N_{2(g)} + 6H_2O_{(g)}$ $\Delta H = -1268$ kJ mol^{-1}

$H_{2(g)} + \frac{1}{2}O_{2(g)} \longrightarrow H_2O_{(g)}$ $\Delta H = -285.8$ kJ mol^{-1}

W21.21 Calculate the heat of formation of calcium carbonate, $CaCO_{3,}$ given the following data:

$2Ca_{(s)} + O_{2(g)} + 2CO_{2(g)} \longrightarrow 2CaCO_{3(s)}$ $\Delta H = -640$ kJ mol^{-1}

$C_{(s)} + O_{2(g)} \longrightarrow CO_{2(g)}$ $\Delta H = -393$ kJ mol^{-1}

W21.22 Calculate the heat of reaction for:

$C_2H_{2(g)} + HCN_{(g)} \longrightarrow C_3H_3N_{(g)}$

given that the heats of formation of $C_2H_{2(g)}$, $HCN_{(g)}$ and $C_3H_3N_{(g)}$ are 233 kJ mol^{-1}, 114.5 kJ mol^{-1} and 194.5 kJ mol^{-1} respectively. [LCH]

W21.23 The heats of formation of water, $H_2O_{(l)}$, and sulfur dioxide, $SO_{2(g)}$, are -286 kJ mol^{-1} and -297 kJ mol^{-1} respectively. Use these values, together with the values of the heats of reaction given below, to calculate the heat of formation of sulfuric acid, $H_2SO_{4(l)}$.

$2SO_{2(g)} + O_{2(g)} \longrightarrow 2SO_{3(g)}$ $\Delta H = -196$ kJ mol^{-1}

$SO_{3(g)} + H_2O_{(l)} \longrightarrow H_2SO_{4(l)}$ $\Delta H = -133$ kJ mol^{-1} [LCH]

22 Some Families of Organic Compounds

W22.1 Chloroform is no longer used as an anaesthetic in hospitals. A less toxic and less flammable compound commonly called halothane, $F_3CCHClBr$, is now used. (The systematic name for halothane is 2-bromo-2-chloro-1,1,1-trifluoroethane.) Draw the structural formula of a molecule of this compound.

W22.2 Name the following compounds:

(a) CCl_4 ____________________

(b) CH_3CHCl_2 ____________________

(c) CH_2ClCH_2Cl ____________________

(d) $CH_3CH_2CHClCH_3$ ____________________

(e) $CH_2ClCH_2CH_2CH_2Cl$ ____________________

W22.3 Draw the structural formulas of the following compounds:

(a) Chloromethane

(b) 1,1-dichloroethane

(c) 1-chloro-2-methylpropane

(d) 2-chloropropane

(e) 1,2-dichlorobutane

W22.4 Name the alcohol found in alcoholic drinks. Give two other uses for this alcohol.

____

____

Write down the names and structural formulas of the isomers of C_4H_9OH.

Write a brief note on fermentation.

Wine is produced by fermentation alone but whiskey is produced by distilling fermented liquids. Why is distillation necessary to produce whiskey?

Explain why the solubility of alcohols in water decreases with chain length.

Describe what you would observe when a quantity of:

(a) methanol is added to an equal quantity of (i) water and (ii) cyclohexane.

(b) butan-1-ol is added to an equal quantity of (i) water and (ii) cyclohexane.

W22.5 (a) What is the carbonyl group?

(b) Name an aldehyde that is a gas at room temperature.

(c) By what name was ethanal formerly known?

(d) What is the bond angle in a molecule of methanal?

(e) Why is hydrogen bonding not possible between molecules of ethanal?

(f) The boiling points of aldehydes and ketones are not as high as those of the corresponding alcohols. What is the reason for this?

(g) What is formalin?

(h) Describe the smell of benzaldehyde.

(i) A student looked up a chemistry data book and found the boiling points of butane, butanal and butan-1-ol. The student then wrote down the numbers in the wrong order. Which of the following boiling points corresponds to each substance: 117 °C, –0.5 °C, 76 °C? Explain your reasoning.

(j) What is the common name for propanone? Give one common use for this substance.

(k) Why does the compound ethanone not exist?

(l) Why is the compound $CH_3COCH_2CH_3$ called butanone and not butan-2-one?

W22.6 (a) Ethanoic acid has a much higher boiling point than ethanol. What is the reason for this?

(b) Would you expect ethanoic acid to be soluble in water? Explain your reasoning.

(c) Give one use for cellulose acetate.

(d) Name the compound $CH_3COOCH_2CH_3$. Describe briefly how you would make a sample of this ester on a test-tube scale in the laboratory.

(e) Many esters are volatile liquids. What is the reason for their volatility? How would you describe their smell? Give two uses for esters.

W22.7 Explain the meaning of the term 'aromatic compound'.

What evidence led chemists to believe that benzene does not consist of alternating double and single bonds.

With the aid of suitable diagrams, describe the bonding in a molecule of benzene.

Why is benzene no longer used as an organic solvent?

Draw the structural formula of methylbenzene and give two uses of this compound.

Name five aromatic compounds that are useful to us in our everyday lives.

23 Types of Reactions in Organic Chemistry

W23.1 (a) Why do alkanes only undergo substitution reactions?

____

(b) Write down the equation of the reaction between methane and chlorine.

____

(c) Using a suitable example, explain the term *homolytic fission*.

____

____

(d) What is a photochemical reaction? ______________________________

____

(e) The chlorination of methane is termed a *free radical* substitution reaction. Explain the term in italics. ______________________________

____

(f) When ethane reacts with chlorine to form chloroethane, it is found that adding a certain lead compound increases the rate of the reaction. Give the name or formula of this lead compound.

____

(g) What is observed when a test-tube containing some cyclohexane and bromine is held near a source of ultraviolet light for a few minutes? Explain this observation.

____

____

____

W23.2 'The formation of an ester may be considered either as a condensation reaction or a substitution reaction'. Using an appropriate example, explain this statement.

What is meant by the term *saponification*?

With reference to the laboratory preparation of soap, answer the following questions:

(a) Write down an equation to represent the reaction that is taking place.

(b) Why is it necessary to carry out a distillation reaction as part of the preparation of soap?

(c) Why is it necessary to *quickly* transfer the mixture to brine?

(d) What experimental technique was used to separate the soap from the brine?

(e) Write down an equation to indicate what happens when soap reacts with hard water.

(f) Explain briefly why soap has a cleansing action on the skin.

W23.3 Explain the meaning of the terms (i) heterolytic fission and (ii) carbonium ion.

By means of balanced chemical equations, show the reactions of ethene (i) with bromine and (ii) with hydrogen chloride. Write down the name of each product and give one use for each of them.

Write a short note on the differences between margarine and butter.

The reaction between ethene and hydrogen chloride may be described as an *ionic addition* reaction. Explain the meaning of this term.

Outline the mechanism of the reaction between ethene and hydrogen chloride.

W23.4 (a) What is meant by the term *polymer*? Polypropene is an example of a polymer that is commonly used in our everyday lives. State two uses of this polymer and draw the structural formula of (i) the monomer and (ii) the repeating unit of the polymer.

(b) Explain the meaning of the term *elimination reaction*. Write the equation of a reaction that may be described as an elimination reaction. List the bonds broken and the bonds formed in the example you have chosen.

Why do elimination reactions result in the formation of a double bond in one of the products of the reaction?

W23.5 (a) How and under what conditions are aldehydes and ketones reduced to alcohols?

(b) Ethanol is a toxic substance in the body and is converted to another substance in the liver. Name this other substance.

(c) What is the colour of Fehling's A solution? What compound is dissolved in water to make up this solution?

(d) What is the colour of Fehling's B solution? Name the two chemicals dissolved in water to make up this solution.

(e) Given reagent bottles of Fehling's A solution and Fehling's B solution, describe how you would make up Fehling's reagent for use in the school laboratory.

(f) A student observed a brick-red precipitate being formed when a sample of an aldehyde was added to Fehling's reagent and the solution was warmed. Give the name and formula of this red precipitate.

W23.6 (a) A small piece of sodium is added to a sample of ethanol in a test-tube. Describe what is observed and write a balanced equation for the reaction.

(b) The reaction of sodium with ethanol is less vigorous than the reaction of sodium with water. What may be concluded about the acidity of ethanol from this observation?

(c) What name is given to the ion formed when a carboxylic acid loses a proton? Write a brief note on the structure of this ion and account for its stability.

(d) Name the gas given off when ethanoic acid is added to sodium carbonate. How would you test for the presence of this gas?

(e) What gas is evolved when ethanoic acid is added to magnesium metal? How would you identify this gas?

W23.7 (i) Give the names and structural formulas of the starting material, S, and the product, P, of the following reaction scheme:

$$S \xrightarrow{Al_2O_3} CH_2{=}CH_2 \xrightarrow{Br_2} P$$

(ii) Name the reagent X required to bring about the first conversion indicated below and give the products A, B and C of the second set of reactions:

$$CH_3CHO \xrightarrow{X} CH_3COOH \xrightarrow{Mg} A$$

$$\xrightarrow{NaOH} B$$

$$\xrightarrow{Na_2CO_3} C$$

(iii) Identify the reagent X and name the type of reaction Y indicated in the following reaction scheme:

$$CH_3CH_2OH \xrightarrow{X} CH_2{=}CH_2 \xrightarrow{Y} -(-CH_2CH_2-)_n-$$

Give the name of each of the above compounds.

W23.8 A student prepared a sample of benzoic acid from phenylmethanol (benzyl alcohol) using potassium permanganate as an oxidising agent. The student was instructed by the teacher to recrystallise the benzoic acid that resulted from the preparation.

(a) Describe the appearance of the crystals prepared by the above method.

(b) What is meant by the term recrystallisation?

(c) Why is it possible to recrystallise benzoic acid using water as a solvent?

(d) In the first stage of the recrystallisation experiment, the student was instructed to dissolve the crystals in the **minimum** of hot water. Why is it important to use the minimum of hot water?

(e) In the second stage of the experiment, the solution was filtered through a heated funnel. Why is this stage necessary? What is the purpose of heating the funnel?

(f) The hot filtration was carried out using a fluted filter paper. What is the advantage of fluting the filter paper?

(g) Why is it important that the hot filtration be carried out quickly?

(h) Explain the meaning of the term *filtrate*.

(i) In the third stage of the experiment, the benzoic acid solution was placed in ice. However, the student had difficulty in obtaining crystals. What two actions would help to start the crystallisation process?

(j) In the fourth stage of the experiment, the student carried out a cold filtration using the apparatus shown in Fig. W23.1 but forgot to label the diagram. Fill in the name of each item on the diagram.

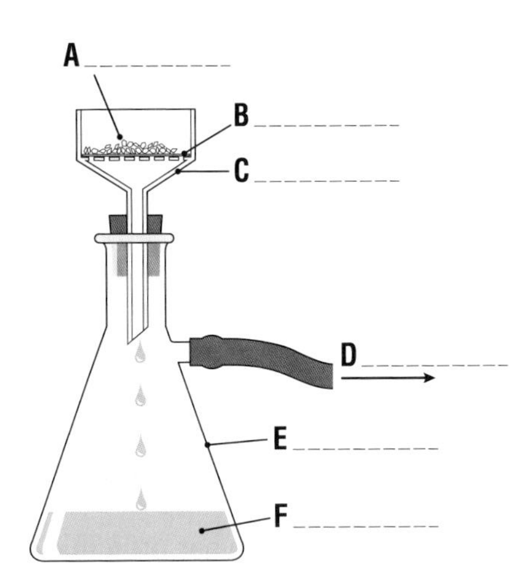

Fig W23.1

(k) State one advantage of vacuum filtration over gravity filtration.

(l) When drying the crystals, one group of students allowed them to air dry in the school laboratory and another group of students placed them in a desiccator. Give one advantage of the use of the desiccator compared to air drying.

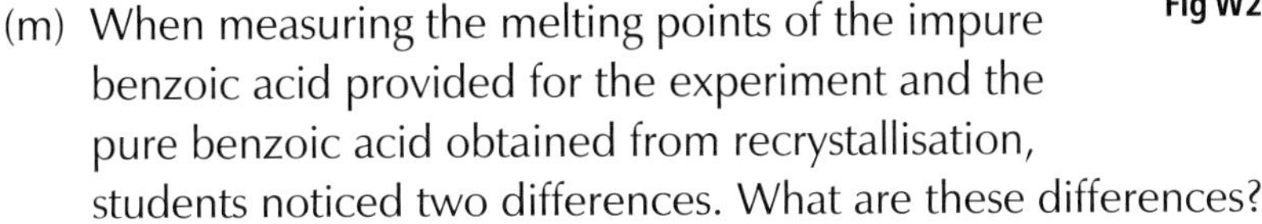

(m) When measuring the melting points of the impure benzoic acid provided for the experiment and the pure benzoic acid obtained from recrystallisation, students noticed two differences. What are these differences?

W23.9 Organic solids are frequently purified by recrystallisation.

An impure sample of benzoic acid contained small quantities of the two solids: salt (**NaCl**, white and soluble) and charcoal (**C**, black and insoluble).

The diagrams illustrate the five main stages in the recrystallisation of the impure benzoic acid from water.

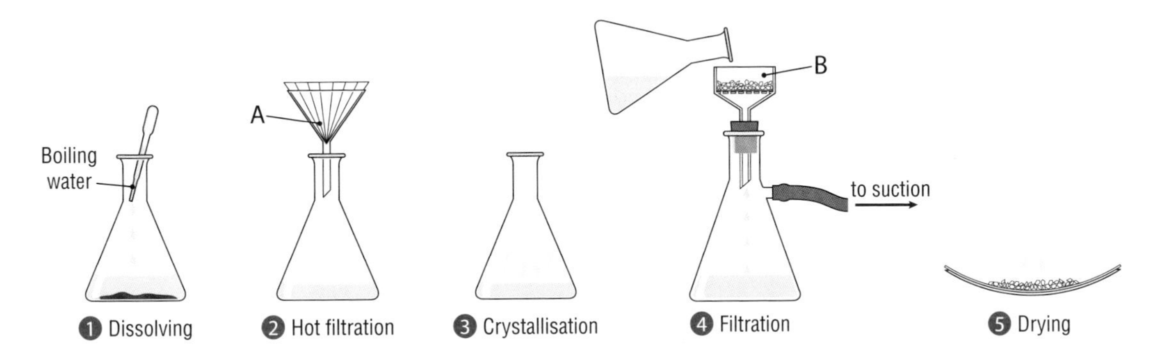

Fig W23.2

(a) What precaution should have been taken at Stage 1 to ensure the maximum yield of pure benzoic acid crystals at Stage 5?

(b) What solid was collected (i) at **A**, (ii) at **B**?

(c) Explain what should have been done at Stage 3 to ensure the maximum yield at Stage 5.

(d) Comparing the solubilities of benzoic acid and salt (**NaCl**) in hot and in cold water, explain how benzoic acid is separated from the salt in this procedure.

(e) Describe how the benzoic acid was dried at Stage 5.

(f) Describe with the aid of a labelled diagram how the melting points of the impure benzoic acid and of the recrystallised, dried benzoic acid could be measured.

How would you expect the melting point values of the two samples to differ?

(g) Give **one** common use of benzoic acid or of its salts. [LCH]

W23.10 (a) With regard to chromatography, explain the terms *mobile phase* and *stationary phase*.

(b) On what general principle are all forms of chromatography based?

(c) Explain, with the aid of a diagram, the principle of operation of the instrument used for gas chromatography. Give one use of gas chromatography.

(d) What do the letter HPLC stand for? State the principle on which HPLC is based and outline the processes involved in using a HPLC instrument.

(e) On what principle is ultraviolet spectrometry based? Give one use for this analytical technique.

24 Stoichiometry II

W24.1 One of the ores of iron is iron pyrites, FeS_2. When this ore is roasted in air, it forms sulfur dioxide (which is used to manufacture sulfuric acid). The equation for the reaction is:

$$4FeS_2 + 11O_2 \longrightarrow 2Fe_2O_3 + 8SO_2$$

When 5000 g of iron pyrites are roasted in excess oxygen, it is found that 2725 g of sulfur dioxide are formed. Calculate the percentage yield of sulfur dioxide.

W24.2 To prepare ammonia in the laboratory, a student mixed together 20 g of ammonium chloride and 20 g of calcium hydroxide. The balanced equation for the reaction is:

$$2NH_4Cl + Ca(OH)_2 \longrightarrow 2NH_3 + CaCl_2 + 2H_2O$$

Calculate the maximum amount of ammonia (to the nearest gram) that could have been obtained in the reaction.

W24.3 A student prepared ethanoic acid, CH_3COOH, from ethanol, C_2H_5OH, according to the following equation:

$$3C_2H_5OH + 2Cr_2O_7^{2-} + 16H^+ \longrightarrow 4Cr^{3+} + 3CH_3COOH + 11H_2O$$

It was found that 28.5 g of ethanoic acid were obtained from 24 g of ethanol. The ethanol was the limiting reactant. Calculate the percentage yield of ethanoic acid, giving your answer correct to the nearest whole number.

W24.4 Two experiments were carried out to prepare ethanal and propanone. In experiment A, ethanal was prepared by reacting an excess of ethanol, C_2H_5OH, with acidified sodium dichromate(VI) solution. In experiment B, propanone was prepared by a similar method using an excess of propan-2-ol, C_3H_7OH. In both experiments 11.92 g of sodium dichromate(VI) crystals ($Na_2Cr_2O_7.2H_2O$) and about 10 cm^3 of concentrated sulfuric acid dissolved in 25 cm^3 of water were used. After purification of the products, the yields obtained were 2.75 g of ethanal and 5.15 g of propanone.

The equation for the reaction carried out in experiment A is:

$$3C_2H_5OH + Cr_2O_7^{2-} + 8H^+ \longrightarrow 3CH_3CHO + 2Cr^{3+} + 7H_2O$$

The equation for the reaction carried out in experiment B is:

$$3C_3H_7OH + Cr_2O_7^{2-} + 8H^+ \longrightarrow 3CH_3COCH_3 + 2Cr^{3+} + 7H_2O$$

Calculate the percentage yields of ethanal and propanone, giving your answers correct to the nearest whole number. [LCH]

W24.5 To 6.6 cm³ of ethyl ethanoate (density = 0.9 g/cm³), 30 cm³ of 20% (w/v) sodium hydroxide solution were added and the mixture was boiled in a suitable apparatus for about 45 minutes. The mixture was then distilled. The solution remaining in the flask was cooled and excess dilute sulfuric acid was added in order to liberate the ethanoic acid. The ethanoic acid was recovered by further distillation.

The reactions may be represented:

$$CH_3COOC_2H_5 + NaOH \longrightarrow CH_3COONa + C_2H_5OH$$

$$2CH_3COONa + H_2SO_4 \longrightarrow 2CH_3COOH + Na_2SO_4$$

(a) What is meant by a 20% (w/v) solution of sodium hydroxide? How many (a) grams, (b) moles, of sodium hydroxide are contained in 30 cm³ of this solution?

(b) Show clearly that the sodium hydroxide is in excess in the reaction with ethyl ethanoate.

(c) Following further purification, 3.1 g of pure ethanoic acid were obtained. Calculate the percentage yield. [LCH]

W24.6 A student carried out the preparation of benzoic acid by oxidising 5 cm³ of phenlymethanol (benzyl alcohol) with excess potassium permanganate according to the following equation:

$$3C_6H_5CH_2OH + 4KMnO_4 \longrightarrow 3C_6H_5COOH + 4MnO_2 + H_2O + 4KOH$$

After recrystallisation of the impure benzoic acid crystals was carried out, it was found that 3.15 g of pure benzoic acid crystals were obtained. Calculate the percentage yield of benzoic acid. (Density of phenylmethanol = 1.04 g/cm³)

W24.7 A volume of 8 cm³ of phenylmethanol (density = 1.04 g/cm³) was oxidised under alkaline conditions using a concentrated solution of potassium permanganate containing 23.7 g of dissolved $KMnO_4$. Benzoic acid was isolated from the reaction mixture and then purified by recrystallisation.

A mass of 6.1 g of pure benzoic acid was obtained. The equation for the oxidation reaction is:

$$3C_6H_5CH_2OH + 4KMnO_4 \longrightarrow 3C_6H_5COOH + 4MnO_2 + H_2O + 4KOH$$

(a) Which of the reactants, the phenylmethanol or the potassium permanganate, was in excess?

(b) Calculate the percentage yield of benzoic acid correct to the nearest whole number.

W24.8 A solution containing 8.16 g of potassium permanganate ($KMnO_4$) was used to oxidise 2.5 cm³ of phenylmethanol (density = 1.04 g/cm³) under alkaline conditions. The benzoic acid produced was found, after recrystallisation, to have a mass of 1.21 g. The equation for the oxidation reaction that took place is:

$$3C_6H_5CH_2OH + 4KMnO_4 \longrightarrow 3C_6H_5COOH + 4MnO_2 + H_2O + 4KOH$$

Calculate the percentage yield of benzoic acid correct to the nearest whole number.

Industrial Chemistry: Case Studies 25

25.1 Introduction

In this chapter we will study some aspects of industrial chemistry. We will first consider some of the general principles involved. We will then study three Irish chemical industries in detail and investigate how the general principles apply to these case studies. For your examination, you need only have knowledge of **one** of these case studies.

As you are aware from what has been studied in this course so far, chemistry makes an enormous contribution to our society. It provides us with fuels, metals, medicines, soaps, detergents, paints, inks, dyes and – most important of all – water that is fit to drink. Chemistry also provides us with many important materials such as plastics, synthetic fibres, semi-conductor devices and liquid crystals. In addition, chemistry helps us to increase crop yields with the aid of fertilisers, herbicides and pesticides. All of the substances listed above are produced by the chemical industry.

Not only does the chemical industry make a major contribution to the quality of our lives, but it is also of vital importance to the economy of our country. The chemical industry provides stable and well-paid employment as well as contributing thousands of millions of euro to our national economy.

The chemical industry in Ireland can be traced back to 1819 when James Muspratt started manufacturing chemicals in Dublin and then moved to Liverpool where he established a chemical plant to manufacture sodium carbonate (washing soda). The modern chemical industry in Ireland started in 1969 when Pfizer Pharmaceuticals established a plant at Ringaskiddy, Co. Cork, to manufacture citric acid and, at a later stage, pharmaceuticals, Fig. 25.1.

Fig. 25.1 Ireland's modern chemical industry was established in 1969 with the arrival of Pfizer Pharmaceuticals to Ringaskiddy, Co. Cork.

The Irish chemical industry produces a wide range of materials with a particular emphasis on pharmaceuticals. A study of industrial chemistry enables us to see the many practical applications of various concepts met earlier in this course e.g. rates of reaction, chemical equilibrium and use of catalysts.

25.2 General Principles of Industrial Chemistry

The chemical industry makes money by carrying out chemical reactions on raw materials and selling the final products. These chemical reactions are carried out in chemical plants that have been constructed for this specific purpose. The size of a chemical plant depends on the particular product being manufactured and on the demand for this product. A product may be manufactured using a **batch process**, a **continuous process** or a **semi-continuous process**.

In a **batch process**, the reactants (feedstock) are allowed to react for a fixed time inside a vessel (batch reactor). The reaction takes place under controlled conditions of temperature and pressure for the required time. When the reaction is complete, the product is removed, allowing another batch to be produced in the batch reactor. Batch processes are commonly used in the pharmaceutical industry, Fig. 25.2.

Fig. 25.2 This photograph shows a typical batch reactor for manufacturing pharmaceuticals.

In a **continuous process**, the raw materials are continually fed in at one end of the plant and the product is continually removed at the other end of the plant. An example of a continuous process is the manufacture of ammonia, Fig. 25.3.

Fig. 25.3 The manufacture of ammonia is an example of a continuous process. This photograph shows an ammonia plant in Sluiskil, the Netherlands.

In the past, ammonia was manufactured by Irish Fertiliser Industries (IFI) at Marino Point, Cobh, Co. Cork, but sadly this plant is now closed. In the manufacture of ammonia, nitrogen gas and hydrogen gas are continuously passed over a catalyst in a reactor to form ammonia which is continuously removed from the reactor. Continuous processes are commonly used in the manufacture of large-scale quantities of materials and a typical plant could produce thousands of tonnes of ammonia each day.

A **semi-continuous** process is a combination of a batch process and a continuous process. The first stage involves a batch process to make the product. The second stage involves a continuous process where the product is purified using feed from several batch reactors. Examples of semi-continuous processes are the brewing industry and the manufacturing of soft drinks. In each case the product is manufactured by a batch process and the bottling and addition of carbon dioxide is carried out continuously.

The advantages and disadvantages of batch and continuous processes are summarised in Tables 25.1 and 25.2.

Advantages of Batch Process	Disadvantages of Batch Process
1. Since small quantities are being made, the capital cost of plant is not too high.	1. Filling and emptying the reactor is time-consuming.
2. The same vessel can be used for a range of products.	2. Contamination from batch to batch is more likely.
3. It is easy to cater for slow reactions.	3. The process may be difficult to control in the case of an exothermic reaction.

Table 25.1 Some advantages and disadvantages of the batch process.

Advantages of Continuous Process	Disadvantages of Continuous Process
1. It is very suitable for large scale production.	1. Very high capital costs to build the plant.
2. Long periods of use are possible before shutdown is needed for maintenance.	2. The plant is 'tailor made' – less flexibility in terms of products manufactured
3. There is low risk of contamination since only one product is being made.	3. If plant is not run at full capacity, it may not be cost effective to manufacture the product.

Table 25.2 Some advantages and disadvantages of the continuous process.

All of the three case studies on the Leaving Certificate chemistry syllabus are continuous processes.

The Leaving Certificate chemistry syllabus specifies that you must have knowledge of the characteristics of effective and successful industrial chemical processes. You must then study one of the three industries, specified on the syllabus for an in-depth case study, using these characteristics.

In all, there are ten general characteristics of industrial chemical processes:

1. **Feedstock**. The term feedstock simply means the reactants used in the industrial process. Feedstock is produced from raw materials. The raw materials may have to be treated to ensure that they are sufficiently pure to be used as feedstock.

2. **Rate**. The best conditions of temperature, pressure and catalyst are selected for the process to occur at the optimum rate. It is also necessary to find the conditions that enable the plant to be run in the most economical way. It is often necessary to come to a compromise when deciding the conditions under which the reaction is carried out.

3. **Product yield**. The conditions – temperature, pressure, catalyst – must be chosen to ensure a reasonable yield of product in a reasonable time. As discussed in Chapter 17 of the textbook when studying the Haber process, if the temperature is too low, the rate of reaction is too slow, i.e. even though there is a high yield of ammonia at low temperature, the ammonia is formed too slowly. At high temperature, the rate of reaction is increased but the yield of ammonia is reduced. Therefore, when choosing the reaction conditions, there has to be a compromise between rate and yield.

4. **Co-products**. In some chemical processes, instead of just one product being formed, two or more products may be formed. The other products formed, along with the main product being manufactured, are called co-products. These co-products are not unexpected as they always appear in the balanced chemical equation describing the process.

   In some cases, unwanted side reactions may occur at the same time as the main reaction. These side reactions give rise to unwanted products called **by-products**. Side reactions reduce the yield of the required product.

5. **Waste disposal and effluent control**. The formation of co-products and by-products means that these have to be separated from the main product. If any of these materials are hazardous, they will have to be treated before disposal and this will add to the cost of running the plant. Waste can only be disposed of when it is in a condition that will not harm the environment. These waste-disposal conditions are laid down in the appropriate legislation. Costs are incurred in treating any waste water or gaseous emissions from the plant. However, co-products and by-products can also be valuable materials and the sale of these can prove very profitable for the company.

6. **Quality control**. All modern chemical plants have laboratories that continuously monitor the quality of feedstock and products to ensure that these meet the required specifications. The use of instrumentation in quality control is very common.

7. **Safety**. This is a priority in the chemical industry and all aspects of health and safety are covered by legislation. Many safety features are incorporated in the location and layout of chemical plants. There is frequent on-site training of staff, and continuous monitoring of potential hazards. When you visit the site of a chemical industry, you will notice many safety features such as the availability of safety glasses, eye washes, breathing apparatus and first aid centres.

8. **Costs**. Production costs in a chemical plant are of two types – fixed costs and variable costs. Fixed costs are those costs that have to be paid regardless of the rate of production of the plant, i.e. whether the plant produces one tonne of product or 1000 tonnes of product per day. Examples of fixed costs are costs of labour, plant depreciation and repayment of loans. Variable costs depend directly on the rate of production of the plant, i.e. its level of output. Examples of variable costs are the costs of raw materials, costs of effluent treatment and disposal and distribution costs.

   Various ways of reducing costs are employed in chemical plants, e.g. recycling of unreacted feedstock, using catalysts, selling useful co-products and by-products, keeping lengths of piping to a minimum, using optimum temperatures and pressures for reactions, and using heat exchangers to transfer heat generated in one part of the plant to another part of the plant where heat is needed.

9. **Site location**. The location of a chemical industry at a particular site depends on a number of factors. There must be good road or rail connections to the plant to allow the raw materials to be transported into the plant and the products distributed from the plant. Deep-sea access can be important if the products are being manufactured for export. The availability of a large supply of cooling water is often an important factor. Other important factors are the availability of a skilled workforce, scope for plant expansion, local availability of raw materials and facilities for disposal and treatment of waste.

10. **Plant construction materials**. The construction materials used in a chemical plant are generally unreactive and resistant to corrosion. Materials are chosen that do not react with the feedstock, products, solvents or catalysts used in the production process. In general, glass-lined vessels and stainless steel components are commonly used.

Using the above characteristics, you are required to study **one** of the following three chemical industries:

(i) The manufacture of ammonia and urea by IFI at Cobh, Co. Cork.

(ii) The manufacture of nitric acid and fertilisers by IFI at Arklow, Co. Wicklow.

(iii) The manufacture of magnesium oxide by Premier Periclase at Drogheda, Co. Louth.

While the first two industries listed above are no longer in operation, the chemical processes that took place in them are still of relevance in understanding the general characteristics of continuous processes.

25.3 The Manufacture of Ammonia and Urea by IFI at Cobh

Ammonia is the basic ingredient used to manufacture all fertilisers containing nitrogen compounds. Some of the main uses of ammonia are shown in Fig. 25.4.

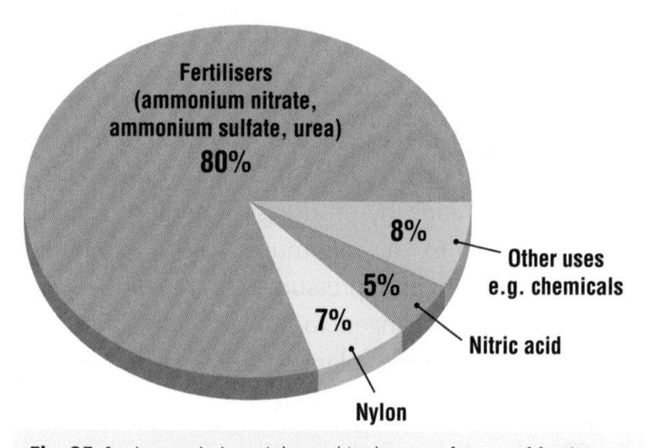

Fig. 25.4 Ammonia is mainly used in the manufacture of fertilisers.

Ammonia is manufactured by passing hydrogen and nitrogen over an iron catalyst.

$$N_2 + 3H_2 \overset{Fe}{\rightleftharpoons} 2NH_3$$

This process is called the Haber process or, more correctly, the Haber–Bosch process after the chemist (Fritz Haber) and the chemical engineer (Carl Bosch) who developed the process, Fig. 25.5.

Fig. 25.5 Fritz Haber and Carl Bosch developed the process to manufacture ammonia from nitrogen and hydrogen.

The process was developed in Germany prior to World War I to ensure that Germany would be able to manufacture fertilisers and explosives. (Before this, the main source of nitrogen-containing compounds in Germany was sodium nitrate which was imported from Chile.)

A flow chart summarising the main stages in the manufacture of ammonia is given in Fig. 25.6.

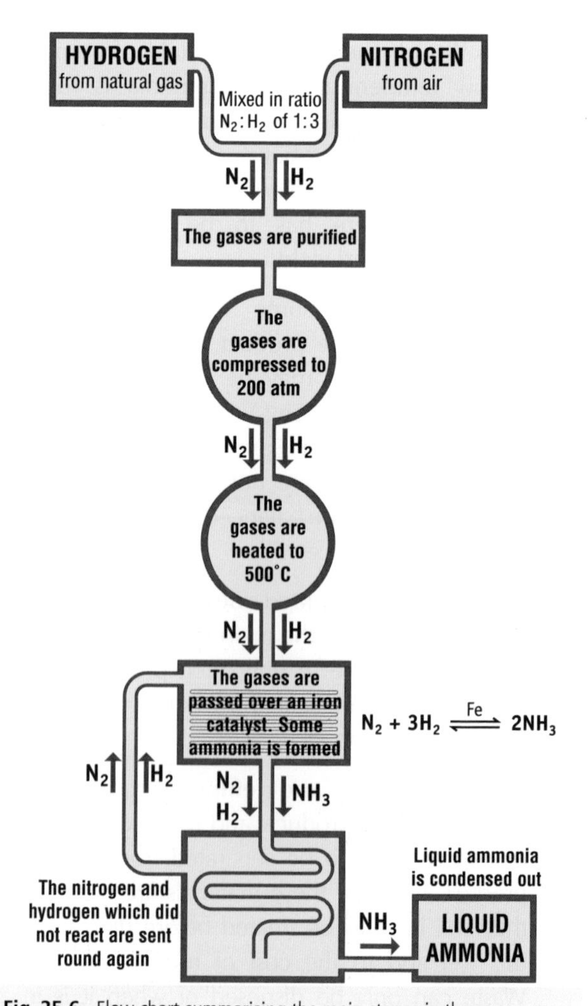

Fig. 25.6 Flow chart summarising the main stages in the manufacture of ammonia.

We now consider this chemical industry under the headings outlined at the beginning of the chapter.

1. **Feedstock**. Nitrogen and hydrogen are the feedstock for the manufacture of ammonia. The hydrogen comes from natural gas. The nitrogen comes from the air.

   The hydrogen is obtained from the natural gas in a process called **methane-steam reforming**. In this reaction, natural gas (methane) is reacted with steam at high temperature to form carbon monoxide and hydrogen according to the following equation:

   $$CH_4 + H_2O \rightleftharpoons CO + 3H_2$$

   The carbon monoxide formed in the above reaction then reacts with more steam to form carbon dioxide and more hydrogen:

   $$CO + H_2O \rightleftharpoons CO_2 + H_2$$

   This reaction is called the **Shift Reaction** as the carbon monoxide is removed by the equilibrium being shifted from left to right. It is necessary to remove the carbon monoxide as it would poison the catalyst, i.e. the carbon monoxide would become adsorbed on the iron catalyst. Thus, in the Shift Reaction the carbon monoxide is converted to carbon dioxide (which is easily removed from the system). Not only does the Shift Reaction remove carbon monoxide, but also more hydrogen is produced for the manufacture of ammonia.

   Overall, the yield of hydrogen is quite high (about 70%) since it is formed in both reactions.

   The nitrogen gas is formed by burning the unreacted methane (from the methane-steam reforming stage) in air that is injected into the reactor. Burning the methane in air forms carbon dioxide and steam:

   $$CH_4 + 2O_2 \rightleftharpoons CO_2 + 2H_2O$$

   This reaction is called **secondary reforming**. Thus, the oxygen in the air is removed and this leaves almost pure nitrogen. This nitrogen is later used to synthesise ammonia.

2. **Rate**. A high pressure of about 200 atm and a temperature of around 500 °C give a satisfactory rate. Also, by keeping the particle size of the iron catalyst small, the rate of reaction is increased.

3. **Product yield**. The yield of ammonia in the ammonia-synthesis reactor is about 17%. On leaving the reactor, the ammonia is liquefied by refrigeration. The unchanged reactants are re-circulated. A typical ammonia plant produces about 20,000 tonnes of ammonia each day.

4. **Co-products**. Since the Haber process involves the formation of just one product (NH_3), there are no co-products. However, in the secondary reforming reaction shown above, carbon dioxide is formed. This carbon dioxide is a very useful by-product and is used for two purposes: (i) to manufacture urea in another part of the plant and (ii) to be sold to soft drinks manufacturers and breweries to put the "fizz" into drinks.

   After the Shift Reaction has taken place, the carbon dioxide is removed by reacting it with potassium carbonate (K_2CO_3) solution. This forms a solution of potassium hydrogencarbonate:

   $$CO_2 + H_2O + K_2CO_3 \longrightarrow 2KHCO_3$$

The potassium hydrogencarbonate is pumped to the urea plant where the pressure on the solution is reduced and the hydrogencarbonate dissociates back into carbon dioxide and potassium carbonate. We will now see how carbon dioxide (a by-product) is combined with ammonia (the main product) to form urea.

Synthesis of urea

Urea is an excellent fertiliser since its nitrogen content is so high (> 46%), Fig. 25.7.

Fig. 25.7 Urea is a very good fertiliser because of its high nitrogen content.

Urea has the structural formula shown in Fig. 25.8.

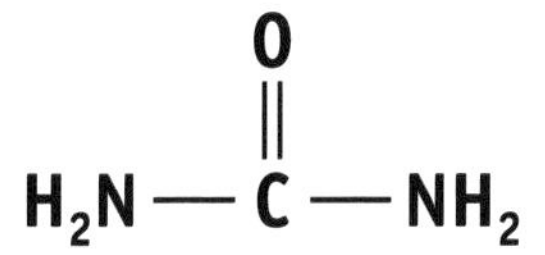

Fig. 25.8 Structural formula of the urea molecule.

Urea is manufactured by combining ammonia with carbon dioxide. The formation of urea takes place in two steps. An intermediate compound called ammonium carbamate, NH_2COONH_4, is first formed:

$$CO_2 + 2NH_3 \longrightarrow \underset{\text{ammonium carbamate}}{NH_2COONH_4}$$

The ammonium carbamate then loses water to form urea.

$$NH_2COONH_4 \longrightarrow \underset{\text{urea}}{NH_2CONH_2} + H_2O$$

Overall, the formation of urea may be represented as:

$$CO_2 + 2NH_3 \longrightarrow \underset{\text{urea}}{NH_2CONH_2} + H_2O$$

5. **Waste disposal and effluent control**. All emissions and effluents from the plant are monitored for the presence of substances such as ammonia or dust from urea. The level of emissions has to comply with the license issued to the plant by the Environmental Protection Agency. The level of emissions from ammonia plants is usually very low due to the recycling of materials back into the production process.
6. **Quality Control**. This is carried out at various stages of the production process using gas chromatography and infra-red spectrometry, Fig. 25.9. In addition, sensors are used throughout the plant to monitor variables such as temperature, pressure, pH and flow rates of gases. All of this information is monitored from a central control room.

Fig. 25.9 This gas chromatography apparatus may be used to analyse the mixture of gases in the ammonia reactor.

7. **Safety**. All those working in the plant have undertaken training courses in safety. A fire-fighting team is on standby at all times. All of the normal safety equipment (breathing apparatus, goggles and first aid kits) is available on site.
8. **Costs**. The costs involved in running the plant are: (i) purchase of natural gas (variable), (ii) electricity – the plant has a high electrical consumption to drive the turbines for the compressors that keep the gas mixtures under the appropriate pressure (variable), (iii) purchase of large quantities of fresh water (millions of litres are used each day for cooling purposes, variable) and (iv) wages for the people who work at the plant (fixed).
9. **Site location**. The site at Cobh was chosen for a number of reasons:
   (i) The Cork–Cobh railway line was very near the plant. This was ideal as ammonia was transported to the IFI plant in Arklow by train.
   (ii) The site was next to a deep-water harbour for easy export of ammonia and urea by ship.
   (iii) The site was near to the location of natural gas off Kinsale.
   (iv) There was a plentiful supply of skilled personnel (engineers, chemists and technicians) as the plant was only 20 km from Cork City, which has a university and an Institute of Technology.
10. **Plant construction materials**. Stainless steel, specifically designed and custom made, was used throughout the plant. This was to ensure that corrosion was kept to a minimum.

Test Yourself: Attempt questions 25.1 and 25.4–25.6.

25.4 The Manufacture of Nitric Acid by IFI at Arklow

The IFI plant at Arklow manufactured nitric acid using ammonia (from IFI in Cobh). This nitric acid was then reacted with more ammonia to form ammonium nitrate, an important constituent of fertilisers.

$$\underset{\text{ammonia}}{NH_3} + \underset{\text{nitric acid}}{HNO_3} \longrightarrow \underset{\text{ammonium nitrate}}{NH_4NO_3}$$

A typical nitric acid manufacturing plant is shown in Fig. 25.10

Fig. 25.10 Nitric acid is manufactured in this chemical plant at Porsgrunn, Norway.

The ammonium nitrate that is formed in the above reaction is mixed with limestone to form a fertiliser commonly referred to as **calcium ammonium nitrate (CAN)**. Fertilisers play a vital role in food production. It has been estimated that one bag of calcium ammonium nitrate fertiliser (50 kg) would produce enough wheat to feed over 400 people for a day.

A flow chart summarising the main stages in the manufacture of nitric acid is given in Fig. 25.11.

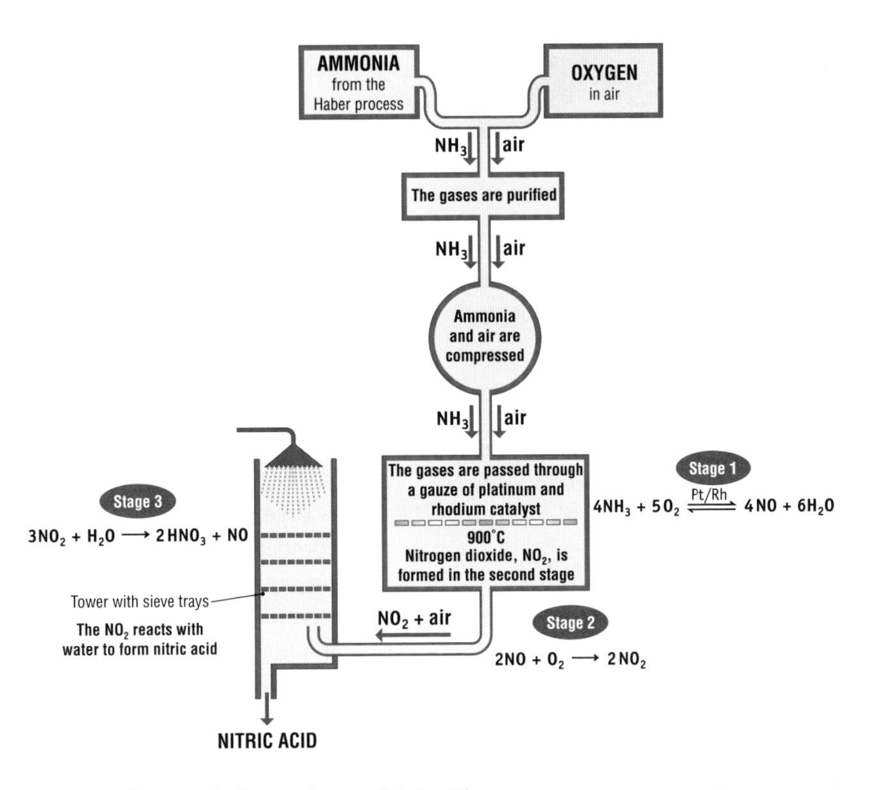

Fig. 25.11 Flow chart summarising the stages in the manufacture of nitric acid.

We now consider this chemical industry under the headings outlined at the beginning of this chapter.

1. **Feedstock**. To manufacture nitric acid, three chemicals are needed: ammonia, oxygen (from the air) and water. The ammonia produced by IFI in Cobh was transported by train to Arklow. Special pressurised containers must be used when transporting ammonia. When ammonia was off-loaded from the trains, it was stored in two large pressurised spherical containers, Fig. 25.12.

Fig. 25.12 These spherical containers are used to store ammonia in the nitric acid plant in Posgrunn, Norway.

This ammonia was used to manufacture nitric acid. As stated previously, the nitric acid was then used to manufacture ammonium nitrate. A small portion of the nitric acid manufactured was sold to industry.

There are three stages involved in the manufacture of nitric acid:

(i) **The oxidation of ammonia to nitrogen monoxide**. This reaction is carried out by passing the ammonia over a platinum/rhodium catalyst, Fig 25.13, at a temperature of around 900 °C.

The following reaction occurs:

$$4NH_3 + 5O_2 \xrightarrow{Pt/Rh} 4NO + 6H_2O$$

This reaction is exothermic and keeps the catalyst red-hot at approximately 900 °C. The catalyst consists of layers of platinum–rhodium mesh that must be replaced approximately every eight weeks. This is because the high temperature causes the coating of platinum and rhodium to vaporise off the gauze.

Fig. 25.13 A platinum–rhodium catalyst is used to convert ammonia into nitrogen monoxide.

(ii) **The oxidation of nitrogen monoxide to nitrogen dioxide**. This is carried out by introducing more air into the reactor.

$$2NO + O_2 \longrightarrow 2NO_2$$

(iii) **The absorption of nitrogen dioxide in water**. The nitrogen dioxide made in the second step is then absorbed in water to form nitric acid.

$$3NO_2 + H_2O \longrightarrow 2HNO_3 + NO$$

Thus the feedstock for the manufacture of nitric acid consists of ammonia, oxygen and water.

The nitric acid prepared is then reacted with ammonia to make ammonium nitrate.

$$NH_3 + HNO_3 \longrightarrow NH_4NO_3$$

As can be seen from the above equation, the feedstock for the manufacture of ammonium nitrate consists of ammonia and nitric acid. Pure ammonium nitrate is not sold as fertiliser because of its properties as an explosive. (About 90% of all explosives contain ammonium nitrate.) Instead, the ammonium nitrate is mixed with ground limestone to form calcium ammonium nitrate.

Pure ammonium nitrate has a nitrogen content of 35% (i.e. % N = $\frac{28}{80}$ × 100). Sufficient calcium carbonate is mixed with this to produce a fertiliser with a nitrogen content of 27.5%.

2. **Rate**. All reactions proceed at a reasonably fast rate. The high temperature and the catalyst – dispersed on gauze to give a large surface area – ensure a satisfactory rate in stage (i) page 83.
3. **Product yield**. The yields of both nitric acid and ammonium nitrate are very high (around 95%).
4. **Co-products**. There are no co-products formed.
5. **Waste disposal and effluent control**. The main pollutants generated in the above processes are the oxides of nitrogen and effluents containing ammonia and nitrates. With the aid of modern technology, these emissions are kept to a minimum. The level of pollutants in the air is continuously monitored by the plant as required by its air pollution license. All effluents from the plant are automatically analysed for levels of ammonia and nitric acid. Plants usually have an Ammonia Recovery Unit installed, and this recycles the ammonia and the ammonium nitrate back into the process. Thus, the amount of waste generated is kept to an absolute minimum.
6. **Quality Control**. The feedstock and products are continuously analysed in a laboratory located in the plant. Similarly, at various stages of the manufacturing process, samples are analysed to ensure that the required specifications are met. This analysis ensures that the nitrogen content of the final fertiliser product is correct. Another important specification is that the fertiliser must flow freely so that it can be easily spread by the farmer.
7. **Safety**. Safety is a top priority for nitric acid plants as large quantities of ammonia are stored on site. Companies manufacturing nitric acid must take all precautions to ensure the highest levels of safety. Each member of staff receives training in the area of site safety. In keeping with the requirements of Health and Safety legislation, detailed documentation has to be produced outlining all areas of risk and management of safety.
8. **Costs**. The operating costs of the plant are (i) the cost of ammonia (variable), (ii) the cost of the catalyst (variable), (iii) the cost of limestone (variable), (iv) labour costs (fixed), (v) maintenance costs (variable) and (vi) the cost of electric power (variable).
9. **Site location**. The plant was located in Arklow for a number of reasons:
   (i) The site was close to the Avoca river, which supplied the plant with fresh water for cooling purposes.
   (ii) The site was near a local harbour for ease of exporting products.
   (iii) The rail link connection to the main Dublin–Rosslare line made obtaining ammonia and the distribution of fertiliser products very easy.
10. **Construction materials**. Most of the material from which the plant was constructed consisted of stainless steel. This was necessary because of the corrosive nature of the reactants and products.

Test Yourself: Attempt questions 25.2 and 25.4–25.6.

25.5 The Manufacture of Magnesium Oxide by Premier Periclase at Drogheda

Premier Periclase established its plant at Drogheda in 1980, Fig. 25.14. This plant manufactures magnesium oxide (MgO) from seawater. Magnesium oxide (magnesia) occurs as the mineral **periclase**. This substance has a very high melting point (2800 °C) and this makes it very useful as a heat-resistant material for lining furnaces. Materials with very high melting points used to line furnaces are commonly called refractory materials. The periclase manufactured in Drogheda is exported to be made into refractory bricks which are commonly used in steel-making plants.

Fig. 25.14 The Premier Periclase plant at Drogheda manufactures magnesium oxide from sea water.

A flow chart summarising the main stages in the manufacture of magnesium oxide is given in Fig. 25.15.

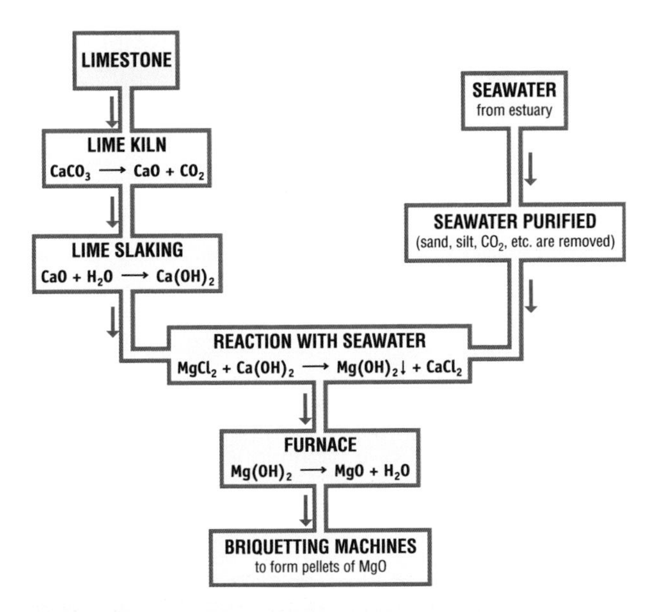

Fig. 25.15 Flow chart summarising the main stages in the manufacture of magnesium oxide.

The production of magnesium oxide from seawater can be divided into four stages:

(i) **The conversion of limestone to lime.** In the first stage, limestone is converted into lime by heating the limestone in a large oven called a kiln.

$$\underset{\text{limestone}}{CaCO_3} \xrightarrow{\text{heat}} \underset{\substack{\text{lime}\\\text{(quicklime)}}}{CaO} + CO_2$$

(ii) **The conversion of lime into slaked lime**. In the second stage, water is added to the lime from the first stage to form a substance commonly called slaked lime. The chemical name for slaked lime is calcium hydroxide. A solution of calcium hydroxide in water is commonly called limewater.

$$\underset{\substack{\text{calcium}\\\text{oxide}}}{CaO} + H_2O \longrightarrow \underset{\substack{\text{calcium hydroxide}\\\text{(slaked lime)}}}{Ca(OH)_2}$$

(iii) **The reaction of slaked lime with seawater to form magnesium hydroxide**. In the third stage, the calcium hydroxide from step (ii) reacts with seawater. The magnesium chloride found in seawater reacts with the calcium hydroxide to form a precipitate of magnesium hydroxide.

$$\underset{\substack{\text{magnesium}\\\text{chloride}}}{MgCl_2} + Ca(OH)_2 \longrightarrow \underset{\substack{\text{magnesium}\\\text{hydroxide}}}{Mg(OH)_2} \downarrow + CaCl_2$$

(iv) **The conversion of magnesium hydroxide to magnesium oxide**. In the fourth stage, magnesium hydroxide from step (iii) is heated in a large furnace to form magnesium oxide. The magnesium oxide powder is then made into briquettes and heated to 2300 °C to make the final high-density pellets (Fig. 25.16).

$$\underset{\substack{\text{magnesium}\\\text{hydroxide}}}{Mg(OH)_2} \xrightarrow{\text{heat}} \underset{\substack{\text{magnesium}\\\text{oxide}}}{MgO} + H_2O$$

Fig. 25.16 These high-density pellets of magnesium oxide are commonly referred to as periclase.

We now consider this chemical industry under the headings outlined at the beginning of the chapter.

1. **Feedstock**. The feedstock is seawater and limestone. Seawater is taken from the Boyne estuary. Limestone is taken from a quarry at Mullaghcrone, near Drogheda. The limestone is of very good quality (98% pure calcium carbonate).
2. **Rate**. The conversion of limestone to lime is a slow reaction. The other three reactions proceed at a fast rate.
3. **Product yield**. A litre of seawater yields only about 2 g of magnesium oxide. Hence the company needs to have large quantities of seawater available. (About 150,000 m^3 of seawater are pumped each day through large underground pipes four miles upstream from the plant).
4. **Co-products**. No co-products are produced.
5. **Waste disposal and effluent control**. All emissions from the plant are carefully monitored for the presence of dust. Particles of dust in chimney stacks are removed by filtration or electrostatic precipitators. In addition, the effluents from the plant are analysed with regard to concentration of suspended solids and pH levels. The seawater that has been used in the plant is treated to bring its pH and suspended solid level in line with normal seawater. It is then pumped out to sea, 1500 m from the shore.
6. **Quality Control**. The quality control laboratory carries out a detailed chemical analysis of all reactants and products at every stage of the production process. Techniques commonly used are acid–base titrations and X-ray analysis.
7. **Safety**. The company places a high priority on safety in the workplace. All employees receive induction and ongoing training in health and safety. Personal protective equipment is used where required and includes safety helmets, boots, goggles and clothing. Ear protection – in the form of ear muffs and ear plugs – is also provided where high noise levels exist.
8. **Costs**. The main costs involved in running the plant are (i) energy for operating kilns, furnaces and pumps (variable), (ii) labour costs (fixed), (iii) maintenance costs (variable), (iv) extraction and preparation of raw materials (variable), (v) administration (fixed).

   The plant was set up on the site of a former Irish Cement Works plant. By being able to utilise some of the plant, equipment and kilns of the cement works, the cost of setting up the plant was less than would otherwise have been the case.
9. **Site location**. The location at Drogheda is ideal for a number of reasons:
   (i) The site is close to a plentiful supply of seawater.
   (ii) The site is close to a limestone quarry.
   (iii) The plant is built next to the river Boyne for easy export of the product.
   (iv) There is a good road network to allow easy transport of limestone to the plant.
10. **Construction materials**. Many of the buildings on the site are made from steel with cladding on the outside. Lime is stored in large concrete silos. The seawater and calcium hydroxide are reacted together in a large concrete reactor. The kiln used to convert limestone to lime is made of steel on the outside and refractory bricks on the inside to withstand the high temperature. Similarly, refractory bricks are used in the furnaces where the magnesium hydroxide is converted to magnesium oxide.

Test Yourself: Attempt questions 25.3–25.6.

Summary

- The chemical industry provides us with many important materials that we require.
- Products are made by the chemical industry using either a batch process or a continuous process.
- In a batch process, the products are made in a large vessel and the product is then removed, allowing another batch to be produced in the vessel.
- In a continuous process, the raw materials are continuously fed in at one end of the plant and the product is continuously removed at the other end of the plant.

- The ten characteristics of industrial chemical processes are feedstock, rate, product yield, co-products, waste disposal and effluent control, quality control, safety, costs, site location and plant construction materials.
- Ammonia is manufactured by reacting nitrogen and hydrogen. The nitrogen comes from the air and the hydrogen comes from natural gas. Hydrogen is formed in the methane-steam reforming reaction and in the Shift Reaction. Nitrogen is formed by burning methane in air to remove the oxygen from it. Carbon dioxide is formed as a by-product. The carbon dioxide is combined with ammonia to form urea which is used as a fertiliser.
- Nitric acid is manufactured using ammonia, oxygen and water. There are three stages involved in the manufacture of nitric acid: oxidation of ammonia to nitrogen monoxide, oxidation of nitrogen monoxide to nitrogen dioxide, absorption of nitrogen dioxide in water to form nitric acid. The nitric acid is then reacted with ammonia to form ammonium nitrate. Ammonium nitrate is combined with ground limestone to form calcium ammonium nitrate which is used as a fertiliser.

Magnesium oxide is manufactured by Premier Periclase at Drogheda. It is used for making heat-resistant materials for lining furnaces. There are four stages in the manufacture of magnesium oxide: the conversion of limestone to lime, the conversion of lime to slaked lime, the reaction of slaked lime with seawater to form magnesium hydroxide and the conversion of magnesium hydroxide to magnesium oxide.

EXAM EDGE Use Chapter 25 Exam Edge to study the sample answers to questions that have been asked on past Leaving Certificate Chemistry examinations on the topics covered in this chapter.

Questions

25.1

(a) Ammonia is made by passing.........................and hydrogen over a catalyst of.........................

(b) The feedstock for the manufacture of ammonia consists of.........................and.........................

(c) Hydrogen is obtained from natural gas in a process called......................... The balanced equation for this reaction is:

....

(d) Carbon monoxide is removed from the system in a reaction called the Shift Reaction. It is necessary to remove the carbon monoxide because...

....

(e) In secondary reforming, methane is burned in air. Why is this process carried out?

....

(f) Name the two scientists who invented the process for the manufacture of ammonia.

1...

2...

(g) Carbon dioxide is formed as a by-product. Give two uses for this product.

1...

2...

(h) Write down an equation to show the formation of urea from the reaction between ammonia and carbon dioxide

....

(i) Give two reasons for choosing this site as the location for the plant.
1..
2..

25.2 (a) The feedstock for the manufacture of nitric acid consists of ammonia and two other chemicals. Name these chemicals. 1................................ 2................................

(b) Name the source of ammonia that was used by the plant and describe how it was transported to the plant..

(c) Name the three stages involved in the manufacture of nitric acid and write a balanced chemical equation for each stage.
1..
2..
3..

(d) Nitric acid is used to manufacture ammonium nitrate. For what purpose is ammonium nitrate used? ....

(e) Write a balanced chemical equation to represent the formation of ammonium nitrate from ammonia and nitric acid.
....

(f) Another substance is normally mixed with ammonium nitrate before it is sold. Name this other substance..

(g) Explain why the substance mentioned in (f) is mixed with ammonium nitrate.
....

(h) Calculate the nitrogen content of pure ammonium nitrate..

(i) List two costs involved in running a nitric acid plant.
1..
2..

(j) Give two reasons why the plant was located at this particular site.
1..
2..

25.3 (a) The feedstock for the manufacture of magnesium oxide is...

(b) Magnesium oxide occurs as the mineral..

(c) Refractory substances have high...

(d) The chemical formula for limestone is................................and for lime is................................

(e) Limestone is converted into lime by heating in a kiln. The balanced chemical equation to describe this reaction is:..

(f) When water is added to lime a compound called slaked lime is formed. The chemical name for slaked lime is ....

(g) The balanced chemical equation to describe the reaction between calcium oxide and water is:
....

(h) Write down the equation to describe the reaction between magnesium chloride and calcium hydroxide..

(i) The final stage in the formation of magnesium oxide from magnesium hydroxide is carried out by...........................the magnesium hydroxide. The balanced equation to describe this reaction may be written as:
....

(j) Give two reasons why the location of the plant at Drogheda is particularly suitable.
1...
2...

25.4 Distinguish between the terms *batch process* and *continuous process*. Give one advantage and one disadvantage of each type of process.

Give two examples of products produced by the Irish chemical industry.

25.5 Name one industrial process you have studied in detail. With regard to the process you have studied, answer the following questions:

Name the product manufactured by the company.

What feedstock is used in the manufacture of the product?

What co-products (if any) are formed in the process?

List two costs involved in running the plant.

25.6 Write a brief note on the contribution that chemistry makes to our society.

With regard to the chemical industry, explain the meaning of the terms: feedstock, co-products, by-products.

Name one chemical industry you have studied. Give a brief description of this chemical industry under the following headings:

(i) Product or products manufactured.

(ii) Feedstock used.

(iii) Costs involved in running the plant.

(iv) Plant construction materials.

Write chemical equations to describe any two of the processes taking place in the plant.

Name one type of industry in Ireland in which the product is made by a batch process.

With regard to industrial chemistry, write a brief note on (i) product yield, (ii) waste disposal and effluent control, (iii) safety and (iv) costs.

Name a chemical process you have studied in detail. Discuss the reasons why the industry was located at the particular site chosen.

Write chemical equations to describe any three of the processes taking place in the plant.

REVISE CHEMISTRY LIVE

Chapter 25 in Revise Chemistry Live contains a summary of the key points in this chapter.

26 Atmospheric Chemistry

26.1 Introduction

The atmosphere is a layer of gas that extends about 100 km above the surface of the Earth. In recent years, the atmosphere and the chemistry of the atmosphere have been very much in the news. Governments from all over the world have held meetings to discuss topics such as the ozone layer in the atmosphere, the effect of chlorofluorocarbons (CFCs) on the atmosphere and the build up of 'greenhouse gases' in the atmosphere. In this chapter, we will study these and other topics in atmospheric chemistry.

The composition of the atmosphere is quite similar all over the Earth due to the high degree of mixing of the gases in the atmosphere. The mixing is helped by the rotation of the Earth and by the air currents caused by the heating of the Earth by the Sun. The composition (by volume) of dry, unpolluted air is shown in Table 26.1.

Name of Gas	Composition (by Volume)
oxygen	21%
nitrogen	78%
other gases (e.g. noble gases, carbon dioxide)	1%

Table 26.1 The composition of dry, unpolluted air.

26.2 Oxygen – The Reactive Gas

Oxygen is the most reactive gas in the air. When you breathe air into your lungs, the oxygen in the air passes into your bloodstream and is carried to the cells of your body where it takes part in many chemical reactions such as respiration.

Oxygen is an extremely useful gas. It is used in hospitals for people who have difficulty in breathing, e.g. people recovering from heart attacks and strokes and premature babies, Fig. 26.1.

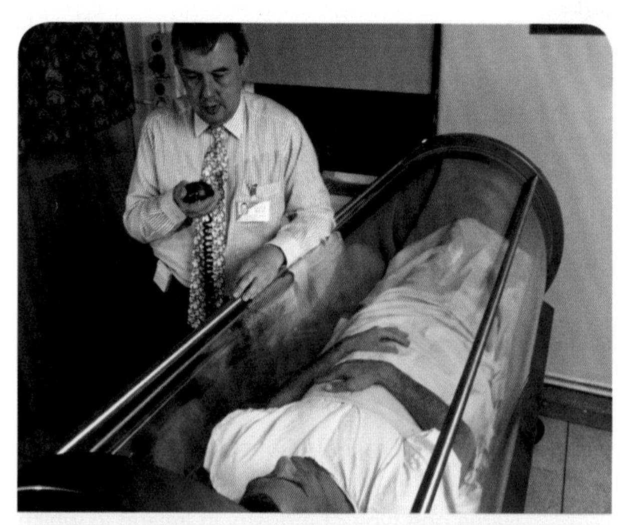

Fig. 26.1 This patient is in a high-pressure oxygen chamber. The chamber contains oxygen at high pressure which causes more oxygen to dissolve in the blood.

A big user of oxygen gas is the steel industry. Oxygen is used to remove carbon and other impurities that make iron brittle. The impurities are removed by burning them out of the molten iron with a controlled blast of oxygen. (This topic is covered in more detail in Chapter 28.) Oxygen is also used in rocket fuels, in producing many industrial chemicals, and in welding and cutting metals e.g. in the oxyacetylene torch. When oxygen is mixed with ethyne (acetylene), the mixture of gases burns very strongly. The flame is so hot that it burns through metals by melting the metal. The flame can also be used to join or weld metals together. The metals to be welded are melted, brought together, and allowed to solidify.

A further use of oxygen is to combat pollution in rivers and lakes. Tankers of oxygen are sometimes used to pump oxygen into the water to help purify the water.

The various uses of oxygen are summarised in Fig. 26.2.

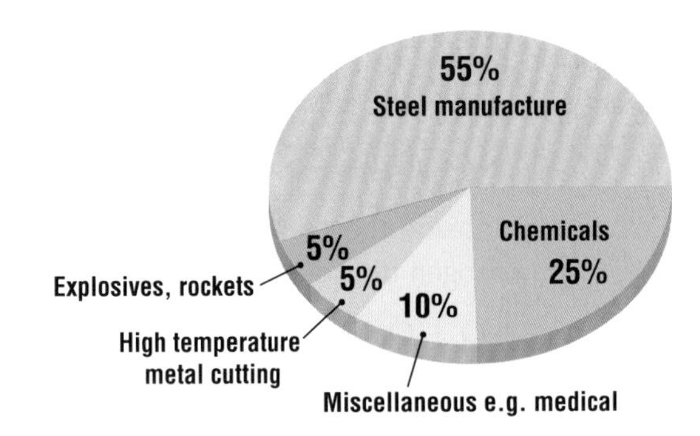

Fig. 26.2 The various uses of oxygen gas.

You may remember from your Junior Certificate that oxygen is prepared in the laboratory by decomposing hydrogen peroxide. However, oxygen is produced in industry by a different method. Industrially, oxygen is manufactured on a large scale by a process involving **liquefaction** of the air, followed by **fractional distillation**. This simply means that the air is first turned into a liquid and the different gases are then allowed to boil off at different temperatures. The principle of the method is summarised in Fig. 26.3.

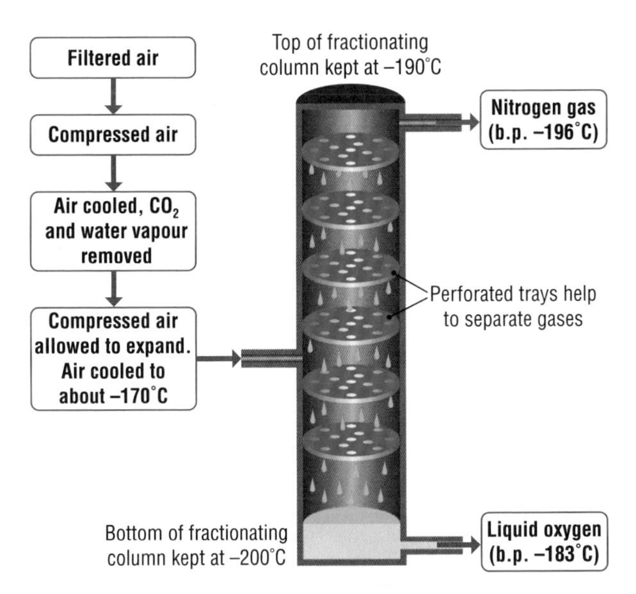

Fig. 26.3 Oxygen and nitrogen may be separated from the air by liquefaction of the air, followed by fractional distillation.

To liquefy the air, it must be cooled to about –200 °C. The first stage of liquefaction involves filtering the air in order to remove dust and other impurities, and then compressing it to a pressure of about 6 atmospheres. Carbon dioxide and water vapour are then removed as these would solidify and block the pipes at a later stage. The air is then cooled to a temperature of about –170 °C. It has been found that one way of cooling a gas is to compress the gas and then allow it to expand suddenly. Therefore, the cold, compressed air is allowed to expand suddenly and the gas is cooled down further to –200 °C.

This very cold air is then fed into a fractionating column. This column is kept well insulated. The top of the column is maintained at a temperature of about –190 °C and the bottom at about –200 °C. The liquid air at the bottom of the column is allowed to warm up and it begins to boil. Nitrogen has the lower boiling point (–196 °C) and begins to boil off first. Oxygen has a higher boiling point (–183 °C) and is taken off at the bottom of the column as liquid oxygen. (The nitrogen gas which comes off at the top of the column is sent to a compressor where it is liquefied.)

Thus, oxygen and nitrogen have been separated from the air and leave the plant as liquid oxygen and liquid nitrogen.

26.3 Nitrogen – The Unreactive Gas

Nitrogen is a colourless, odourless and tasteless gas. It does not tend to take part readily in many chemical reactions, i.e. it is an unreactive gas. The fact that it is unreactive makes it very useful. For example, nitrogen is used in food packaging, e.g. bags of crisps are usually filled with nitrogen. Crisps are made by frying thin slices of potato in cooking oil. If the crisps are left out in the air, the oils become slowly oxidised by the air. This would give an unpleasant taste to the crisps. Packing the crisps in nitrogen prevents them coming in contact with the air. Another advantage of filling the bags with nitrogen is that it creates a pressure within the bag. This pressure provides protection for the crisps and prevents them from being broken.

Since nitrogen is such an unreactive gas, it is ideal for keeping flammable chemicals safe. For example, the storage tanks in ships that deliver crude oil to oil refineries are often flushed out with nitrogen when the oil is being unloaded. The nitrogen forms a 'blanket' above the oil and prevents any of the vapours from igniting. Nitrogen is also used to purge empty road tankers that deliver fuel to petrol stations.

Liquid nitrogen is a very useful substance. It is so cold (temperature below –196 °C) that it is ideal for quick-freezing of food, Fig. 26.4. The fact that the food is frozen so quickly means that bacteria have very little time to multiply and spoil the food. Also, many bacteria need oxygen in order to grow. The presence of nitrogen prevents them getting the oxygen they need.

Fig. 26.4 The liquid nitrogen in the flask is at a temperature of −200 °C. The clouds are formed by the water vapour in the air condensing.

Liquid nitrogen is also used in medicine. Doctors use liquid nitrogen when removing warts. Veterinary surgeons carry the semen of a bull in a special type of vacuum flask filled with liquid nitrogen. This is used in artificial insemination where the semen of one bull may be used to inseminate a large number of cows.

As already seen in Chapter 25, a very important use of nitrogen is in the manufacture of ammonia.

One of the reasons why nitrogen is so unreactive is because of the large amount of energy needed to break the triple bond in the nitrogen molecule, Fig. 26.5. (The bond energy of the N≡N triple bond is 944 kJ mol^{-1}.) In addition, nitrogen is a non-polar molecule and this means that it is only slightly soluble in water.

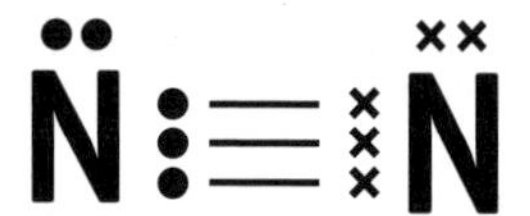

Fig. 26.5 The large amount of energy needed to break the triple bond in nitrogen causes nitrogen to be a very unreactive gas.

We have already seen that nitrogen is the most abundant gas (78%) present in the air. Nitrogen is essential for plant growth as nitrogen is needed to manufacture proteins. However, atmospheric nitrogen, because it is so unreactive, cannot be used by plants. Therefore, it must be changed or 'fixed' into nitrogen compounds (e.g. nitrates) in order to be used by plants.

Nitrogen fixation is the conversion of atmospheric nitrogen to compounds that can be used by plants.

In nature, it is found that nitrogen fixation takes place in two ways. Firstly, during thunderstorms, the discharge of electricity provides enough energy for the nitrogen and oxygen in the air to react together. A substance called nitrogen monoxide, NO, is formed.

$$N_2 + O_2 \longrightarrow 2NO$$

The nitrogen monoxide then reacts with oxygen from the air to form nitrogen dioxide.

$$2NO + O_2 \longrightarrow 2NO_2$$

The nitrogen dioxide then dissolves in rainwater to form nitrous acid, HNO_2, and nitric acid, HNO_3.

$$2NO_2 + H_2O \longrightarrow HNO_2 + HNO_3$$

The nitric acid falls to earth in rainwater and forms nitrate (NO_3^-) compounds in the soil. Plants take in these nitrate compounds through their roots and use them to make proteins. Animals obtain the proteins they need by eating plants or eating other animals.

A second method, by which nitrogen from the atmosphere is converted to compounds that can be used by plants, involves nitrogen-fixing bacteria. It has been found that one family of plants, the **legumes** (e.g. peas, beans, clover), have tiny nodules (swellings) on their roots that contain *rhizobium* bacteria, Fig. 26.6. These bacteria have the ability to fix nitrogen. Thus, cultivation of these types of plants is one way of increasing the amount of nitrogen compounds in the soil. It is not clear how these bacteria succeed in converting atmospheric nitrogen (N_2) into nitrate ions (NO_3^-). A substantial amount of research is taking place in an attempt to discover more about how this conversion occurs.

Since the above two methods of fixing nitrogen occur in nature, they are often referred to as **natural fixation**. However, natural fixation would not provide sufficient fertile soil to grow enough food for our requirements. Hence it is necessary to **artificially** fix

Fig. 26.6 Some plants called legumes have nodules (swellings) on their roots. These nodules contain bacteria that convert nitrogen from the air into nitrogen compounds, which can be used by the plant to grow.

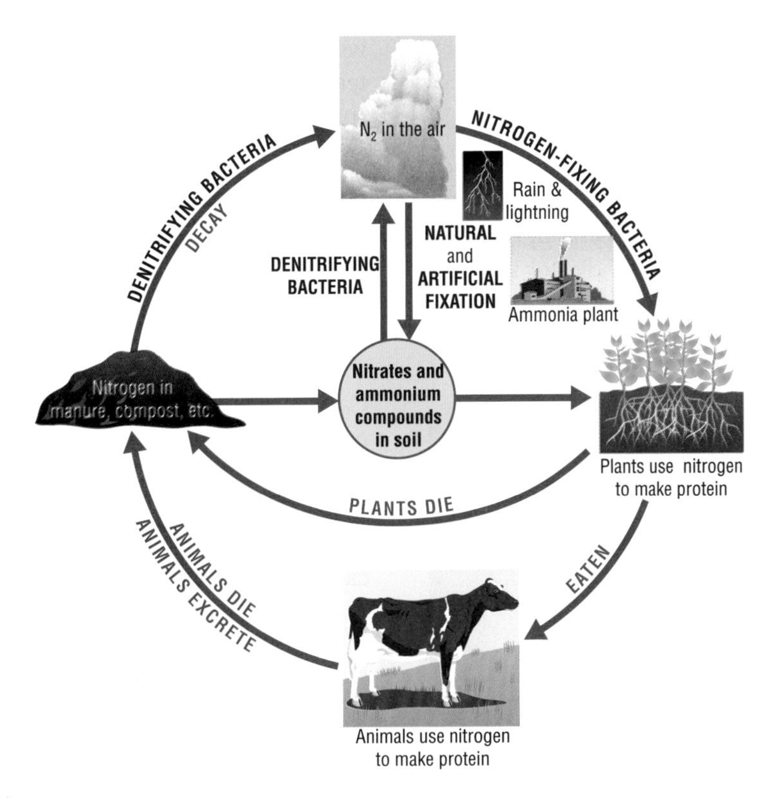

Fig. 26.7 The nitrogen cycle.

nitrogen in industry as studied in the Haber–Bosch process in Chapter 25.

The sequence of events that remove nitrogen from the air and put nitrogen back into the air are summarised in the **nitrogen cycle**, Fig. 26.7.

Ammonium salts are present in the excretion products of animals and the products formed when animals and plants decay. Certain bacteria in the soil which are called **nitrifying bacteria** convert these ammonium salts into nitrates. Also, some bacteria attack nitrates and change them to atmospheric nitrogen. These bacteria are called **denitrifying bacteria**.

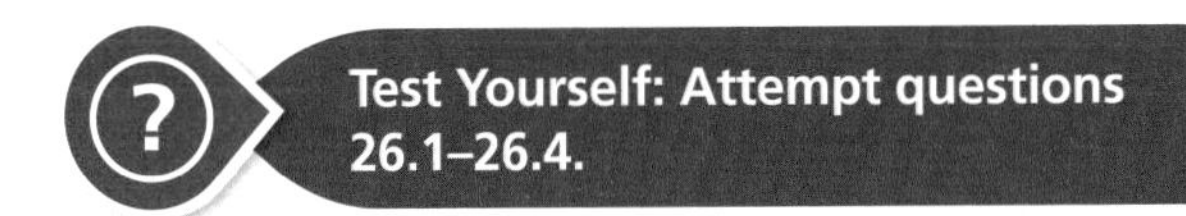

26.4 Inorganic Carbon Compounds

In Chapter 21 we saw that organic compounds are compounds containing carbon. However, a few carbon compounds are not classified as organic compounds. These compounds classed as inorganic are carbon dioxide (CO_2), carbon monoxide (CO), carbonate compounds, e.g. calcium carbonate ($CaCO_3$), hydrogencarbonate compounds, e.g. calcium hydrogencarbonate [$Ca(HCO_3)_2$] and carbide compounds, e.g. calcium carbide (CaC_2).

When powdered carbon is held in a deflagrating spoon and heated over a Bunsen burner, it becomes red hot. If this carbon is then plunged into a jar of oxygen, it glows brightly, and carbon dioxide gas is formed:

$$C + O_2 \longrightarrow CO_2$$

If some water is now added to the gas jar and the jar is shaken, it is found that the carbon dioxide dissolves slightly in water. The solution of carbon dioxide in water changes the colour of litmus paper from blue to red, i.e. the water is acidic. This is because carbon dioxide reacts with water to form a weak acid called carbonic acid, H_2CO_3.

$$CO_2 + H_2O \rightleftharpoons \underset{\text{carbonic acid}}{H_2CO_3}$$

Carbonic acid is a weak acid that dissociates further into either hydrogencarbonate ions or carbonate ions depending on the conditions.

$$H_2CO_3 \leftrightharpoons H^+ + \underset{\text{hydrogen-carbonate ion}}{HCO_3^-} \leftrightharpoons 2H^+ + \underset{\text{carbonate ion}}{CO_3^{2-}}$$

Although pure carbonic acid cannot be isolated, its carbonate and hydrogencarbonate salts are plentiful. Thus, carbon dioxide may exist in its free state as CO_2 or in its combined state as carbonates or hydrogencarbonates. We have seen how to test for the presence of the carbonate and hydrogencarbonate ions in Chapter 6 of the textbook. One of the most common substances found in nature is calcium carbonate, $CaCO_3$, which occurs in the form of marble, chalk or limestone.

Since carbon dioxide forms an acidic solution when dissolved in water, carbon dioxide is said to be an **acidic oxide**. This may be demonstrated quite easily by bubbling carbon dioxide through some litmus indicator solution, Fig. 26.8. Note that litmus indicator solution turns red as the carbon dioxide dissolves to form carbonic acid.

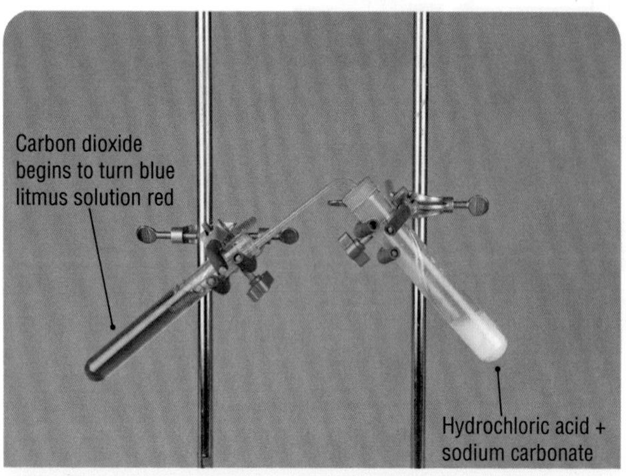

Fig. 26.8 Carbon dioxide is an acidic oxide. The carbonic acid formed when it dissolves in water turns the litmus indicator red.

One of the most common uses of carbon dioxide is to put the 'fizz' in drinks, Fig. 26.9. The fact that carbon dioxide dissolves in water to give a refreshing drink was discovered as far back as 1766 by Joseph Priestly, the discoverer of oxygen, who tasted the solution made by dissolving carbon dioxide in water! For this reason, fizzy drinks are often referred to as carbonated drinks.

Carbon dioxide is also used in fire extinguishers. When carbon dioxide is put under pressure, it turns into a white solid commonly called 'dry ice.' This occurs at a temperature of –78 °C and is used to create a 'mist' for special effects on stage. It is also used to keep objects cold while being transported.

Fig. 26.9 Fizzy drinks are made by dissolving carbon dioxide under pressure in water. The pressure is lowered when the can is opened and bubbles of carbon dioxide form in the drink.

We have seen that carbon dioxide may be produced by burning carbon in air. Carbon dioxide may be conveniently prepared in the laboratory by reacting dilute hydrochloric acid with marble chips:

$$CaCO_3 + 2HCl \longrightarrow CaCl_2 + H_2O + CO_2$$

Carbon dioxide is also produced during a process called **fermentation**. Fermentation is one of the methods used to produce ethanol. When fermentation occurs, the action of enzymes (biological catalysts) in yeast helps to break glucose down into ethanol and carbon dioxide.

$$\text{glucose} \xrightarrow{\text{yeast}} \text{ethanol} + \text{carbon dioxide}$$

$$C_6H_{12}O_6 \xrightarrow{\text{yeast}} 2C_2H_5OH + 2CO_2$$

The ethanol is then separated from the fermented mixture by distillation. It may be easily shown that the gas that is given off is carbon dioxide by setting up the apparatus shown in Fig. 26.10. A solution of glucose in water (about 10 g per 100 cm^3) is placed in the conical flask. About three spatula measures of yeast are added. The flask is stored in a warm place for a few days and the mixture is allowed to ferment. The gas evolved turns the limewater milky.

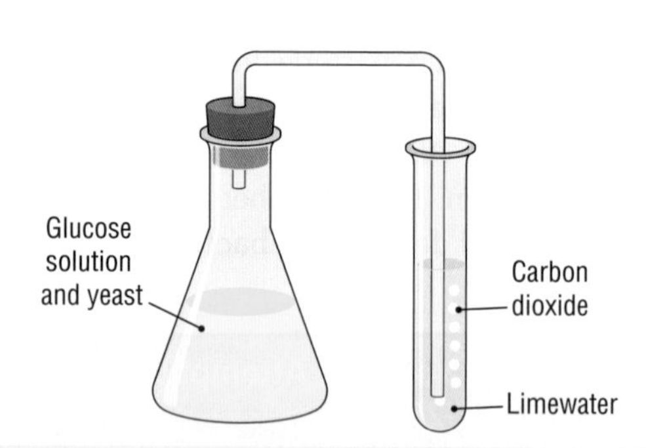

Fig. 26.10 Carbon dioxide is given off when fermentation takes place.

We have seen above that, when carbon is burned in a plentiful supply of oxygen, carbon dioxide is formed. However, if there is a limited supply of oxygen, carbon monoxide (CO) is formed instead, e.g. in car engines as a result of incomplete combustion of motor fuels. Carbon monoxide is also formed when cigarettes are smoked. The tobacco at the end of the cigarette burns in a plentiful supply of oxygen and carbon dioxide is formed. However, the tobacco further along the cigarette burns in a limited supply of oxygen and carbon monoxide is formed.

$$C + \frac{1}{2}O_2 \longrightarrow CO$$
carbon monoxide

Carbon monoxide is a colourless gas that has no smell. It is a highly poisonous gas. If it is inhaled, it reacts with the haemoglobin in the blood and reduces the ability of the blood to carry oxygen. Even low levels of carbon monoxide are harmful to people with heart disease. Since carbon monoxide is odourless, it is particularly difficult to detect. It is very important to ensure that there is always a good air supply whenever a fuel is being burned. If the air supply is poor, it is possible that there may not be enough oxygen to oxidise the carbon monoxide to carbon dioxide. From time to time you hear of fatal accidents occurring as a result of this problem, e.g. gas heaters being used in confined areas such as caravans.

When studying catalytic converters in Chapter 16, we learned that carbon monoxide is converted to carbon dioxide by catalytic converters in cars. However, in large cities there is always a considerable build-up of carbon monoxide in the atmosphere. Not all cars have catalytic converters and, in some cases, the catalytic converters may not be hot enough (e.g. in short city journeys) to function efficiently. The lifetime of carbon monoxide in the atmosphere is not very long – about four months. It is removed from the atmosphere by being converted to carbon dioxide. Catalytic converters merely help to speed up this conversion.

Carbon monoxide does not dissolve in water and does not react with either acids or bases. For this reason it is said to be a **neutral oxide**.

26.5 The Carbon Cycle

The percentage of carbon dioxide in the atmosphere is fairly constant at 0.03%. Studying Fig. 26.11 will help you to understand why this is the case. The **carbon cycle** shows us how carbon (in carbon dioxide and other compounds) is recycled through various processes.

Carbon dioxide is removed from the atmosphere by photosynthesis. This is the method by which plants make food. It may be summarised as:

carbon dioxide + water ⟶ glucose + oxygen

$$6CO_2 + 6H_2O \longrightarrow C_6H_{12}O_6 + 6O_2$$

The glucose produced during photosynthesis is converted by the plant into starch and other materials needed by the plant.

The carbon dioxide in the atmosphere is also removed from the atmosphere by the gas dissolving in oceans, rivers, lakes and rainwater. As already discussed, carbonic acid is formed when carbon dioxide dissolves in water. Some of the carbonic acid is used to form carbonate rock, e.g. calcium carbonate (limestone).

Carbon dioxide is added to the atmosphere in the process of respiration. This is the method by which all living things get energy from food. It may be summarised as follows:

glucose + oxygen ⟶ carbon dioxide + water

$$C_6H_{12}O_6 + 6O_2 \longrightarrow 6CO_2 + 6H_2O$$

All living things carry out respiration and this produces a lot of carbon dioxide, e.g. each of us breathes out about 500 litres of carbon dioxide daily.

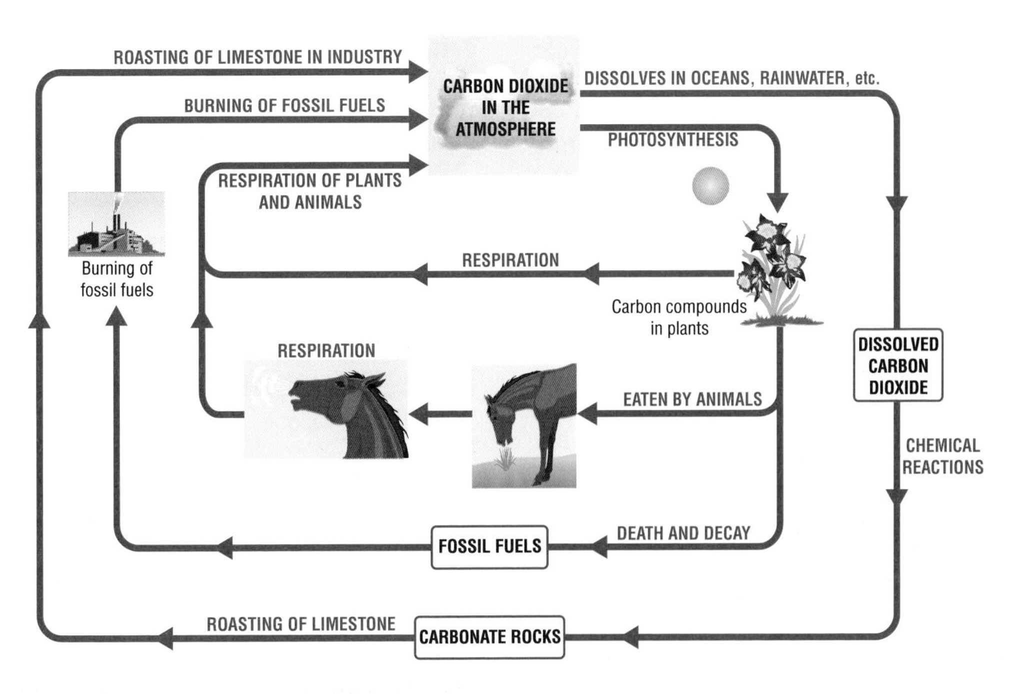

Fig. 26.11 The carbon cycle.

If we examine the equations for respiration and photosynthesis, we see that they are simply the reverse of each other. As long as there is a balance between the two processes, we need not be concerned about running out of food and oxygen or that high levels of carbon dioxide will build up in the atmosphere. However, if we look at the carbon cycle, it is clear that the burning of fossil fuels also gives rise to carbon dioxide in the atmosphere. In recent years, scientists have expressed concern at the increasing levels of carbon dioxide in the atmosphere. They are worried that this may lead to what is commonly called 'global warming.' This is discussed in the next section.

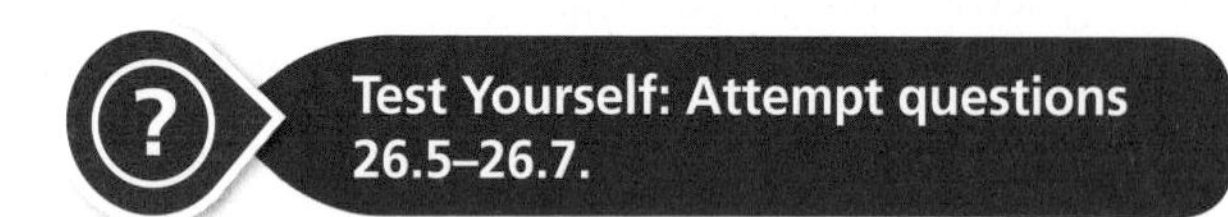

26.6 The Greenhouse Effect

We are all aware that a garden greenhouse helps to trap some of the energy radiated from the Sun. Thus the plants inside the greenhouse are kept at a higher temperature than they would be if kept outside the greenhouse. Similarly, the Earth's atmosphere acts like a greenhouse. Radiation from the Sun (mainly visible and ultraviolet radiation) falls on the Earth and warms up the Earth. The Earth loses some of this heat as it cools down. However, the atmosphere helps to trap some of the energy being lost, i.e. the atmosphere helps to keep the Earth warm, Fig. 26.12. This trapping of the Sun's energy by the atmosphere is called the **greenhouse effect**. This effect is a completely natural occurrence. Without the greenhouse effect a lot of heat energy would be lost from the Earth into outer space. This would cause the average temperature of the air just above the surface of the Earth to fall from about 15 °C to about –15 °C (the temperature it would be if there were no atmosphere). The greenhouse effect is necessary for us – without it the Earth would be covered by a thick sheet of ice and life on Earth could not exist! The Moon is approximately the same distance from the Sun as the Earth. It has no atmosphere surrounding it and the average surface temperature is about –18 °C.

It is found that some gases in the atmosphere are particularly good at absorbing the heat energy (mainly infra-red radiation) given off as the Earth cools down. Such gases are commonly referred to as **greenhouse gases**. Carbon dioxide and water vapour are the main greenhouse gases. The other significant greenhouse gases are methane, dinitrogen oxide (nitrous oxide) and CFCs. Nitrogen and oxygen, the most abundant gases in the atmosphere, are not greenhouse gases as they do not absorb the infra-red radiation emitted by the Earth.

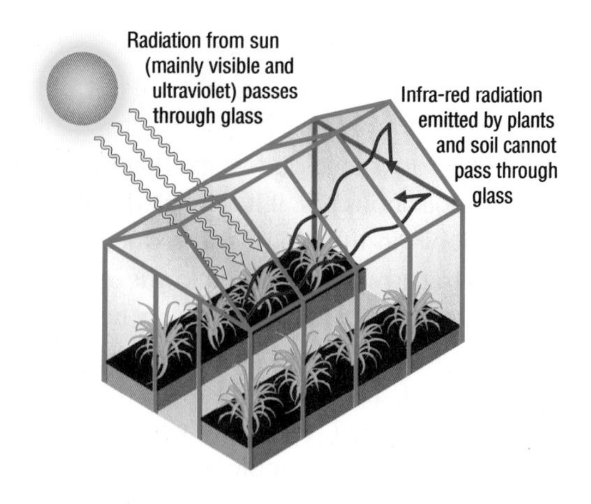

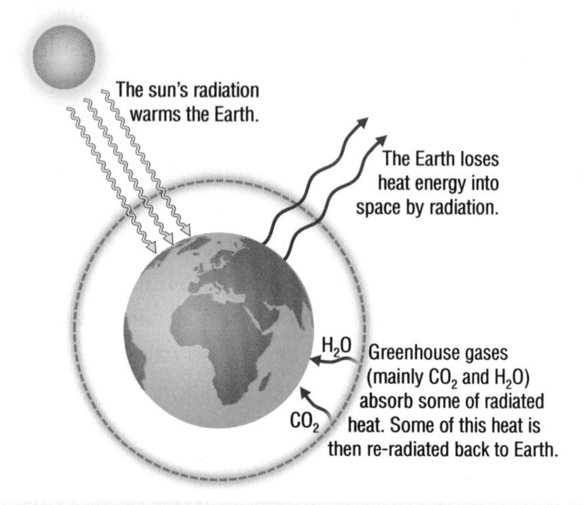

Fig. 26.12 The Earth's atmosphere acts like a greenhouse. It helps to trap some of the heat being lost from the Earth as it cools down.

The greenhouse factor is a measure of the greenhouse effect caused by a particular gas, relative to the same amount of carbon dioxide, which is taken as the standard and is assigned a value of 1.

From Table 26.2 we see that a molecule of methane has the same effect as 30 molecules of carbon dioxide.

Gas	Greenhouse Factor
Water vapour	0.1
Carbon dioxide	1
Mathane	30
N_2O	160
CFCs	21,000–25,000*

Table 26.2 The main greenhouse gases and their corresponding greenhouse factors. (*The actual value depends on the particular CFC.)

It is of great concern to scientists that increasing concentrations of greenhouse gases in the atmosphere may be causing the Earth to get warmer. This occurrence is called the **enhanced greenhouse effect**. The extra warming that results from the enhanced greenhouse effect is called **global warming**.

The concentration of carbon dioxide in the atmosphere plotted against time since 1958 is shown in Fig. 26.13. The levels of carbon dioxide in the Earth's atmosphere are rising as a result of more fossil fuels being burned due to increasing industrialisation. The rise in levels of carbon dioxide became particularly obvious in the 1970s and has caused considerable debate about the effect of the carbon dioxide increase on the Earth's climate. Over the past 100 years, the amount of fossil fuels being burned has increased by about 4% each year. It has been estimated that the burning of fossil fuels produces an average of about 16,000 tonnes of carbon dioxide per year.

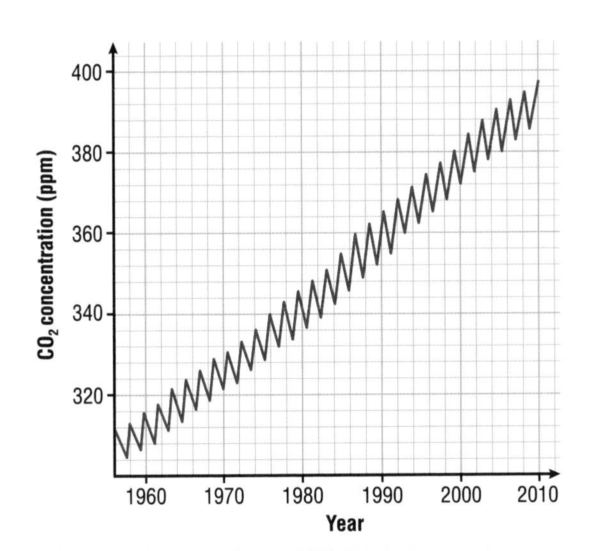

Fig. 26.13 Accurate measurements of the concentration of carbon dioxide in the atmosphere have been made in Hawaii since 1958. The rising levels are giving cause for concern.

You will observe that within any one year the levels rise and fall. This is because, as plants grow in the spring and summer, photosynthesis uses up carbon dioxide causing the level in the atmosphere to fall. In the winter and autumn, the level of carbon dioxide rises again as less photosynthesis is occurring as plants decay.

The contribution of greenhouse gases to global warming is shown in Fig. 26.14.

Water vapour is also a greenhouse gas and has a greater overall effect than carbon dioxide due to its higher concentration. (You may have noticed that, if there are no clouds in the sky, the nights can be very chilly. This is because heat is rapidly escaping from the Earth as there is little water vapour to redirect the escaping infra-red radiation back to the Earth.) However, the global concentration of water vapour is not affected to any great extent by human activities. The amount of water vapour in the atmosphere depends on temperature and is controlled by evaporation and condensation in the water cycle.

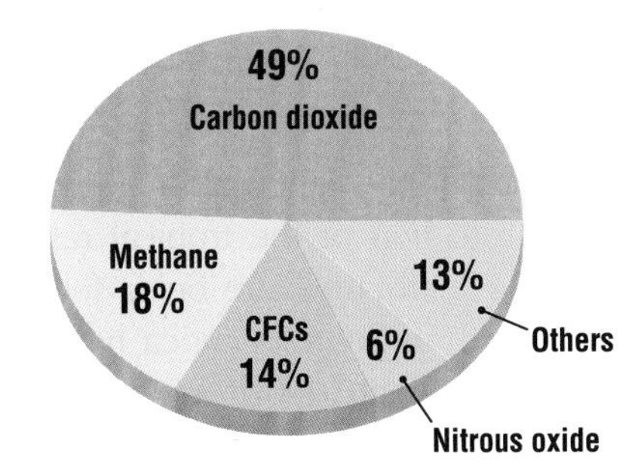

Fig. 26.14 The contribution of the main greenhouse gases to global warming.

On the other hand, it is found that the rate of 'turnover' of carbon dioxide in the atmosphere is quite slow. This 'turnover' rate of carbon dioxide is referred to as the **residence time** for carbon dioxide. Although the sea can dissolve a lot of carbon dioxide, the top few hundred metres of sea water mixes very slowly with deeper waters. This means that, when carbon dioxide dissolves in seawater, it can take hundreds of years before it penetrates deep down in the ocean and is precipitated as calcium carbonate. Thus, although the oceans will eventually dissolve much of the increased levels of carbon dioxide in the atmosphere, this will take a long time. It is estimated that carbon dioxide has a residence time of about 100 years, i.e. the average molecule of carbon dioxide remains in the atmosphere for about 100 years. Photosynthesis is the process that removes carbon dioxide from the atmosphere at the greatest rate. However, this cannot keep pace with the rate at which carbon dioxide is being released into the atmosphere by burning fossil fuels.

The concentration of other greenhouse gases in the atmosphere are also affected by human activity, e.g. methane (from natural gas leakage, landfill rubbish dumps, swamps, paddy fields and ruminants), dinitrogen oxide (e.g. from car-exhaust fumes, use of nitrogenous fertilisers) and CFCs (from fridges, foams and aerosol sprays). Although there are only very small amounts of CFCs in the atmosphere, each molecule has a big effect since CFCs have a large greenhouse factor. Therefore, it is important that steps are taken to limit the amounts of these substances released into the atmosphere.

It has been calculated that the residence times of other greenhouse gases such as CFCs and dinitrogen oxide (N_2O) are similar to that of carbon dioxide – about 100 years. In contrast, methane has a residence time of only about 10 years as methane is broken down naturally in the atmosphere.

International agreements have pledged to limit carbon dioxide emissions. There is still much debate as to the best way to achieve this and different countries adopt different methods of reducing these emissions. In industrialised countries, alternative energy sources would have to be developed. In developing countries it could be difficult to insist on a reduction in the use of fossil fuels as this could delay industrialisation of these countries.

A very effective step in the fight against global warming would be the protection of the tropical rain forests. Unfortunately, too many trees are being felled in the world. For example, in South America huge areas of tropical forests have been cut down for timber and to provide land for farming. Therefore, fewer trees are available to take carbon dioxide from the air by photosynthesis. In addition, the clearing of forests is often accompanied by burning large quantities of wood and this increases the level of carbon dioxide in the atmosphere. This problem must be tackled by growing a lot more trees, as carbon dioxide is removed from the air in the process of photosynthesis. However, large areas of forest would need to be planted each year, and it would take many years before a significant contribution to reducing levels of carbon dioxide would be made. For example, an electric power company in the USA agreed to plant 52 million trees in Guatemala to absorb the carbon dioxide produced by a new power station built by the company.

Implications of the enhanced greenhouse effect

It is expected that enhanced global warming will have three main effects:

(a) **Rise in sea level**: It is predicted that the Earth's surface, the atmosphere and the oceans will probably become a few degrees warmer as a result of these human-made emissions of greenhouse gases. Since water expands as the temperature increases, it is expected that sea levels will rise. It is also expected that sea levels could be affected by the melting of glaciers in the Arctic and Antarctic regions. It has been predicted by some scientists that the sea level will have risen by about 18 cm by the year 2030. This could be quite serious and could adversely affect the homes and livelihoods of people in low-lying countries such as the Netherlands and Bangladesh.

(b) **Climate changes**: It is expected that, as the temperature of the atmosphere is increased, more violent weather disturbances will be observed – storms will be more frequent and more violent. This is because more energy will be contained in the air and water vapour at the Earth's surface. Climate conditions in general will become more extreme, and data from climate conditions in the past will be less reliable.

(c) **Agriculture:** One possible advantage of the enhanced greenhouse effect is that the rate of photosynthesis in crops may be increased due to increased levels of carbon dioxide in the atmosphere. However, weeds will also grow faster! It is likely that climate changes could counteract the benefit of crops growing more quickly, e.g. increased rainfall could lower crop yields and make harvesting more difficult.

Example 26.1

Question

Distinguish between the terms 'greenhouse effect' and 'enhanced greenhouse effect.'

Answer

The greenhouse effect is a natural phenomenon involving the trapping of the Sun's energy by the atmosphere. Some gases in the atmosphere are particularly good at absorbing the heat energy given off as the Earth cools down. Thus, the greenhouse effect is a property of the Earth's atmosphere.

The enhanced greenhouse effect refers to the extra effect of human-made emissions of greenhouse gases (e.g. carbon dioxide, methane and CFCs) which have taken place since the growth of industrialisation.

Test Yourself: Attempt questions 26.8–26.9.

26.7 Atmospheric Pollution

The pollution of the atmosphere has been taking place since the earliest times. However, it is only in the recent past that we have become aware of it. One of the reasons for our concern is the increasing levels of pollution of the atmosphere. More people are now living on Earth than ever before. This means more homes, more cars, more industries and more power stations – and, consequently, more pollution.

Air pollution is a situation that exists when a constituent in the air is present to the extent that there is a significant hazard to present or future health or to the environment.

Gases released into the air spread throughout the atmosphere by diffusion. Not all gases released by human activities damage the environment. In this section we will consider those gases that give rise to acid rain. In the next section we will look at the damage being done to the ozone layer.

Acid rain arises because some air pollutants have acidic properties. Sulfur dioxide and nitrogen dioxide are the main pollutants that give rise to acid rain. Normal rainwater is slightly acidic with a pH of about 5.6. This is because, as discussed above, carbon dioxide dissolves in water to form a solution of the weak acid, carbonic acid. However, acid rain can have a pH of from 2–5.

One of the main gases responsible for the formation of acid rain is sulfur dioxide, SO_2. Some sulfur dioxide in the air comes from natural sources e.g. volcanoes or rotting vegetation. However, it is estimated that about 85% of the sulfur dioxide in the air over Europe comes from the burning of fossil fuels (mainly coal). Coal and other fossil fuels contain small amounts of sulfur. When these fuels are burned in our homes and industries, the sulfur in the fuels combines with the oxygen in the air to form sulfur dioxide.

$$\text{sulfur} + \text{oxygen} \longrightarrow \text{sulfur dioxide}$$
$$S + O_2 \longrightarrow SO_2$$

The reaction that occurs when sulfur dioxide – from natural sources or industrial gaseous emissions – dissolves in water may be represented as:

$$\text{sulfur dioxide} + \text{water} \longrightarrow \text{sulfurous acid}$$
$$SO_2 + H_2O \longrightarrow H_2SO_3$$

Sulfur dioxide reacts with oxygen in the air to form sulfur trioxide.

$$\text{sulfur dioxide} + \text{oxygen} \longrightarrow \text{sulfur trioxide}$$
$$2SO_2 + O_2 \longrightarrow 2SO_3$$

The sulfur trioxide then dissolves in rainwater to form sulfuric acid.

$$\text{sulfur trioxide} + \text{water} \longrightarrow \text{sulfuric acid}$$
$$SO_3 + H_2O \longrightarrow H_2SO_4$$

Sulfurous acid is also oxidised to sulfuric acid.

$$\text{sulfurous acid} + \text{oxygen} \longrightarrow \text{sulfuric acid}$$
$$2H_2SO_3 + O_2 \longrightarrow 2H_2SO_4$$

Sulfur dioxide may be made very simply in the laboratory by burning a small quantity of sulfur on a deflagrating spoon in a gas jar of oxygen. Some water containing a few drops of litmus indicator is then added. The litmus indicator turns red, Fig. 26.15.

Fig. 26.15 Sulfur dioxide is formed when sulfur is burned in oxygen. The sulfur dioxide is an acidic gas as is shown by the litmus indicator turning a red colour.

Although sulfur dioxide is thought to be the biggest single cause of acid rain, the oxides of nitrogen also play a part in its formation. The main oxides of nitrogen in the atmosphere are nitrogen monoxide, NO, and nitrogen dioxide, NO_2. These oxides of nitrogen are produced naturally and are also human-made. The main natural sources of oxides of nitrogen are soil bacteria and lightning discharges. Oxides of nitrogen are also produced when fossil fuels are burned at high temperatures in power stations and in car engines. At high temperature, the nitrogen in the air combines with oxygen to form nitrogen monoxide. In car engines, the high temperature is produced by the spark plug.

$$\text{nitrogen} + \text{oxygen} \longrightarrow \text{nitrogen monoxide}$$
$$N_2 + O_2 \longrightarrow 2NO$$

The nitrogen monoxide then combines with oxygen in the air to form nitrogen dioxide.

$$\text{nitrogen monoxide} + \text{oxygen} \longrightarrow \text{nitrogen dioxide}$$
$$2NO + O_2 \longrightarrow 2NO_2$$

The nitrogen dioxide then dissolves in rainwater to form a mixture of nitrous acid and nitric acid.

$$\text{nitrogen dioxide} + \text{water} \longrightarrow \text{nitrous acid} + \text{nitric acid}$$
$$2NO_2 + H_2O \longrightarrow HNO_2 + HNO_3$$

The formation of acid rain is illustrated in Fig. 26.16 on page 100.

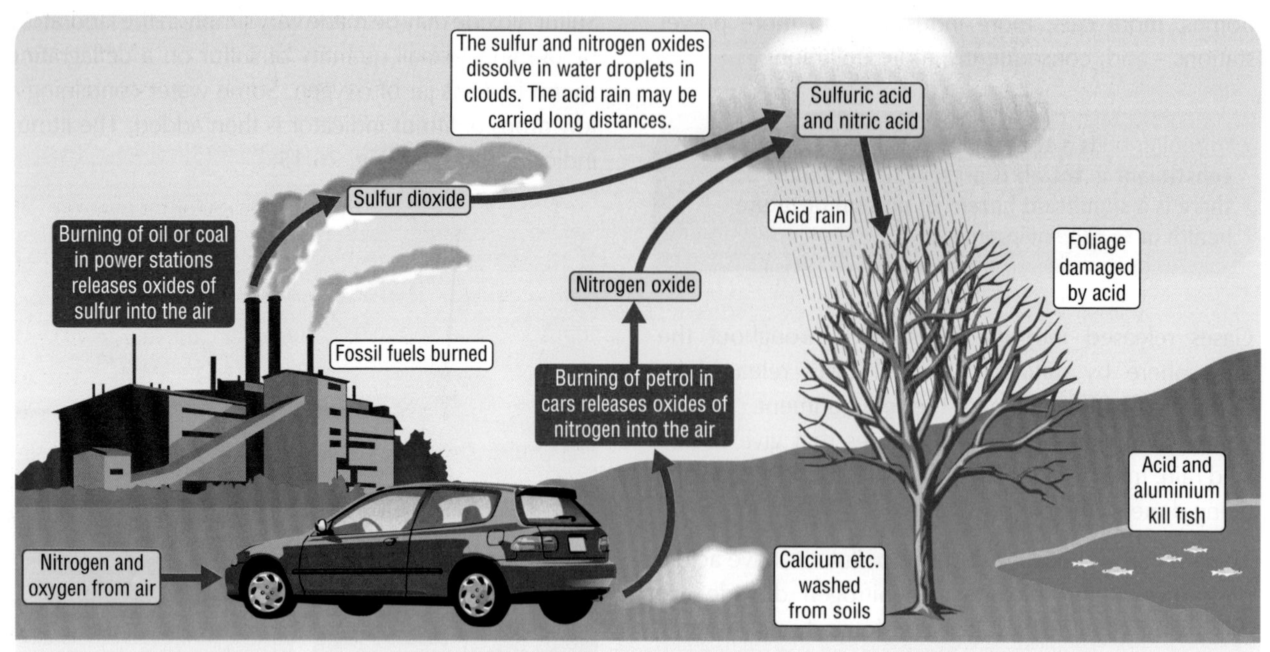

Fig. 26.16 Acid rain is formed when sulfur dioxide and oxides of nitrogen dissolve in water. Acid rain contains sulfuric acid and nitric acid.

Acid rain is generally recognised as being the cause of extensive damage to trees in Europe and in many other parts of the world. It is also thought to be responsible for the death of fish in many lakes – particularly in the Scandinavian countries where the prevailing winds carry the acid rain from other countries. Also, acid rain causes many metals to become more soluble, e.g. aluminium ions become leached out of soil and dissolve in lakes. The aluminium compounds interfere with the operation of fish gills and they become blocked, killing off the fish. Lakes are more affected by acid rain than rivers since the acidity builds up in lakes killing off the fish. In rivers, the level of acidity is diluted by the movement of the flowing water.

Since acid rain affects the growth of trees, this has caused major damage to forests. Countries such as Germany and the Czech Republic have had serious problems with defoliation of trees. Acid rain washes out essential nutrients such as calcium and magnesium from the soil. Therefore, trees cannot absorb these nutrients through their roots and go into decline. It is thought that much of this acid rain comes from the highly industrialised areas of England and Germany. Most of the acid rain in Canada is thought to come from the USA.

Acid rain also damages limestone buildings – the acid reacts with the calcium carbonate which crumbles away. Objects made of metals (e.g. bridges, cars, ships) are also damaged by acid rain since many metals are corroded by acid.

Up to recent times, acidic gases from power plants and industries were simply discharged through tall chimneys. This protected the local community but merely transferred the problem of acid rain to another area perhaps hundreds of kilometres away. Coal-fired power stations are a major source of sulfur dioxide. In recent years, many of these power stations have installed 'scrubbing systems' to remove sulfur dioxide from the gases in the chimney-stack before they leave the power station. For example, in Moneypoint in Co. Clare, limestone is used as a 'scrubber' (i.e. a sulfur remover) to remove the sulfur dioxide from the chimney gases. As the gases pass up the chimney, jets of wet powdered limestone are sprayed on them. The following reaction occurs:

limestone + sulfur dioxide ⟶ calcium sulfite + carbon dioxide

$$CaCO_3 + SO_2 \longrightarrow CaSO_3 + CO_2$$

The calcium sulfite reacts with oxygen to form calcium sulfate (gypsum) which is removed as a sludge. Calcium sulfate can be used to make plaster for the building industry.

Test Yourself: Attempt questions 26.10–26.11.

26.8 The Ozone Layer

Trioxygen, O_3, is a form of oxygen more commonly known as ozone. The word ozone comes from a Greek word meaning 'to smell,' as ozone is a pungent, pale blue gas that condenses to a deep blue liquid at –112 °C. About 25 km above the Earth's surface, there is a layer of ozone surrounding the Earth, Fig. 26.17. The ozone is actually present in tiny amounts. The maximum concentration of ozone (only about 10 ppm) is in a region 25–50 km from the surface of the Earth. If it were all collected at ground level, it would form a

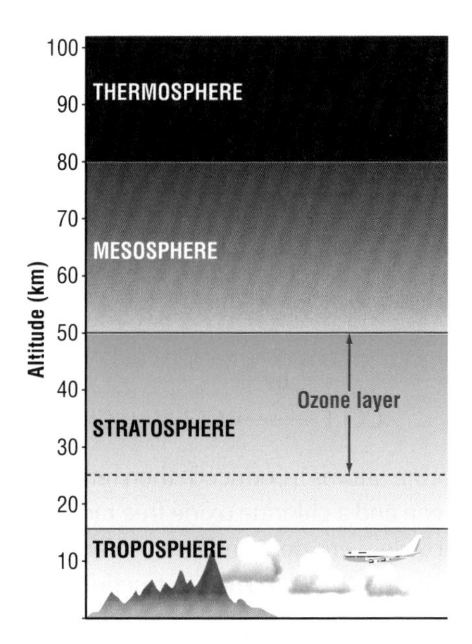

Fig. 26.17 The ozone layer is in the stratosphere and absorbs much of the harmful ultraviolet radiation from the Sun.

layer only 3 mm thick at atmospheric temperature and pressure! In this upper part of the atmosphere (called the stratosphere), ozone performs a very important task. It absorbs much of the harmful ultraviolet radiation coming from the Sun. There is no life in the stratosphere because this ultraviolet radiation is so damaging that it would destroy living tissue.

Ozone is formed in the stratosphere by the reaction between an oxygen atom and an oxygen molecule. The oxygen atoms are formed when ultraviolet light of particularly high energy breaks the oxygen molecule into oxygen atoms:

$$O_2 \xrightarrow{uv} O^\bullet + O^\bullet$$

This is an example of **photodissociation**, i.e. the breaking of a bond using radiation. Oxygen atoms are very reactive since they have an unpaired electron. (They are often referred to as oxygen **free radicals** and are represented by $^\bullet$ written after the symbol. This dot represents the unpaired electron.) As soon as the oxygen atoms are formed, they react with the oxygen molecules in the atmosphere to form ozone.

$$O^\bullet + O_2 \longrightarrow O_3 \qquad \textbf{Production of ozone (1)}$$

This reaction is the source of all the ozone in the stratosphere.

The energy to break the oxygen molecules into oxygen atoms may also be provided by an electric discharge, i.e. by electricity passing through the air. Very often it is possible to get the sharp smell of ozone near photocopiers or electric motors. The high voltage causes the oxygen molecules to split into oxygen atoms which then form ozone as shown in the above reaction.

When the ozone formed in the above reaction absorbs ultraviolet radiation, **photodissociation of the ozone** occurs, i.e. the above reaction is reversed and the ozone is decomposed:

$$O_3 \xrightarrow{uv} O_2 + O^\bullet \qquad \textbf{Decomposition of ozone (2)}$$

Most of the oxygen atoms produced in this reaction then react with O_2 molecules to re-form ozone.

Reaction (2) is responsible for the very important screening effect of ozone since it absorbs much of the harmful ultraviolet radiation. Excessive exposure to ultraviolet light can cause skin cancer. As stated above, the ozone layer extends from about 25–50 km above the Earth's surface, and this layer of ozone helps to protect us from much of the harmful ultraviolet radiation coming from the Sun.

Note: Some of the oxygen atoms produced in reaction (2) destroy ozone molecules by converting them to oxygen molecules:

$$O^\bullet + O_3 \longrightarrow 2O_2 \qquad \textbf{Removal of ozone (3)}$$

The oxygen molecules are then broken down by ultraviolet light to form oxygen atoms (free radicals) which lead to the production of ozone as shown in reaction (1).

Thus, we can see from reactions (1)–(3) that ozone is being made and destroyed all the time. Ozone is not formed below the stratosphere because there is insufficient high-energy ultraviolet light available in the lower atmosphere to produce the O atoms necessary to form ozone as shown in reaction (1). This high-energy ultraviolet light has already been absorbed by O_2 and O_3 in the stratosphere.

At one stage it was thought that the rate at which ozone was being made was the same as the rate at which it was being used up, i.e. that the concentration of ozone in the atmosphere was constant. However, in 1984 a group of scientists working with the British Antarctic Survey discovered that ozone concentrations over the Antarctic were lower than expected. It was discovered that there was a large decrease in ozone over the Antarctic during the spring (August–October at the South Pole). This is commonly referred to as a 'hole' in the ozone layer. Since then, evidence has been gathered that there is also an ozone 'hole' above the Arctic and a general depletion of ozone in other areas around the globe.

Information gathered by NASA satellites demonstrated that chlorine atoms are mainly responsible for destroying the ozone layer. Substances called chlorofluorocarbons (CFCs) are responsible for producing chlorine atoms in the atmosphere and causing much of the damage to the ozone layer. CFCs are prepared from alkanes by carrying out substitution reactions as discussed in the section 22.2.1 of Chapter 22.

26.9 CFCs

Chlorofluorocarbons are a family of compounds that contain chlorine, fluorine and carbon. Two examples of CFCs are shown in Fig. 26.18. CFCs were invented as far back as 1930 in the USA as replacements for ammonia in fridges – ammonia is a toxic, corrosive and pungent gas. The American engineer, Thomas Midgley, demonstrated their lack of toxicity and flammability to the American Chemical Society in a rather spectacular manner. He inhaled some dichlorodifluoromethane CCl_2F_2 (commonly referred to as CFC-12 and used in fridges in the past) and blew out a candle with it!

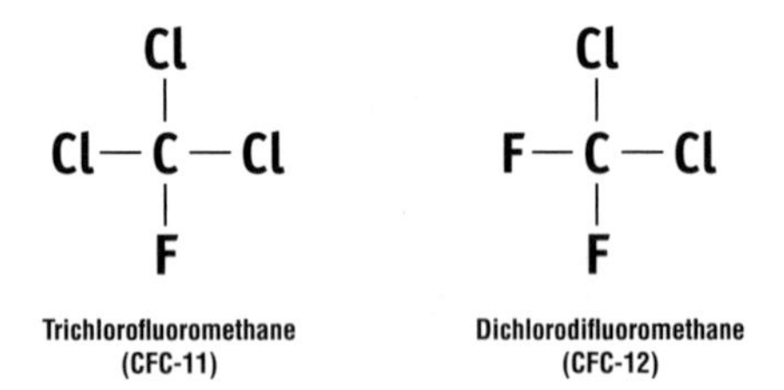

Fig. 26.18 Two examples of CFCs. Each CFC is given a number to identify it and to avoid the need to write the full name.

CFCs had all the right properties for use as refrigerants in fridges, freezers and air conditioners. CFCs have low boiling points, low toxicity, low flammability and are very unreactive. Lots of different CFCs have been developed for different purposes. Some of the original uses of CFCs are shown in Fig. 26.19.

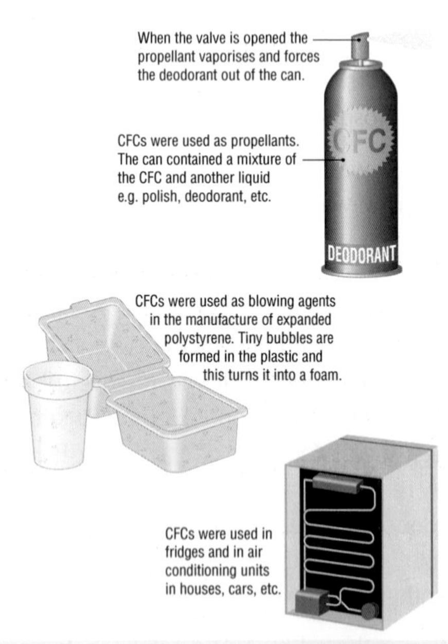

Fig. 26.19 Some of the original uses of CFCs. In most cases, CFCs in these items have being replaced by alternative compounds that do not damage the ozone layer. However, old fridges and air conditioning units may still contain CFCs.

Although CFCs are ideal for the purposes for which they were intended, one of the problems with them is that they are too unreactive. As stated earlier, it is estimated that CFCs have a lifetime (residence time) in the lower atmosphere of about 100 years. This allows plenty of time for them to be transported into the upper atmosphere (stratosphere) where they become reactive. When they reach the stratosphere they are broken down by the high level of ultraviolet radiation there.

One example of a reaction in which a CFC is broken down is:

$$CCl_3F \xrightarrow{uv} CCl_2F^{\bullet} + Cl^{\bullet}$$

The chlorine atoms produced then attack ozone to form oxygen and a chlorine oxide free radical. (Traces of chlorine oxide were detected over Antarctica by NASA scientists in the 1970s.) The destruction of an ozone molecule by a chlorine atom may be represented as follows:

$$O_3 + Cl^{\bullet} \longrightarrow O_2 + ClO^{\bullet} \qquad \text{(i)}$$

The chlorine oxide is very reactive (it is a radical) and attacks an oxygen atom as follows:

$$ClO^{\bullet} + O^{\bullet} \longrightarrow Cl^{\bullet} + O_2 \qquad \text{(ii)}$$

Reaction (ii) releases more chlorine atoms to attack further ozone molecules as in reaction (i) above. Thus, the cycle continues and a chain reaction occurs.

The chlorine atom, used up in reaction (i), is regenerated in reaction (ii). Every time reaction (i) occurs, an ozone molecule is destroyed. It has been estimated that a single chlorine atom can destroy tens of thousands of molecules of ozone.

The damage that CFCs cause to the ozone layer was predicted way back in the 1970s by some research scientists in the University of California, USA. In fact, the USA, Canada, Norway and Sweden all banned CFCs for use in aerosols in the 1970s. It was not until 1987 that an international conference in Montreal decided to place restrictions on the production and release of CFCs into the atmosphere. Three years later, a Revised Montreal Protocol decided on a total phasing out of CFCs by the year 2000. However, we must remember that CFCs are still present in large quantities in fridges and air conditioners, and there is always a danger of leakage from ageing appliances. Also, even if all emissions of CFCs were stopped immediately, it is estimated that the ozone layer could continue being damaged for at least 20 years due to the large quantities of CFCs already there.

The hole in the ozone layer is worst above the Antarctic because of the unique climate there. The size of the hole is enormous – it covers an area about the size of the USA and is as deep as Mount Everest is high. Strong winds (the Roaring Forties) cut off the air around the Antarctic from the rest of the air mass around the Earth and this keeps the hole in the ozone layer confined to the Antarctic.

Nitrogen monoxide also reacts with ozone in the stratosphere and destroys the ozone. The nitrogen monoxide comes from some biological reactions in bacteria on Earth, from the combination of nitrogen and oxygen due to the action of lightning , and from the exhaust fumes of high-altitude, supersonic aircraft.

ozone + nitrogen monoxide ⟶ oxygen + nitrogen dioxide

$$O_3 + NO \longrightarrow O_2 + NO_2$$

However, even though nitrogen monoxide does help in the depletion of ozone, it is CFCs that are believed to be the main cause of damage to the ozone layer.

We have seen in reaction (i) that chlorine atoms attack ozone molecules and destroy them. Fortunately, there are other molecules in the atmosphere, which react with Cl atoms and prevent the concentration of chlorine atoms building up. Otherwise, ozone would be destroyed at a very fast rate.

Methane is an important example of a molecule that reacts with chlorine atoms. Some of the methane released from the Earth reaches the stratosphere where it reacts with chlorine atoms as follows:

methane + chlorine atom ⟶ methyl radical + hydrogen chloride

$$CH_4 + Cl^{\bullet} \longrightarrow CH_3^{\bullet} + HCl$$

The hydrogen chloride is eventually removed in raindrops. This gets rid of some of the chlorine atoms from the atmosphere.

Although ozone has a beneficial effect in the upper atmosphere (stratosphere), it is detrimental to human health in the lower atmosphere (troposphere). It is thought to trigger asthma attacks and bronchitis.

26.10 CFC Substitutes

As the problems with CFCs were discovered, work began on finding other substances to replace them. It was not possible to simply stop using them as the uses of CFCs in fridges, in materials for insulation of houses, etc. make our lives a lot more comfortable. In addition, a lot of jobs were dependent on CFC applications.

The ability of a molecule to destroy ozone depends on its percentage of chlorine and on its lifetime in the atmosphere. Compounds that were proposed as replacements for CFCs all contain hydrogen atoms bonded to carbon. For this reason, these replacement compounds are called **hydrochlorofluorocarbons (HCFCs)** since they contain hydrogen, chlorine, fluorine and carbon. The presence of the C–H bond means that these molecules are broken down by radicals naturally present in the lower atmosphere (troposphere). Hence these molecules do not reach the ozone in the stratosphere. An example of a HCFC molecule is chlorodifluoromethane, $CHClF_2$, which is the propellant being used in many aerosols advertised as 'ozone friendly,' Fig. 26.20. This is commonly referred to as HCFC-22.

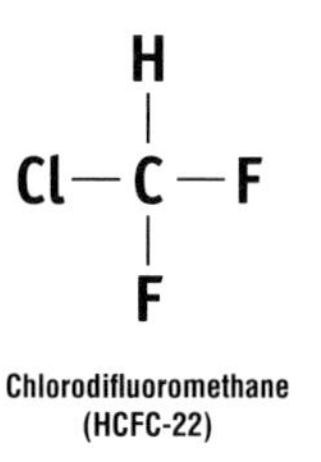

Fig. 26.20 This compound is one of the replacements for CFCs. It is an example of a hydrochlorofluorocarbon (HCFC).

Unfortunately, HCFCs are not the perfect solution as they do destroy some ozone since they contain chlorine. However, they destroy a lot less ozone than CFCs, e.g. it has been calculated that the long-term ozone-damaging effect of HCFC-22 is only about 5% of that of CFC-11. Other HCFCs, however, can have a damaging effect of up to 33% of the damage caused by CFCs. Another problem with HCFCs is that, like CFCs, they are greenhouse gases and contribute to global warming.

Considerable research is taking place to develop substitutes for CFCs and HCFCs which have no chlorine in their molecules. Such compounds are called hydrofluorocarbons, HFCs. These are hydrogen-containing fluoroalkanes, e.g. CH_2FCF_3.

We are fortunate that the hole in the ozone layer over the Antarctic was discovered. This has given us a warning of what might happen if the ozone layer continues to be damaged, enabling us to take steps to minimise this damage.

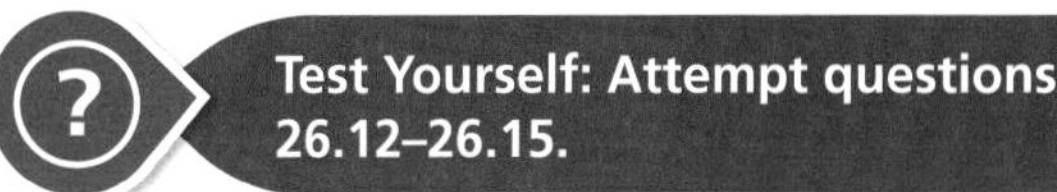

Summary

- Oxygen and nitrogen are the two main gases in the atmosphere.
- Oxygen is a reactive gas and is manufactured by the liquefaction and fractional distillation of air.
- Nitrogen is an unreactive gas and is also manufactured by the liquefaction and fractional distillation of air.
- Nitrogen fixation is the conversion of atmospheric nitrogen to compounds that can be used by plants.
- Carbon dioxide may exist in its free state as CO_2 or in its combined state as carbonates or hydrogencarbonates.
- The carbon cycle shows how carbon is recycled through various processes.
- The greenhouse effect is a natural phenomenon involving the trapping of the Sun's energy by the atmosphere.
- Increasing concentrations of certain gases in the atmosphere are causing the Earth to get warmer. This is called the enhanced greenhouse effect or global warming.
- Sulfur dioxide and nitrogen dioxide are the main pollutants that give rise to acid rain.
- The ozone layer helps to protect us from much of the harmful ultraviolet radiation coming from the Sun.
- CFCs produce chlorine atoms that damage the ozone layer.
- Nitrogen monoxide also damages the ozone layer.
- Methane helps to limit the damage to the ozone layer by reacting with chlorine atoms.
- CFCs are now being replaced with HCFCs.

EXAM EDGE **Use Chapter 26 Exam Edge to study the sample answers to questions that have been asked on past Leaving Certificate Chemistry examinations on the topics covered in this chapter.**

Questions

26.1 Fill in the blanks in the following:

Air is a .... of gases. Most of the air (99%) consists of just two gases .... and .... The gas which is present in the greatest amount in ordinary air is .... A molecule of oxygen gas is represented by .... and of nitrogen gas by .... Only one gas in the air will allow substances to burn in it. This gas is .... Oxygen and nitrogen may be separated from the air by .... because they have different .... Nitrogen is needed by plants to make .... Most plants cannot take nitrogen directly from the .... Some nitrogen is naturally 'fixed' during a .... and some is fixed by .... in the nodules of certain plants called .... An example of such a plant is .... Bacteria which convert ammonium salts into nitrates are called .... bacteria, and bacteria which attack nitrates and change them to atmospheric nitrogen are called .... bacteria.

26.2 Name (a) the most abundant and (b) the most reactive gas in the air. What advantage has pure oxygen over air for use in hospitals? Give two other uses of oxygen gas.

Give a brief description of the method by which oxygen is manufactured industrially. Your description should include a labelled diagram.

26.3 State two uses of nitrogen gas and two uses of liquid nitrogen. Explain the meaning of the term 'nitrogen fixation.' Discuss the two methods by which nitrogen fixation takes place in nature.

Distinguish between the terms 'natural fixation' and 'artificial fixation' of nitrogen.

Using a diagram, describe the sequence of events by which nitrogen is added to and removed from the air. What name is commonly given to this sequence of events?

26.4 Write a brief note on nitrogen-fixing bacteria, nitrifying bacteria and denitrifying bacteria. Draw a diagram of the nitrogen cycle and show where these processes occur.

A farmer wishes to obtain a good yield of barley without using a fertiliser. Suggest what she could plant in the field the previous year to ensure a good yield.

26.5 Give the names and formulas of two compounds containing carbon but which are normally classified as inorganic compounds.

How would you demonstrate that carbon dioxide is an acidic oxide? 'Carbon dioxide is evolved during fermentation.' Explain the underlined term and describe an experiment to demonstrate that the gas evolved during fermentation is carbon dioxide.

Write down the names of two processes that add carbon dioxide to the atmosphere. Suggest a place where you would expect the level of carbon dioxide to be higher than average.

Why is it dangerous to leave a car engine running in a closed garage?

26.6 What is 'dry ice?' Why do ice-cream sellers prefer dry ice to ordinary ice?

If a gas heater is used in a bathroom, it is important to leave the window open. Why is this precaution necessary?

With the aid of a diagram, write a brief account of the carbon cycle. Your account should include a description of the methods by which carbon dioxide is added to the atmosphere and removed from the atmosphere.

Explain how the carbon dioxide in the air is converted to carbohydrate in your body.

'Respiration may be considered as being the opposite reaction to photosynthesis.' Explain this statement.

26.7 Name two common sources of carbon monoxide. How does carbon monoxide act on the body? In a recent newspaper article, it was reported that a man living in a caravan was found dead sitting in a chair next to a portable gas heater. The pathologist's report showed that he had died from carbon monoxide poisoning. Explain how this occurred.

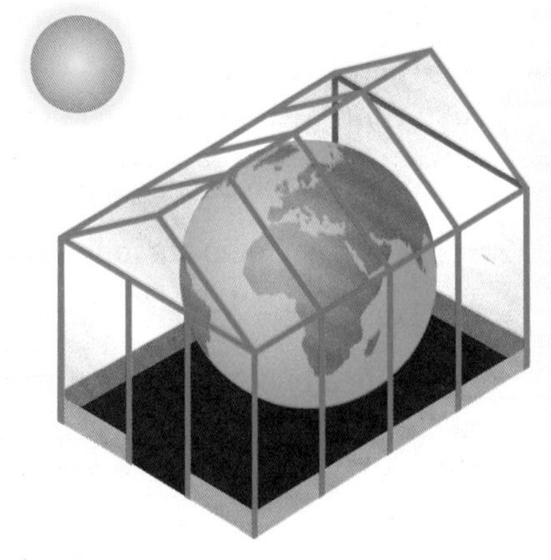
Fig. 26.21

26.8 The levels of carbon dioxide in the atmosphere are increasing.

Give two reasons why this is happening.

(a) Explain how the atmosphere around the Earth acts like the glass in a greenhouse, Fig. 26.21.

(b) What is meant by the enhanced greenhouse effect?

(c) Why is the enhanced greenhouse effect causing concern to scientists?

(d) Name any two greenhouse gases.

(e) Suggest two steps that could be taken to stop the increase in the levels of greenhouse gases in the atmosphere.

26.9 'The greenhouse effect is of great benefit and the Earth would be a very different place without it.' Discuss this statement.

Explain the term *greenhouse gas* and give two examples of such gases. Give one harmful effect and one beneficial effect of global warming.

Why do tropical forests and jungles play such a large part in ensuring a balance between the levels of carbon dioxide and oxygen in the atmosphere?

At night time, the temperature of desert areas can drop considerably. Explain this phenomenon.

Discuss briefly two possible implications of global warming.

26.10 Explain what is meant by the term *acid rain.* Name the two main pollutants responsible for acid rain. Discuss the origins of these pollutants and describe, using the appropriate equations, how acid rain is formed.

Why do power stations that burn fossil fuels always have high chimneys? Are these chimneys a solution to the problems caused by their emissions. Explain your answer.

Why do lakes suffer more than rivers from the effects of acid rain?

26.11 Explain how coal-fired power stations give rise to acid rain. Give one disadvantage of building such a power station close to an area of high population. Discuss the measures being taken to remove some of the pollutant gases from chimney stacks.

Name two problems caused by acid rain. In Europe, Scandinavia is particularly affected by acid rain. Explain the reason for this.

26.12 (a) Distinguish between the stratosphere and the troposphere. In which of these regions is the ozone layer located?

(b) Why is excessive exposure to ultraviolet light dangerous?

(c) Write down the equations showing (i) the production and (ii) the decomposition of ozone.

(d) Where was the 'hole' in the ozone layer discovered in 1984?

(e) What element is mainly responsible for the destruction of ozone in the atmosphere?

26.13 (a) Write down the formula for ozone.

(b) Where is the ozone layer situated in the atmosphere?

(c) Why is there no life in the stratosphere?

(d) Explain how ozone is formed in the atmosphere.

(e) Write a brief note on the important role played by ozone in the stratosphere.

(f) Why is ozone not formed below the stratosphere?

26.14 (a) What problem is caused by the use of CFCs?

(b) Write an equation to describe how a CFC might be broken down in the stratosphere.

(c) Although CFCs are no longer made, they are still a cause for concern. Why is this?

(d) Why are aerosol cans so widely used? An aerosol can is labelled 'ozone friendly.' What does this mean?

(e) What do the letters HCFC represent?

(f) What do you think should be done with a fridge when it is no longer functioning?

26.15 What do the letters CFC represent? Give the name and structural formula of one such compound. Give two uses of this class of compounds. List two advantages of these compounds.

Describe, with the aid of relevant equations, how CFCs damage the ozone layer.

Nitrogen monoxide is also responsible for the destruction of ozone. Explain how this occurs.

How does methane help to lessen the damage being caused to the ozone layer?

REVISE CHEMISTRY LIVE

Chapter 26 in Revise Chemistry Live contains a summary of the key points in this chapter.

27 Materials: Crystals, Metals and Addition Polymers

27.1 Introduction

You may recall from Chapter 1 of the textbook that we referred to the fact that the most obvious impact of chemistry in our lives is the huge variety of new materials that we see all around us. In fact, chemistry is often defined as a branch of science concerned with the structure and composition of materials and the changing of one substance into another. In this course we have already seen many examples where one substance is changed into another. We now take a closer look at the structure and composition of some materials.

In everyday speech, the word 'material' has a number of different meanings. However, to a scientist or an engineer, the word 'material' refers to a substance that is used to make things. Those of you who take up careers in engineering will spend a considerable amount of time studying the properties of various materials e.g. metals, semiconductors, plastics and concrete. In this course we will study just three types of materials: crystals, addition polymers and metals.

27.2 Crystals

You have already come across crystals of various substances in this course, e.g. hydrated copper sulfate, washing soda, sodium chloride, sodium thiosulfate and sodium dichromate. In fact, it is quite common for many solid compounds to exist in a crystalline form (Fig. 27.1). But what is a crystal? A crystal may be defined as follows:

A crystal is a solid particle with a regular shape consisting of faces intersecting at definite angles. There is an ordered arrangement of particles within the crystal.

Fig. 27.1 These sulfur crystals clearly show the fact that crystalline substances have faces at definite angles to each other.

A particular substance always forms crystals of the same basic shape. In the early days of chemistry, there was speculation that the regular shape of crystals suggested a regular arrangement of particles within the crystal. This speculation was proved to be correct when William Bragg and his son Lawrence used X-rays to determine the arrangement of particles within crystals (Fig. 27.2). William and Lawrence Bragg received the Nobel Prize in physics in 1915 for their work. (The Braggs are the only father-son combination to have received a Nobel Prize. Lawrence Bragg was only 25 when he received the award – the youngest person ever to receive a Nobel Prize.)

Fig. 27.2 William Bragg and his son Lawrence Bragg developed a system of using X-rays to determine the arrangement of particles (atoms, ions or molecules) inside a crystal.

The technique of using X-rays to determine crystal structure is called **X-ray crystallography**. This technique involves passing X-rays through a crystal of the substance and studying the diffraction pattern formed. (Those of you studying physics for your Leaving Certificate know all about diffraction. For those of you not studying physics, a diffraction pattern simply means the way that X-rays are scattered when they pass through a crystal.) It is then possible to work out how the particles inside the crystal are arranged in order to give rise to this particular pattern.

The arrangement of particles inside a crystal is often referred to as the **crystal lattice**. The crystal lattice always consists of a structure that repeats throughout the crystal. This repeating structure is called the **unit cell**. For example, using X-ray crystallography it was discovered that a crystal of sodium chloride consists of an arrangement of sodium ions and chloride ions in which the repeating structure (unit cell) is the cube shown in Fig. 27.3. The points occupied by the sodium ions and chloride ions are called **lattice points**. Thus, in a crystal of sodium chloride, the unit cell repeats itself millions and millions of times in every direction to give a three-dimensional crystal structure. For this reason, crystals of salt look like small cubes when examined with the aid of a microscope.

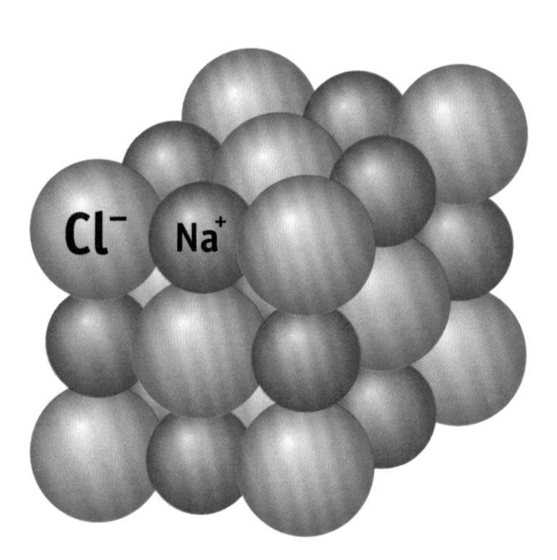

Fig. 27.3 The unit cell of the sodium chloride crystal lattice is a cube consisting of Na^+ ions and Cl^- ions.

Another important person in the area of X-ray crystallography is Dorothy Hodgkin (Fig. 27.4). She carried out research into the crystal structures of complex organic molecules. She spent several years working on the structure of vitamin B_{12}. This is a relatively large molecule of molecular formula $C_{63}H_{90}CoN_{14}O_{14}P$. (Don't even try to remember this formula!) Vitamin B_{12} consists of dark red crystals and its crystal structure was finally solved by Dorothy Hodgkin with the aid of computers. She was awarded the Nobel Prize in chemistry in 1964 for determining the structure of vitamin B_{12} using X-ray crystallography. She was also part of the team that determined the structure of the penicillin molecule.

Fig. 27.4 Dorothy Hodgkin received the Nobel Prize in chemistry in 1964. She received this award for determining the structure of vitamin B_{12} using X-ray crystallography.

Note: A solid that does not have a crystal structure is said to be **amorphous**. The word amorphous means 'without order'. Examples of amorphous materials are glass, rubber and many types of plastic materials. In these substances, the particles are not arranged in an ordered, regular structure but rather in a random fashion.

Crystalline solids are classified into four groups depending on the units that occupy the lattice points. These four groups are ionic crystals, molecular crystals, covalent macromolecular crystals and metallic crystals. We will now discuss the physical properties of each of these four types of crystal.

(a) Ionic Crystals

(i) **Units present and binding forces**. Examples of ionic crystals are NaCl, KI and MgO. In ionic crystals the lattice points are occupied by ions as shown in Fig. 27.3. The binding force is the electrostatic attraction between the positive and negative ions.

(ii) **Melting points**. Melting point is a measure of how much energy is required to overcome the attractive forces holding the crystal lattice together. Since, in ionic crystals there is a strong electrostatic attraction, ionic crystals tend to have high melting points, e.g. the melting point of sodium chloride is 801 °C.

(iii) **Hardness**. Ionic crystals tend to be hard and brittle. This is caused by the strong electrostatic attraction between the ions. When a force is applied to the crystal, the repulsion between like charges tends to shatter the crystal.

(iv) **Electrical conductivity**. Since the ions occupy fixed positions in the crystal lattice, ionic crystals cannot conduct electricity in the solid state. However, if the crystals are melted or dissolved in water, the ions are now free to move. These moving ions now help to carry the electric current through the molten material or solution. (This will be studied in more detail in Chapter 28.)

(v) **Solubility**. Most ionic crystals dissolve in water since there is an attraction between the positive and negative ions and the polar water molecules. This is illustrated in Fig. 5.36 page 61 of the textbook. Ionic crystals are usually insoluble in non-polar solvents since there is very little attraction between the ions and the non-polar solvent molecules.

(b) Molecular Crystals

(i) **Units present and binding forces**. Examples of molecular crystals are iodine, solid carbon dioxide, naphthalene, sulfur (S_8), solid HCl and ice. In a molecular crystal, the lattice points of the crystal lattice are occupied by molecules, e.g. in a crystal of iodine, there is an I_2 molecule at each lattice point (Fig. 27.5). The bonding **within** each molecule is, of course, a single covalent bond. However, the binding forces **between** the iodine molecules are weak van der Waals forces. In the case of polar molecules like HCl, the binding forces are dipole–dipole interactions. In the case of ice, the binding forces are hydrogen bonds.

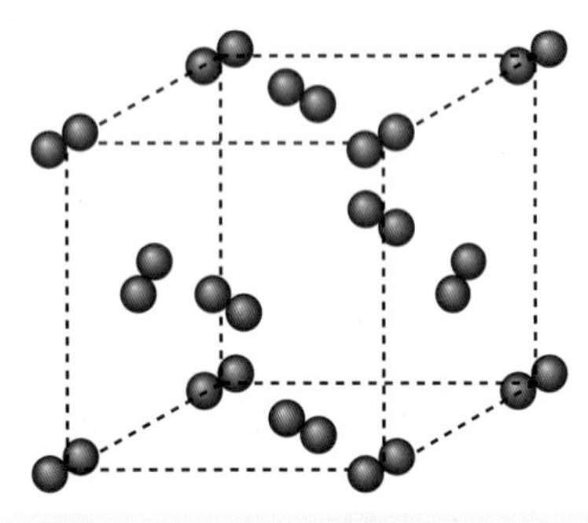

Fig. 27.5 Iodine is an example of a molecular crystal. The lattice points are occupied by I_2 molecules. There is an I_2 molecule at each corner of the cube and an I_2 molecule in the centre of each face.

(ii) **Melting points**. The melting points of molecular crystals are low due to the weak van der Waals forces between the molecules, e.g. the melting point of iodine is 114 °C and that of naphthalene is 80 °C.

(iii) **Hardness**. Molecular crystals are usually quite soft due to the weak van der Waals forces between the units in the crystal lattice.

(iv) **Electrical conductivity**. Since there are no ions or free electrons present, molecular crystals do not conduct electricity.

(v) **Solubility**. The solubility depends on the nature of the molecules at the lattice points. For example, crystals of iodine are insoluble in water since they are non-polar and there is no attraction between the non-polar iodine molecules and the polar water molecules. However, iodine is soluble in non-polar solvents such as hexane. On the other hand, crystals of HCl will dissolve in water due to the polar nature of the HCl molecule giving rise to hydrogen bonding between HCl and water.

(c) Covalent Macromolecular Crystals

(i) **Units present and binding forces**. These are also known as giant molecular crystals. Examples of covalent macromolecular crystals are diamond and quartz (silicon dioxide, SiO_2). In these structures, covalent bonds join the atoms together to form a giant interlocking network. For example, diamond consists entirely of carbon atoms and each tetrahedral carbon atom is joined to four other carbon atoms by single covalent bonds (Fig. 27.6). Examine a model of this in your school laboratory. The whole structure is really one molecule – hence the term 'macromolecular' is used to describe it.

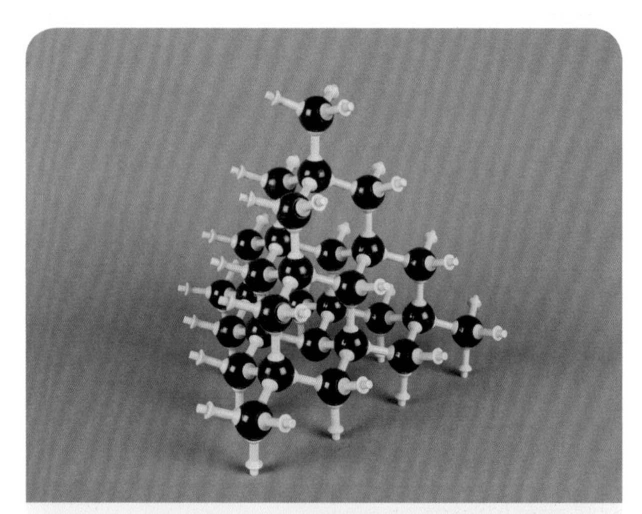

Fig. 27.6 This model shows that the crystal structure of diamond consists of a network of carbon atoms. Each carbon atom is joined to four other carbon atoms by single covalent bonds.

Similarly, the structure of quartz consists of a three-dimensional network of silicon and oxygen atoms joined together by single covalent bonds (Fig. 27.7).

(ii) **Melting points**. The melting points of covalent macromolecular crystals are high due to the strong covalent bonding within the crystal. For example, the melting point of diamond is 3500 °C.

(iii) **Hardness**. Covalent macromolecular crystals are generally very hard because of the giant, interlocking structures described above. Diamond is the hardest naturally-occurring substance known to humans.

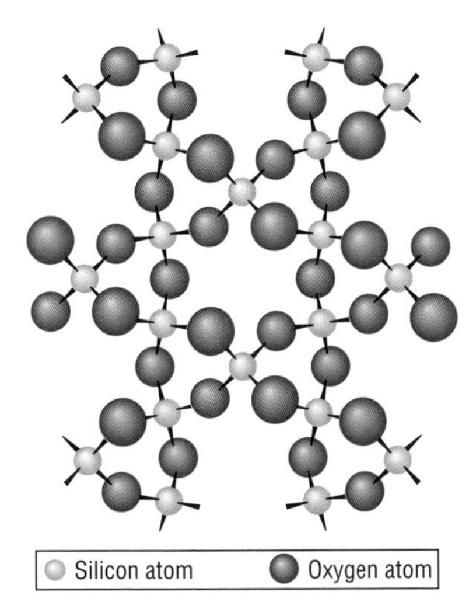

Fig. 27.7 Quartz is an example of a covalent macromolecular crystal. The structure consists of a three-dimensional arrangement of silicon and oxygen atoms joined together by single covalent bonds. Note that each tetrahedral silicon atom is joined to four oxygen atoms and that each oxygen atom is joined to two silicon atoms.

For this reason, diamond is found in drill bits and in tools for cutting and grinding (Fig. 27.8).

Fig. 27.8 Due to their great hardness, diamonds are used in drill bits for oil exploration.

(iv) **Electrical conductivity**. Since there are no ions or free electrons present, covalent macromolecular crystals do not conduct electricity.

(v) **Solubility**. Since the lattice is held so strongly together by the network of covalent bonds, covalent macromolecular crystals do not dissolve in water or in non-polar solvents.

Diamond is said to be an allotrope of carbon.

Allotropes are different physical forms of the same element.

Carbon exists in at least three different physical forms, i.e. it has three well-known allotropes. These allotropes are diamond, graphite and buckminsterfullerene.

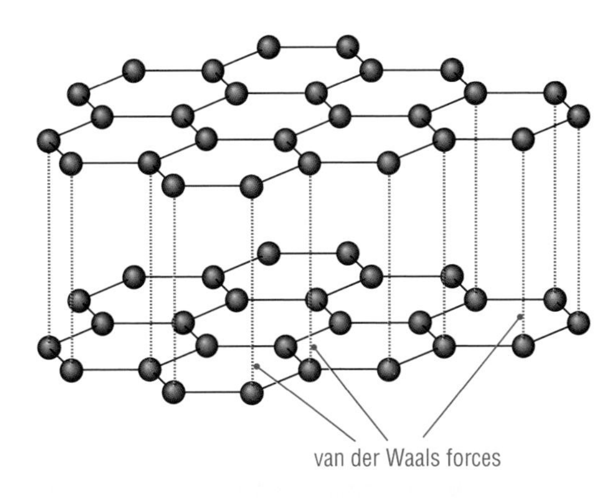

Fig. 27.9 Graphite consists of flat sheets of carbon atoms. The sheets are held in place by weak van der Waals forces.

The structure of graphite is completely different from that of diamond. Graphite consists of flat sheets or layers of carbon atoms arranged in hexagons with all bond angles of 120°. Within each sheet, each carbon atom is joined by covalent bonds to just three other carbon atoms, Fig. 27.9. The layers are too far apart from each other to be joined by covalent bonds. Instead, they are held in place by weak van der Waals forces. For this reason, the layers can slide over each other within the crystal.

The 'lead' in your pencil consists of graphite. When you write with a pencil, layers of graphite are left behind on the page. Graphite is also used as a lubricant – especially in environments where intense heat would cause oil to boil away.

Graphite is a good, cheap electrical conductor. Since each carbon atom is only joined to three other carbon atoms, this means that there is a 'spare' electron from each carbon atom in the layer. These electrons help graphite to conduct electricity and hence graphite is used as an electrical conductor in motors and batteries (Fig. 27.10). Graphite is the only non-metal that conducts an electric current.

Another allotrope of carbon was discovered in 1985. It was found that carbon atoms could link together to form

Fig. 27.10 Graphite is a good electrical conductor and is used in the electrodes of dry-cell batteries.

Fig. 27.11 Buckminsterfullerene is an allotrope of carbon. It consists of sixty carbon atoms arranged in the shape of a football.

a molecule that looked like a football! This molecule has 60 carbon atoms and was nicknamed 'buckyball' at first and is now called **buckminsterfullerene** (Fig. 27.11). This name was given to it because it resembled the structures designed by Buckminster Fuller, an American architect (Fig. 27.12).

Fig. 27.12 Buckminster Fuller, the American architect after whom buckminsterfullerene is named.

A whole family of spherical carbon molecules, similar to buckminsterfullerene, is now known to exist. These molecules are commonly referred to as fullerenes. A great deal of research is currently taking place on the uses of these fullerenes.

(d) Metallic Crystals

(i) **Units present and binding forces**. As you are already aware, the majority of elements in the Periodic Table are metals, e.g. copper, silver, gold, aluminium, iron, magnesium and nickel. X-ray crystallographic studies show that most metals are composed of spheres packed as close together as possible – rather like oranges in a crate. If you were to try to pack oranges as efficiently as possible, you would find that a system where each orange is in contact with six others is very efficient (Fig. 27.13).

Fig. 27.13 Each sphere is in contact with six other spheres. This is a very efficient way of packing spheres together and is commonly found in metals.

You could then put a second layer on top of the first so that the spheres in the second layer fit into the gaps in the first layer (Fig. 27.14). Similarly, a number of other layers can be added to give the overall crystal structure of the metal. You may have polystyrene spheres in your school laboratory to help you visualise this.

Fig. 27.14 The crystal structure of metals may be compared to the way that oranges pack together.

The structure of the atomium (Fig 27.15) is based on the crystal lattice of iron magnified 165 billion times! It's well worth visiting it the next time you are in Brussels.

But what holds the metal together? Chemists imagine metals as consisting of **positive metal ions** formed when metal atoms lose one or more outer electrons. These outer electrons become delocalised all over the positive metal ions and form a **sea of electrons**.

Fig. 27.15 The atomium was built in Brussels for the 1958 World Fair. It represents the crystal lattice of iron. The spheres are packed closely together to represent the structure of this crystal lattice. The atomium is 102 metres in height and each sphere has a diameter of 18 metres.

The attraction between the positive metal ions and the sea of electrons forms the **metallic bond**, i.e. holds the metal together. The sea of electrons is often compared to a type of cement that binds the positively charged ions together, Fig. 27.16.

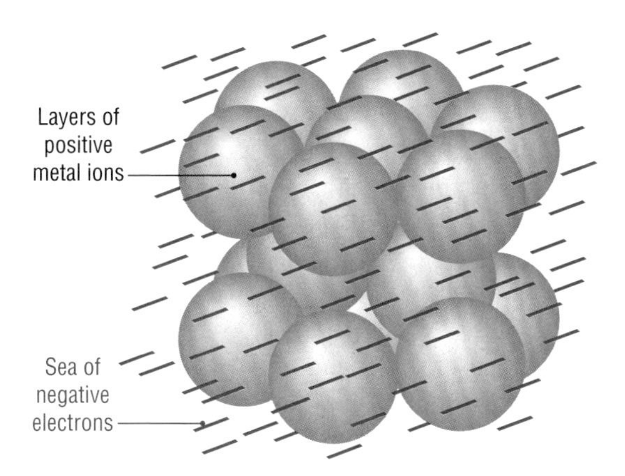

Fig. 27.16 The metallic bond may be visualised as the attraction between the positive metal ions and a sea of electrons.

(ii) **Melting points**. The melting points of metals vary enormously so it is hard to generalise, e.g. the melting point of tungsten is 3410 °C but the melting point of mercury is –39 °C. The strength of the metallic bond varies from metal to metal as it depends on factors such as the size of the ion and the amount of charge on the ion.

(iii) **Hardness**. No general rule can be made regarding hardness as this depends on the strength of the metallic bond. For example, sodium is quite soft and can be cut with a knife but iron is much harder. In general, metals can be hammered into different shapes – they are said to be **malleable**. Also, metals can be pulled into wires – they are said to be **ductile**. Metals have these properties because the layers of metal ions can be forced to slide over one another.

(iv) **Electrical conductivity**. Since the electrons are delocalised over the entire crystal lattice, metallic crystals are excellent conductors of electricity, i.e. the electrons in the electric current can easily pass through the 'sea of electrons' in the metal.

(v) **Solubility**. In general, metals do not tend to be soluble in water or in non-polar solvents as the metallic bond is sufficiently strong to hold the metal ions together in the crystal lattice. However, some metals take part in a chemical reaction with water, e.g. sodium reacts vigorously with water.

27.3 Metals and Non-Metals

There are many differences between the properties of metals and non-metals. These are summarised in Table 27.1.

Property	Metals	Non-Metals
1. Hardness	Usually hard. Most are solid at room temperature.	Usually soft. Most are liquids or gases at room temperature.
2. Lustre	Usually shiny.	Usually dull.
3. Malleability	Can be hammered into different shapes.	Tend to be brittle and soft when solid.
4. Ductility	Can be drawn into thin wires.	Cannot be drawn into thin wires.
5. Heat and electrical conductivity	Very good conductors of heat and electricity.	Poor conductors of heat and electricity.

Table 27.1 Comparing some general properties of metals and non-metals.

There are some exceptions to the generalisations in Table 27.1, e.g. mercury is a liquid at room temperature and lead is a dull metal. Graphite is the only non-metal that is a good conductor of electricity.

In some cases, the metal is mixed with another element to form an alloy. For example, brass is an alloy of copper and zinc. Similarly, bronze is an **alloy** of copper and tin. Alloys can be more useful than the pure metals as the alloy has properties of both metals in the mixture. Steel is an alloy of iron (metal) with carbon (non-metal). Steel contains about 0.15% carbon. The carbon makes the steel harder and tougher than pure iron.

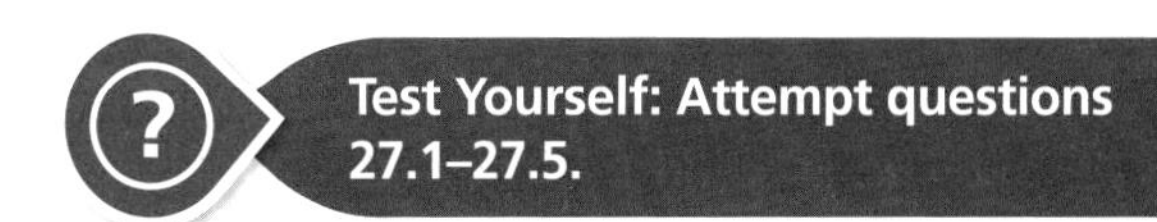

27.4 Addition Polymers

In Chapter 23, we saw that it is possible for molecules with C=C double bonds to undergo **addition reactions** among themselves. For example, we learned that it is possible for molecules of ethene to link with each other to form a long chain of carbon atoms (Fig. 27.17). The compound formed is called poly(ethene) or, more commonly, polythene. This compound is an example of a **polymer**, i.e. a long-chain molecule made by joining together many small molecules. The small molecules from which the polymer is made are called **monomers**. Thus, ethene is the monomer used in the manufacture of the polymer polythene.

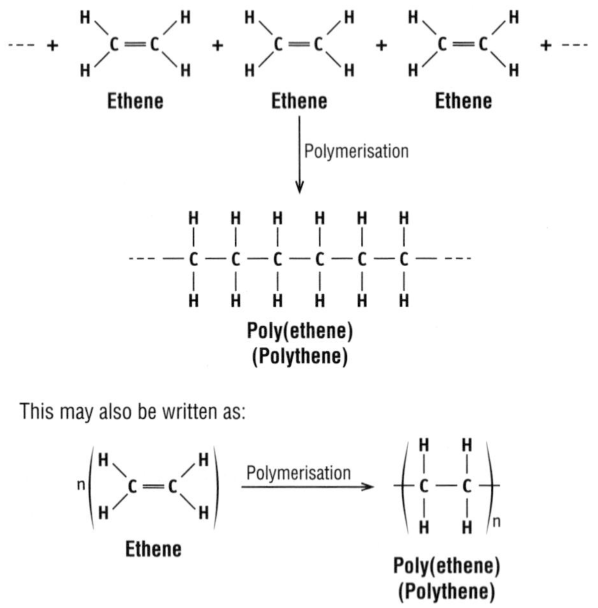

$$\cdots + \underset{\text{Ethene}}{H_2C{=}CH_2} + \underset{\text{Ethene}}{H_2C{=}CH_2} + \underset{\text{Ethene}}{H_2C{=}CH_2} + \cdots$$

Polymerisation

$$\cdots -CH_2-CH_2-CH_2-CH_2-CH_2-CH_2- \cdots$$

Poly(ethene)
(Polythene)

This may also be written as:

$$n\left(H_2C{=}CH_2\right) \xrightarrow{\text{Polymerisation}} \left[\!-CH_2-CH_2-\!\right]_n$$

Ethene → Poly(ethene) (Polythene)

Fig. 27.17 Molecules of ethene undergo addition reactions among themselves to form the addition polymer polythene.

Polythene is more correctly called an **addition polymer** because it is manufactured using an addition reaction. In this course, we will study the following five addition polymers:

(a) poly(ethene)

(b) poly(chloroethene)

(c) poly(propene)

(d) poly(phenylethene)

(e) poly(tetrafluoroethene).

(a) Poly(ethene) or Polythene

Poly(ethene) is the simplest of the addition polymers and, as shown above, it consists of long chains of carbon atoms. It was discovered by accident in 1933 at the ICI plant in Cheshire, England. Two chemists at the plant, Eric Fawcett and Reg Gibson, were carrying out research on the effects of high pressure and temperature on certain reactions. It was found that, when ethene was heated under high pressure, a white waxy solid was formed in the reaction vessel. Tests on this material showed that it had good electrical insulating properties. The material was originally called polyethylene since ethylene was the old name for ethene. The modern name for this compound is **poly(ethene)** or simply **polythene**.

The first time that poly(ethene) was used was in 1939 when it was found to be ideal for insulating underwater cables. (It was not affected by the weather, unlike the rubber that was previously used.) It was used in World War II for insulating cables used in radar equipment. This type of polythene is commonly called **low-density polythene**. The low density is caused by the long chains of carbon atoms becoming branched, coiling around each other and leaving a lot of empty space causing the density to be lowered. After the war, this low-density polythene became more widely used and is now used for food wrapping (transparent film), shopping bags, 'squeezy' bottles for washing-up liquid, milk bottles, rubbish bags and fertiliser bags. (For your examination, you are required to know two uses of each of the polymers on your course.)

In 1953, Karl Ziegler (Fig. 27.18), a German chemist, was carrying out research to try to polymerise ethene at a lower pressure than that used by ICI. He discovered that, by using catalysts consisting of metals bonded to organic groups, he was able to produce polythene using much lower pressures. The types of compounds he used as catalysts are called organometallic compounds, e.g. $Al(C_2H_5)_3$.

The new type of polythene had a higher density than that manufactured by the old method and was called **high-density polythene**. The high-density polythene

Fig. 27.18 Karl Ziegler, a German chemist, discovered how to make high-density polythene using a new type of catalyst.

had very little branching along the chains. Since the chains could then pack more closely, the density of the polythene was increased. High-density polythene is harder and stiffer than low-density polythene. (High-density polythene may be compared to uncooked spaghetti where the lengths can line up side-by-side. The low-density polythene is like the cooked spaghetti where the side chains coil around each other.) It was also found that the high-density polythene had a much higher melting point than low-density polythene. This made it ideal for use as containers when sterilising equipment used in hospitals and food production.

High-density polythene is used for washing-up bowls, food storage containers, buckets, ice-cube trays, petrol tanks in cars, bleach bottles and crates for bottles.

(b) Poly(chloroethene) or Polyvinyl Chloride (PVC)

As in the case of ethene, chloroethene may also undergo polymerisation to form **poly(chloroethene)** (Fig. 27.19). The old name for chloroethene was vinyl chloride. Hence, poly(chloroethene) is also known as **polyvinyl chloride** or **PVC**.

--- + $CH_2=CHCl$ + $CH_2=CHCl$ + $CH_2=CHCl$ + ---

Chloroethene Chloroethene Chloroethene

↓ Polymerisation

--- $-CH_2-CHCl-CH_2-CHCl-CH_2-CHCl-$ ---

Poly(chloroethene)
(Polyvinyl chloride, PVC)

This may also be written as:

$n\,CH_2=CHCl \xrightarrow{\text{Polymerisation}} (-CH_2-CHCl-)_n$

Chloroethene **Poly(chloroethene)** **(Polyvinyl chloride, PVC)**

Fig. 27.19 Chloroethene undergoes polymerisation to form poly(chloroethene). The old name for chloroethene was vinyl chloride. Hence, poly(chloroethene) is also known as polyvinyl chloride or PVC.

The presence of the Cl atom polarises the C – Cl bond. This gives rise to dipole–dipole attractions between the polymer chains making PVC a strong, rigid plastic. For this reason, PVC is used to manufacture window frames, gutters, drain pipes, curtain rails, credit cards, floppy-disc covers and clear corrugated roofing.

It is also possible to turn PVC into a softer and more flexible plastic by adding a material called a **plasticiser**. Plasticisers are small molecules that fit between the polymer chains and allow them to slide over each other. Plasticised PVC is used for manufacturing raincoats, shower curtains, car upholstery, floor coverings, insulation for electric cables, handbags, wallets, toys, hosepipes, oxygen tents, medical tubing for blood transfusions and drips, lifejackets, jackets for emergency services, wellington boots and aprons. The unplasticised form of PVC is normally indicated as uPVC and the plasticised form as pPVC.

Some examples of materials made from PVC are shown in Fig. 27.20.

Fig. 27.20 PVC is used to manufacture a wide variety of materials, e.g. gutters and shower curtains.

(c) Poly(propene) or Polypropylene

As stated in Chapter 23, **poly(propene)**, commonly called **polypropylene**, is made by the polymerisation of propene (Fig. 27.21). Its structure is similar to that of PVC except that a CH_3 group has replaced a Cl atom.

--- + $CH_2=CHCH_3$ + $CH_2=CHCH_3$ + $CH_2=CHCH_3$ + ---

Propene Propene Propene

↓ Polymerisation

--- $-CH_2-CH(CH_3)-CH_2-CH(CH_3)-CH_2-CH(CH_3)-$ ---

Poly(propene)

This may also be written as:

$n\,CH_2=CHCH_3 \xrightarrow{\text{Polymerisation}} (-CH_2-CH(CH_3)-)_n$

Propene **Poly(propene)**

Fig. 27.21 Poly(propene) is made by polymerising propene. Poly(propene) is commonly called polypropylene.

Poly(propene) was first manufactured in 1954 by Giulio Natta, an Italian chemist, using Ziegler catalysts. Ziegler and Natta were awarded the Nobel Prize in chemistry in 1963 in recognition of their outstanding contribution to polymer chemistry. The polymer chains pack closely together in poly(propene) and this causes it to have similar properties to high-density polythene. Poly(propene) is used for making chairs, briefcases, laboratory beakers, toys, bowls, buckets and water pipes for plumbing. Poly(propene) can be turned into fibres to make ropes that do not rot (Fig. 27.22). As a fibre, it is also used for making carpets, curtains, fishing nets and sacks.

Fig. 27.22 Poly(propene) is used to make ropes, fishing nets, clothes lines, etc. Since it is a synthetic polymer it does not rot like natural fibres and can be produced in different colours.

(d) Poly(phenylethene) or Polystyrene

As the name suggests, **poly(phenylethene)** is made by polymerising phenylethene (Fig. 27.23). Phenylethene is simply a molecule of ethene in which one of the hydrogen atoms has been replaced by a benzene ring. Poly(phenylethene) is more commonly known as **polystyrene**. (Styrene was the old name for phenylethene.) The presence of the bulky benzene rings in the polymer chain makes the polymer chains quite rigid and hence polystyrene tends to be brittle.

There are two types of polystyrene that you see around you – **rigid polystyrene** and **expanded polystyrene**. Rigid polystyrene is used for making yoghurt containers, disposable drinking cups, flower pots, cases for CDs and DVDs and cases for ballpoint pens. Expanded polystyrene is made by adding pentane to the polystyrene beads and heating the polymer. Expanded polystyrene is used as packing for fragile objects, ceiling tiles, egg boxes, food trays, burger boxes, insulation in refrigerators and between walls in houses.

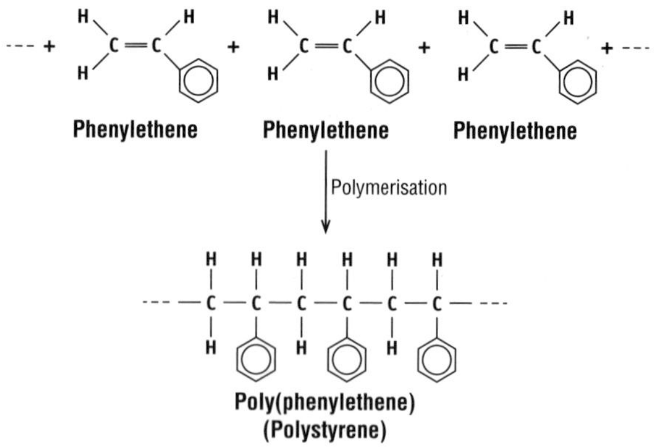

Phenylethene + Phenylethene + Phenylethene

Polymerisation

Poly(phenylethene)
(Polystyrene)

This may also be written as:

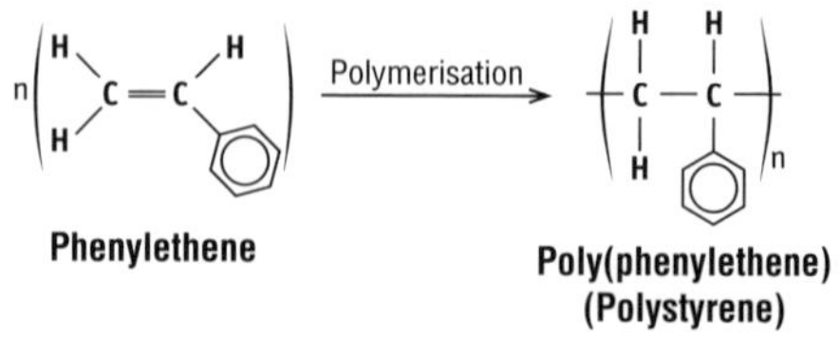

Phenylethene —Polymerisation→ Poly(phenylethene) (Polystyrene)

Fig. 27.23 Poly(phenylethene) is made by polymerising phenylethene. Poly(phenylethene) is commonly called polystyrene.

(e) Poly(tetrafluoroethene) or Teflon

Poly(tetrafluoroethene) often written as **PTFE** and commonly known as **Teflon** is one of the most useful polymers ever made. It was accidentally discovered in 1938 by Roy Plunkett, a chemist working with Du Pont in the USA (Fig. 27.24).

Fig. 27.24 Roy Plunkett, the discoverer of Teflon.

He was carrying out research into the manufacture of refrigerants and was using a cylinder of the gas tetrafluoroethene to try to prepare a non-toxic refrigerant. He opened the valve of the cylinder but, to his surprise, no gas came out. He was puzzled at this because the weight of the cylinder indicated that it should be full of the gas. He knew that the valve was not faulty, as he was able to run a wire through its opening. He called his assistant and together they sawed off the top of the cylinder. Inside, they found the cylinder coated with a white, slippery powder. They immediately realised that the gaseous tetrafluoroethene molecules had polymerised to form this solid material (Fig. 27.25). The polymer is called poly(tetrafluoroethene) and was given the brand name *Teflon* by the Du Pont company.

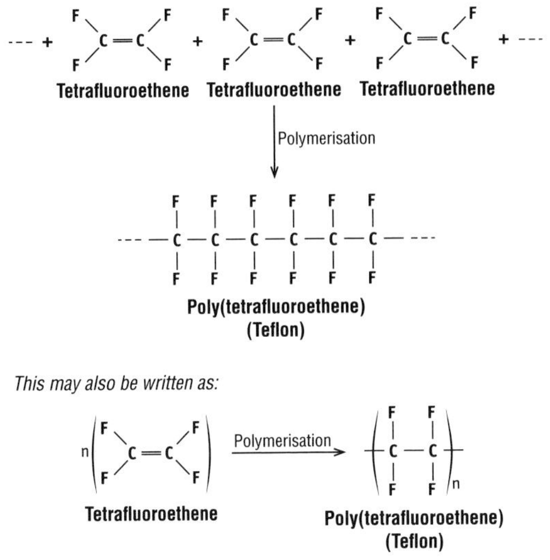

$$--- + F_2C{=}CF_2 + F_2C{=}CF_2 + F_2C{=}CF_2 + ---$$

Tetrafluoroethene Tetrafluoroethene Tetrafluoroethene

Polymerisation

$$---CF_2-CF_2-CF_2-CF_2-CF_2-CF_2---$$

Poly(tetrafluoroethene)
(Teflon)

This may also be written as:

$$n\,(F_2C{=}CF_2) \xrightarrow{\text{Polymerisation}} \left(-CF_2-CF_2-\right)_n$$

Tetrafluoroethene Poly(tetrafluoroethene) (Teflon)

Fig. 27.25 Poly(tetrafluoroethene), commonly referred to as Teflon, is made by polymerising tetrafluoroethene.

Roy Plunkett carried out various tests on Teflon and found it was an extremely inert polymer. It was not affected by acids or bases, would not dissolve in any solvent and was very slippery. These properties made it extremely useful. It began to be made commercially in the 1950s and was used as the coating on 'non-stick' frying pans. It is also used to coat the bottom of snow skis and electric irons and is used as 'plumber's tape' to wrap around the screw threads of pipe joints to enable the joint to be reopened more easily. Because of its resistance to corrosion and its slippery properties, PTFE is used in the taps of burettes in laboratories.

Its most important uses are in the field of medicine. Since it is so inert, it is not rejected by the body and has been widely used for making body parts such as aortas, corneas, knee joints, ear parts, tracheas. It is also used to make heart pacemakers and space suits. It is recommended in the syllabus that you examine some of the physical properties (density, flexibility and hardness) of the polymers polythene, PVC and polystyrene. (Since a hard plastic is more difficult to scratch than a soft one, the hardness of a polymer may be examined by testing how easy it is to scratch the polymer using an iron nail.)

27.4.1 Recycling of Plastics

There can be no doubt about the important role that plastics play in our lives. If you just look around your own home, you will realise how much we have come to depend on plastics. In the kitchen, plastics are used in tabletops, worktops, floor coverings, food containers and numerous appliances. These plastic materials are safe, hygienic, durable and easy to maintain. In your sitting room, the television, mp3 player, DVD player, armchairs and carpets are made with plastics that are tough and hardwearing. Similarly, in the bathroom, shower and bath fittings, plumbing, pipes and floor covering are made with plastics that are resistant to corrosion, hygienic and easy to maintain. In addition, the actual structure of the house contains items such as window frames, guttering, drainpipes and cladding that have excellent resistance against bad weather when made of plastic. The modern car contains a lot more plastic than older models as the use of lightweight plastics in cars is of great assistance in fuel economy. In view of the large amount of plastics that we use, it makes good sense to recycle as many of them as possible. Recycling of plastics is important for a number of reasons:

(i) Recycling of plastics saves one of our most important natural resources – oil.

(ii) Plastic recycling will help to keep the cost of plastics low when oil becomes too costly to be used as a raw material.

(iii) Recycling of plastics will keep down the cost of waste disposal. Plastic materials make up about 20% by volume of domestic refuse.

(iv) Recycling of plastics helps to reduce litter. Since most plastics are non-biodegradable, litter due to discarded plastics is among the worst forms of litter.

(v) Recycling of plastics would help to create employment for people with a wide variety of skills.

Not all plastics can be recycled. About 75% of plastics are classified as **thermoplastics** or **thermosoftening plastics**. These can be softened by heating and remoulded a number of times. All of the plastics studied above are thermoplastics. However, some plastics cannot be softened by heating and cannot be re-moulded, e.g. the plastics used in the manufacture of plugs, sockets and saucepan handles. These types of plastics are called **thermosetting plastics**. Bakelite is an example of a thermosetting plastic.

One of the major problems about recycling plastics is that plastic waste usually contains a mixture of many different plastics. Since each type of plastic has its own particular properties, it is not possible to simply melt them all together. Instead, it is necessary to sort the plastics into their individual types. This sorting is made easier by having a coding system for the common plastics (Fig. 27.26).

PET
poly(ethene terephthalate)

HDPE
high density poly(ethene)

PVC
polyvinyl chloride

LDPE
low density poly(ethene)

PP
poly(propene)

PS
polystyrene

7

Other
(including multi-layer)

Fig. 27.26 The coding system that is used to help separate plastics for recycling.

The symbol labelled PET refers to the type of plastic used to make bottles for fizzy drinks and mineral water.

Expanded polystyrene is one of the plastics with the highest level of recycling. It is estimated that about 60% of it is being recycled in Europe. The **recycling of polystyrene** consists of five stages:

1. **Sorting**. The polystyrene is separated from the other plastics by hand. (In some countries the separation is carried out by each householder using different types of collection bags.)
2. **Shredding**. At the recycling plant, the polystyrene is fed into a machine called a granulator. The granulator chops the plastic into smaller pieces.
3. **Washing**. The plastic is washed with steam and detergent to remove any impurities.
4. **Drying**. All excess water is removed with the aid of warm blow dryers. The material is then passed into a blender for thorough mixing with similar granules.
5. **Re-extrusion**. The dried, shredded polystyrene is fed into a machine called an extruder where it is melted. It is then remoulded into the shape of the required item.

Fig. 27.27 Some products made from expanded polystyrene.

Test Yourself: Attempt questions 27.6–27.10.

Summary

- A crystal is a solid particle with a regular shape consisting of faces intersecting at definite angles. There is an ordered arrangement of particles within the crystal.
- Crystal structures are determined by X-ray crystallography.
- There are four types of crystals: ionic crystals, molecular crystals, covalent macromolecular crystals and metallic crystals.
- Each type of crystal has its own particular properties.
- A polymer is a long-chain molecule made by joining together many small molecules called monomers.
- There are five important addition polymers: poly(ethene), poly(chloroethene), poly(propene), poly(phenylethene) and poly(tetrafluoroethene).
- Each polymer has its own properties and a number of different uses.
- Recycling of plastics is important. There are five stages in the recycling of polystyrene.

EXAM EDGE **Use Chapter 27 Exam Edge to study the sample answers to questions that have been asked on past Leaving Certificate Chemistry examinations on the topics covered in this chapter.**

Questions

27.1

(a) A crystal is defined as ....

(b) Name the two scientists who discovered how the arrangement of particles inside a crystal could be determined ....

(c) What type of radiation is used to determine crystal structures? ....

(d) The arrangement of particles in a crystal is called the ....

(e) The repeating structure of the crystal lattice is called the ....

(f) Name the scientist who determined the crystal structure of vitamin B_{12} ....

(g) Give one example of an amorphous substance ....

(h) Name the four types of crystalline solids:
1.......... 2..........
3.......... 4..........

(i) What is an allotrope? ....
Give one example of an allotrope of carbon ....

(j) What is the origin of the name buckminsterfullerene? ....

27.2

(a) Ionic crystals usually have .... melting points because ....

(b) Write a brief note on the electrical conductivity of ionic crystals ....
....

(c) Give one example of a molecular crystal ....

(d) Write a brief note on the hardness of molecular crystals ....

(e) Would the molecular crystal you have named in (c) above be soluble in water? Explain your answer ....
....

(f) Write a brief note on the structure of diamond..
....

(g) How does the structure of graphite differ from that of diamond? ....
....

(h) Give two uses of graphite ....

(i) A metal may be considered as consisting of .... metal ions in a .... of electrons.

(j) Metals can be hammered into shape, i.e. they are .... Metals can be pulled into wires, i.e. they are ....

(k) A mixture of carbon and iron is called ....

27.3 Compare ionic, molecular, metallic and covalent macromolecular crystals under the following headings, giving a suitable example of each type of crystal: (i) the units present and the binding forces between them, (ii) hardness, (iii) melting point, (iv) electrical conductivity, (v) solubility in water and non-polar solvents. [LCH]

27.4 The following substances are crystalline solids:

ice   iodine   diamond   sodium fluoride

(i) Which one of the four solids exists as ionic crystals? Show the formation of the ionic bonds by means of suitable diagrams. Explain why the substance does not conduct electricity in the solid state but does act as a conductor when in the molten state or when dissolved in a polar solvent.

(ii) Which one of the four solids exists as molecular crystals held together by van der Waals forces? What type of bond holds the atoms together in a molecule of this substance? Explain why the substance is virtually insoluble in water. [LCH]

27.5 Compare and contrast the properties of metals and non-metals with regard to the following: hardness, lustre, malleability, ductility, heat conductivity and electrical conductivity. Metals are usually solid at room temperature. Name a metal that is a liquid at room temperature. Explain the meaning of the term alloy. Give one example of an alloy.

27.6 (a) Name the two types of poly(ethene)...

(b) Why is poly(ethene) called an addition polymer? ....

(c) Poly(chloroethene) is more commonly known as ....

(d) Window frames and drain pipes are often made from ....

(e) What polymer is represented by the letters PTFE?...

(f) High-density polythene has a .... melting point than low-density polythene.

(g) Burette taps are normally made of the polymer..

(h) Disposable drinking cups and flower pots are commonly made from ....

(i) Roy Plunkett discovered ....

(j) What is the difference between uPVC and pPVC? ....
....

27.7 (a) The letters PVC stand for ....

(b) Name the German chemist who discovered how to polymerise ethene at low pressures using organometallic catalysts..........

(c) Teflon is the brand name for ....

(d) Give one advantage of having fishing nets made from poly(propene) ....

(e) Burger boxes are normally made from the polymer ....

(f) Laboratory beakers are made from the polymer ....

(g) The hardness of a polymer may be tested by..........

(h) Give two reasons why it is important to recycle plastics ....

(i) Plastic carrier bags are normally made from the polymer ....

(j) Distinguish between the terms *thermosoftening plastic and thermosetting plastic.*

....

27.8 Explain the meaning of the terms *monomer* and *polymer*.
Using structural formulas, show how ethene is polymerised to poly(ethene). This polymer exists as low-density poly(ethene) and high-density poly(ethene). Outline briefly how each of these forms was discovered. In each case, name the chemist or chemists responsible for the discovery. What is the main structural difference between the two forms? Give one use of low-density poly(ethene) and one use of high-density poly(ethene).

27.9 (a) Show, using structural formulas, how propene is polymerised to poly(propene). This polymer is used to make ropes. What is the advantage of making a rope from this material rather than a natural fibre? Name two other products that are commonly made from poly(propene).

(b) Show, with the aid of structural formulas, how chloroethene may be polymerised to poly(chloroethene).
What is the common name for poly(chloroethene)? Give two uses for this material. How is this material made into a softer and more flexible plastic?

27.10 (a) Show, with the aid of structural formulas, how phenylethene may be polymerised to poly(phenylethene).
By what name is poly(phenylethene) commonly known? This polymer commonly exists in two forms. Name these forms and give one use for each form of poly(phenylethene).
Write a brief note on the recycling of poly(phenylethene).

(b) Show, using structural formulas, how tetrafluoroethene is polymerised to poly(tetrafluoroethene).
By what name is poly(tetrafluoroethene) commonly known?
Write a brief note on the discovery of poly(tetrafluoroethene).
Give two uses of this polymer.

REVISE CHEMISTRY LIVE

Chapter 27 in Revise Chemistry Live contains a summary of the key points in this chapter.

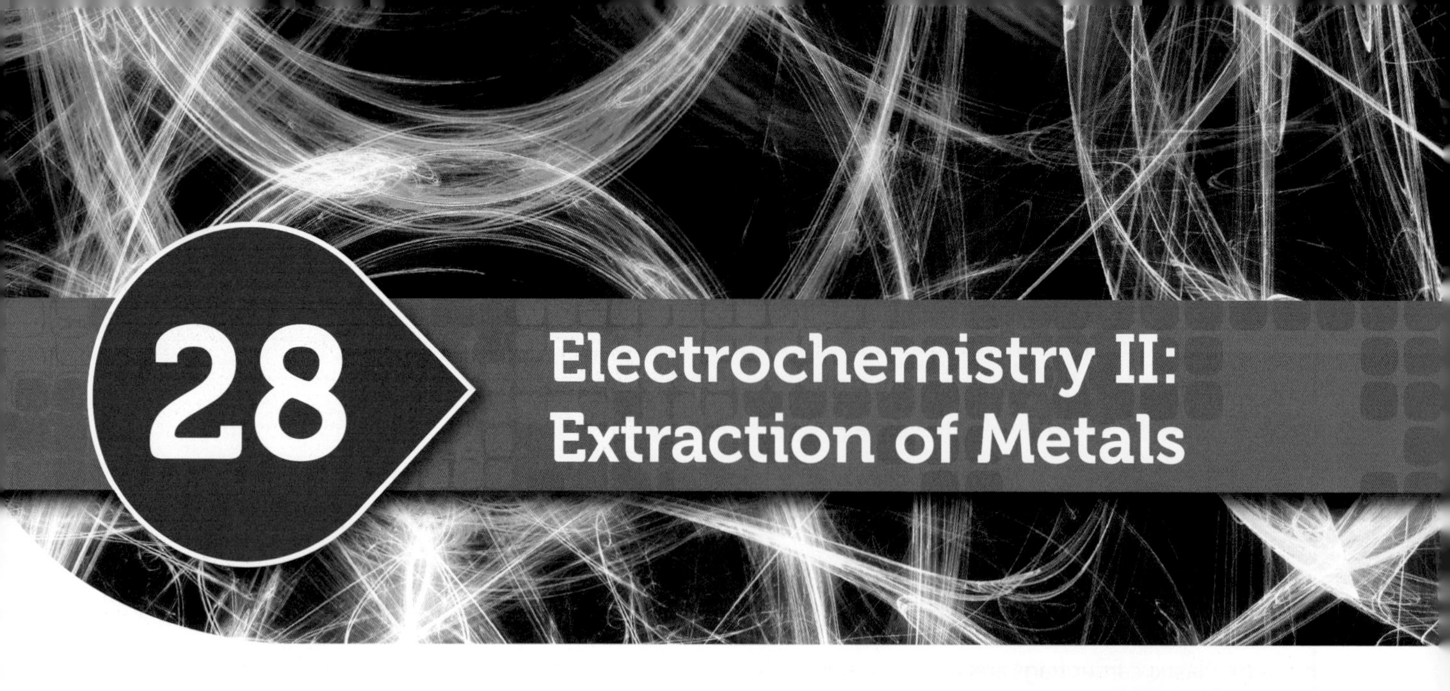

28 Electrochemistry II: Extraction of Metals

28.1 Introduction

In Chapter 20 of the textbook we learned about the electrochemical series. We saw that this was simply a list of metals arranged in order of their electrode potentials, i.e. their tendency to lose electrons. In this chapter we will begin by looking at how the corrosion of a metal depends on its position in the electrochemical series. We will then go on to look at one more example of an electrolysis reaction in the laboratory. You may remember that, in Chapter 20, we saw how electrolysis was used to bring about chemical reactions. We examined what occurred when an electric current was passed through various solutions. In this chapter we will examine what occurs when an electric current is passed through a molten salt.

Having reviewed the electrochemical series and electrolysis, we will then study how electrolysis is used to extract the metals sodium and aluminium from their ores. Finally, we will study how steel is manufactured.

Fig. 28.1 Luigi Galvani produced an electric current using two metals.

28.2 The Electrochemical Series: Corrosion

You may recall from Chapter 20 that an Italian scientist called **Luigi Galvani** (Fig. 28.1) discovered that the muscles in a dissected frog's leg twitched when touched by two different metals. Galvani had discovered a method of producing an electric current using two different metals. More sophisticated instruments than frogs' legs were later developed to detect the flow of an electric current. One of these instruments, the galvanometer, was named in honour of Galvani.

When Galvani made his discovery in 1791, he thought that the twitching of the frog's leg was a property of the living tissue in the frog.

However, three years later a friend of Galvani, another Italian scientist called **Alessandro Volta** (Fig. 28.2),

Fig. 28.2 Alessandro Volta invented the first battery using plates of copper and zinc separated by cardboard soaked in salt solution. The plates were piled on top of each other and hence the first battery was called 'Volta's pile'.

came up with the explanation. Galvani showed that electricity is generated whenever two different metals are placed in a conducting solution. Volta was the first person to construct a battery using various layers of copper and zinc plates with cardboard moistened in salt solution between them. This primitive battery was called 'Volta's pile'.

A more modern version of the voltaic cell is shown in Fig. 20.15 (page 339 in the textbook).

It was Volta's invention of the battery that allowed Humphry Davy and Michael Faraday to carry out their work on electrolysis.

In Chapter 20, we saw that different combinations of metals produce different voltages in a simple cell. We saw that each voltage can be measured relative to a standard hydrogen electrode. By arranging the metals in order of their tendency to lose electrons, we formed a list of metals called the electrochemical series (Table 28.1). Elements near the top of the table have a great tendency to lose electrons to form positive ions. These metals tend to be very reactive. Elements near the bottom of the table have a small tendency to lose electrons. These metals tend to be very unreactive.

Metal	
Potassium	Metals near the top of the series have the greatest tendency to form positive ions in solution, i.e. they are very reactive.
Calcium	
Sodium	
Magnesium	
Aluminium	
Zinc	
Iron	
Lead	**Reactivity Decreasing** ↓
Hydrogen	
Copper	
Mercury	Metals near the bottom of the series tend to be very unreactive.
Silver	
Gold	

Table 28.1 Part of the electrochemical series.

Since metals near the top of the electrochemical series tend to lose electrons readily, these metals corrode easily.

> **Corrosion is any undesired process whereby a metal is converted to one of its compounds.**

You are probably aware that metals such as potassium and sodium have to be stored under oil to prevent them reacting with moisture or oxygen in the air. If a piece of potassium or sodium is removed from the jar of oil and sliced in two, a white powder is seen to form quickly on the metal (Fig. 28.3). The sodium or potassium forms an oxide of the metal, i.e. it corrodes.

Fig. 28.3 Freshly cut sodium has a shiny appearance. However, the sodium quickly tarnishes as the metal reacts with oxygen in the air.

The most common example of corrosion we see around us is the corrosion of iron and steel. As you are aware, if iron and steel are not treated, they will slowly be converted to rust. Rust is an oxide of iron of formula $Fe_2O_3.xH_2O$. (The amount of water of crystallisation can vary.) Rusting requires the presence of both oxygen and water.

As a general rule, the metals high up in the electrochemical series corrode more quickly than those low down in the series. There are some notable exceptions to this. For example, aluminium is quite high in the electrochemical series but does not appear to corrode. In fact, aluminium does corrode but the oxide of aluminium formed, Al_2O_3, sticks firmly to the metal surface and prevents further corrosion.

Stainless steel is an alloy of iron with chromium. The chromium in the steel reacts with air to form a layer of chromium oxide that protects the steel from corrosion.

Corrosion is actually an electrochemical process, i.e. a cell is set up where oxidation occurs at one electrode and reduction at another electrode. For example, when iron corrodes, the first step is the oxidation of iron in the presence of oxygen:

$$Fe \longrightarrow Fe^{2+} + 2e^-$$

Since this is an oxidation reaction, the iron is acting as the anode of the electrochemical cell.

The two electrons lost by the iron atom are accepted by the oxygen molecule to form hydroxide ions:

$$\frac{1}{2}O_2 + H_2O + 2e^- \longrightarrow 2OH^-$$

Since this is a reduction reaction, the oxygen and water are acting as the cathode of the electrochemical cell.

The Fe^{2+} ions and the OH^- ions then come together to form iron(II) hydroxide, $Fe(OH)_2$. This is then oxidised in air to form rust, $Fe_2O_3.xH_2O$. The process is summarised in Fig. 28.4.

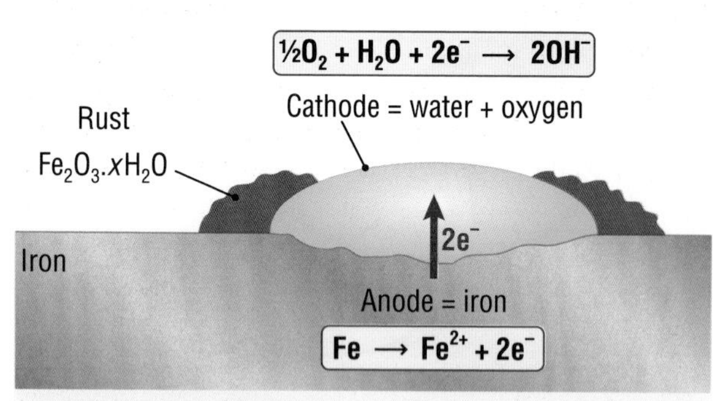

Fig. 28.4 The rusting of iron is an electrochemical process.

Rusting takes place more quickly if a salt such as sodium chloride is present. The reason for this is that the salt makes the water a better conductor and this speeds up the above reactions. Similarly, the presence of acid rain speeds up corrosion, since this speeds up the rate at which Fe^{2+} ions are formed as the iron metal dissolves in the acid rain.

There are many ways of preventing corrosion:

1. **Painting and greasing**. Painting is very useful for large structures such as bridges. However, the painting has to be done fairly frequently as corrosion will take place if the metal is scratched. When this happens, the bare metal is then exposed to air and water. For moving parts of machinery, oil and grease are very useful for preventing corrosion.
2. **Galvanising**. In this case, a coating of zinc is used to cover iron or steel to protect the iron or steel from corrosion. Such iron is called **galvanised iron** (named after Galvani). Since zinc is higher than iron in the electrochemical series, it corrodes in preference to the iron, thus protecting the iron. Items such as metal dustbins, metal buckets and wheelbarrows are made from galvanised iron. In addition, galvanised iron is used in building sheds and barns. The coating of zinc is applied either by dipping the objects in molten zinc or by electrolysis.
3. **Coating of surface with another metal**. In some cases, the iron or steel is coated with a very unreactive metal, e.g. 'tin' cans are made of steel coated with tin. The unreactive tin protects the steel. Chromium is also used as a surface coating, e.g. metal car bumpers, taps and bathroom fittings all consist of steel coated with chromium to prevent corrosion and also to give a nice shiny finish. Chromium is a good metal to use for this purpose as chromium itself is protected by an oxide coating on its surface.
4. **Using sacrificial anodes**. In this method of preventing corrosion, the iron is placed in contact with a metal that is more easily oxidised, e.g. a block of zinc is bolted to iron. In this case, the zinc corrodes rather than the iron, i.e. the zinc is sacrificed to protect the iron. Sometimes, large pieces of zinc are attached to the steel hulls of ships or underground pipes (Fig. 28.5). The zinc is oxidised, i.e. the zinc becomes the anode and the anode is eaten away. The zinc needs to be replaced from time to time. The steel of the hull is therefore the cathode and cannot corrode. This method of protection is also called **cathodic protection** because the steel is being protected by making it the cathode of the cell.

Fig. 28.5 Zinc is bolted onto the steel hull. Since zinc is higher in the electrochemical series, it corrodes in preference to the steel hull. Zinc is the sacrificial anode.

5. **Alloying with another element.** The corrosion of iron may also be prevented by alloying it with other elements. For example, stainless steel is a mixture of iron, chromium and carbon. This gives the stainless steel a very high resistance to corrosion.

28.3 Electrolysis of Molten Salts

In Chapter 20 we learned the meaning of the words *electrolysis, electrode* and *electrolyte*. All of these terms were introduced into the language of chemistry by Michael Faraday (Fig. 28.6). Michael Faraday started his scientific career as Humphry Davy's assistant – washing bottles and beakers! However, Faraday became a far more famous scientist than Davy and made many great discoveries in his lifetime. Not only did he discover the laws of electrolysis (not on the syllabus!), but he also discovered benzene and invented a method of generating electricity. He was a brilliant teacher and became famous for his Christmas lectures at the Royal Institution. If the Nobel Prizes had been in existence during his lifetime, Faraday would certainly have won quite a number of them.

Fig. 28.6 Michael Faraday (1791–1867) made many discoveries in the areas of chemistry and physics – particularly in the study of electrolysis and electricity.

In Chapter 20 we also studied a number of examples of the electrolysis of various solutions. It is far easier to predict what will happen if we electrolyse a molten salt. Consider what happens if we pass an electric current through molten lead bromide (Fig. 28.7). This compound has the formula $PbBr_2$ and is a suitable example to study because its low melting point allows it to be melted

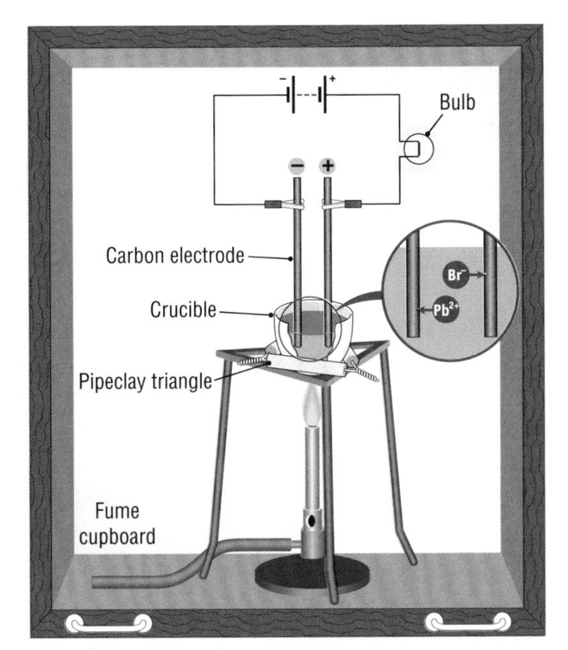

Fig. 28.7 When molten lead bromide is electrolysed, lead metal is formed at the negative electrode and bromine vapour is formed at the positive electrode. Lead metal has been extracted from the lead bromide salt.

using a Bunsen burner. This experiment must be carried out in a fume cupboard due to the dangerous nature of the products formed. Alternatively, you could see the experiment performed on the internet.

When the two graphite electrodes are inserted into the solid lead bromide, the bulb does not light. This shows that no current is passing through the solid compound. However, as the lead bromide is heated and begins to melt, the bulb lights. The Pb^{2+} ions and the Br^- ions are no longer locked in their positions in the crystal lattice but are free to move in the melted lead bromide.

The Pb^{2+} ions are attracted towards the negative electrode where each ion accepts two electrons to form a lead atom. The Br^- ions are attracted towards the positive electrode where each bromide ion gives up an electron to form a bromine atom. Two bromine atoms then join together to form a bromine molecule.

The following are the reactions that occur:

Negative electrode: $Pb^{2+} + 2e^- \longrightarrow Pb$

Positive electrode: $2Br^- \longrightarrow Br_2 + 2e^-$

Thus, lead metal has been extracted from the lead salt by electrolysis. You may recall from Chapter 20 that it was only in 1807 that Humphry Davy discovered the fact that electrolysis can be used to extract a metal from one of it salts. For this reason, many metals were not discovered until after 1807, e.g. magnesium, aluminium and calcium. These three metals are examples of strongly electropositive metals, i.e. metals near the top of the electrochemical series. These metals have a high tendency to lose electrons. These metals are found in the earth in the form of compounds of the metal. Electrolysis is used to extract strongly electropositive metals from their compounds.

We now go on to study the industrial processes for the extraction of sodium metal from sodium chloride and aluminium metal from the ore bauxite.

28.4 Extraction of Sodium from Molten Sodium Chloride

Sodium is used in street lighting and as a coolant in certain kinds of nuclear reactors. Sodium is far too reactive to be found occurring as sodium metal. In nature, sodium is commonly found in the form of sodium chloride. In order to produce sodium metal on an industrial scale, the sodium is extracted from the sodium chloride in a special type of cell called the Downs cell, after J.C. Downs who invented it in 1921 (Fig. 28.8). The cell is about 3 m high and 1.5 m in diameter.

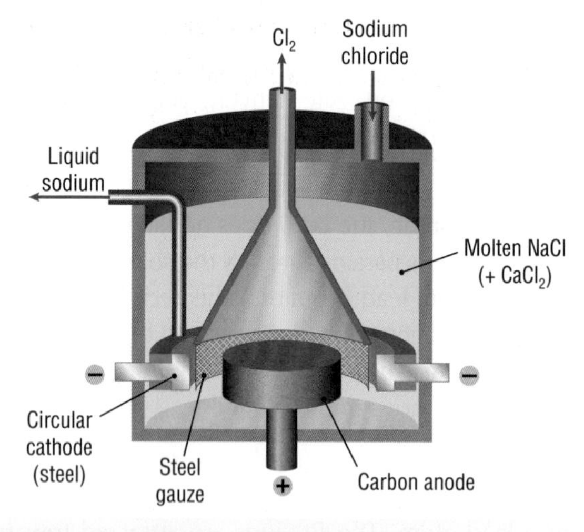

Fig. 28.8 The Downs cell is used to extract sodium from sodium chloride. The sodium metal is formed at the negative electrode.

A mixture of solid sodium chloride and calcium chloride (to lower the melting point of the sodium chloride) is placed in the Downs cell. A large electric current (≈ 30,000 amps) is passed through the cell and this melts the mixture of sodium chloride and calcium chloride and electrolysis takes place as follows:

Negative electrode: $Na^+ + e^- \longrightarrow Na$

Positive electrode: $2Cl^- \longrightarrow Cl_2 + 2e^-$

As shown in Fig. 28.8, the molten sodium is removed using a pipe. The sodium is over 99% pure – the small level of impurity is due to small amounts of calcium metal being formed from the calcium chloride. Chlorine gas is a useful by-product of the process.

The negative electrode is made of steel, as steel is a very good conductor of electricity. The positive electrode is not made of iron – it is made of graphite. Graphite is not as good a conductor as steel, so why is it used? The reason for this is that the chlorine formed at the positive electrode would react with the iron.

Note that the chlorine gas formed at the positive electrode is collected using a hood. This is done to prevent it reaching the negative electrode where it would react with the sodium metal. This mixing is also prevented by means of a steel gauze which separates the two electrodes.

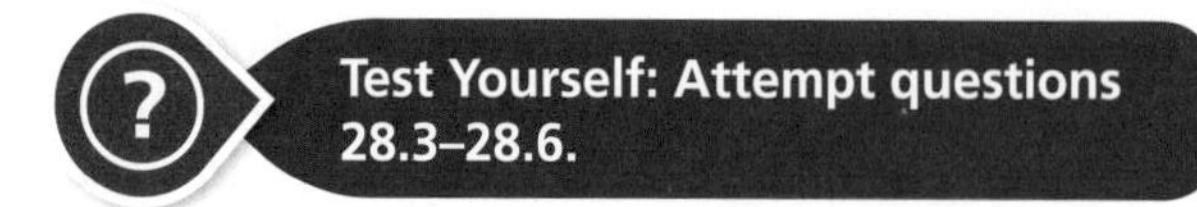

28.5 Extraction of Aluminium from Bauxite

Aluminium is an important metal which has many uses in our lives, e.g. food packaging (aluminium foil), cooking utensils, overhead electricity cables, window frames, aircraft construction, train carriages, ladders and drink cans. The fact that aluminium is an excellent conductor of heat and electricity, has low density, is non-toxic, resists corrosion, and is very malleable makes it ideal for so many applications. Another advantage of aluminium is that it can be recycled and made into new products.

Bauxite is the ore from which aluminium metal is extracted (Fig. 28.9). One of the world's largest deposits of bauxite is found in Guinea, on the west coast of Africa. Bauxite contains about 50% aluminium oxide, Al_2O_3.

Fig. 28.9 Bauxite is the ore from which aluminium is extracted. It contains about 50% aluminium oxide, Al_2O_3.

There are two stages involved in obtaining aluminium metal from bauxite. Firstly, pure aluminium oxide has to be obtained from the bauxite. In the second stage, the pure aluminium oxide has to be electrolysed to obtain aluminium metal from it.

(I) Obtaining Aluminium Oxide from Bauxite

In Ireland, Aughinish Alumina, located on the banks of the Shannon estuary, uses bauxite as the raw material for its chemical plant (Fig. 28.10). The purpose of the plant at Aughinish is to obtain pure aluminium oxide from bauxite. Aluminium oxide is commonly called **alumina**.

Fig. 28.10 Aughinish Alumina, on the Shannon estuary, converts bauxite into pure aluminium oxide.

There are fives stages involved in converting bauxite into aluminium oxide:

1. **Crushing and mixing**. The bauxite is crushed to a fine powder and mixed with hot sodium hydroxide solution. The reason the bauxite is crushed is to ensure that it will react completely with the sodium hydroxide solution.
2. **Digestion**. The mixture of ground bauxite and sodium hydroxide solution is pumped into tall towers called 'digesters'. In these towers it is heated under pressure and the hydrated aluminium oxide in the bauxite reacts with the sodium hydroxide to form a compound called sodium aluminate.

   $$\underset{\text{hydrated aluminium oxide}}{Al_2O_3.3H_2O} + 2NaOH \longrightarrow \underset{\text{sodium aluminate}}{2NaAlO_2} + 4H_2O$$

   As well as aluminium oxide, the bauxite also contains various impurities. These impurities consist mainly of oxides of iron (giving a red colour to the bauxite), oxides of silicon and oxides of titanium. These insoluble impurities do not take part in the above reaction and are removed in the next stage.
3. **Clarification (removal of impurities)**. Flour is added to help the insoluble impurities mentioned above to stick together and precipitate out. These impurities are then filtered off and pumped to the waste storage area. The waste is commonly referred to as 'red mud'.
4. **Precipitation of aluminium oxide**. The sodium aluminate solution is then pumped to precipitation tanks. In these tanks, the solution is cooled and tiny 'seed' crystals of $Al_2O_3.3H_2O$ are added to help the formation of more crystals of this substance.

   $$\underset{\text{sodium aluminate}}{2NaAlO_2} + 4H_2O \longrightarrow \underset{\text{hydrated aluminium oxide}}{Al_2O_3.3H_2O} + 2NaOH$$

   Note that this is simply the reverse of the reaction in step 2.
5. **Removal of water of crystallisation**. The water of crystallisation is removed by heating the hydrated aluminium oxide in a large kiln:

   $$\underset{\text{hydrated aluminium oxide}}{Al_2O_3.3H_2O} \xrightarrow{\text{heat}} \underset{\text{anhydrous aluminium oxide}}{Al_2O_3} + 3H_2O$$

The pure aluminium oxide formed consists of a fine white powder. The whole process of converting the red bauxite to the white aluminium oxide takes 14 days.

Great care is taken to ensure that the environment is not damaged by the presence of the plant. Part of the island on which Aughinish Alumina is built has been designated a wildlife sanctuary and many different species of animals live there. All waste is treated within the plant and the quality of the environment around the plant is continually being monitored.

(II) Extraction of Aluminium Metal from Aluminium Oxide by Electrolysis

The aluminium oxide from Aughinish Alumina is exported to various aluminium smelters around the world. In these smelters it undergoes electrolysis to give aluminium metal. The electrolysis is carried out in large steel containers that are lined with graphite (Fig. 28.11).

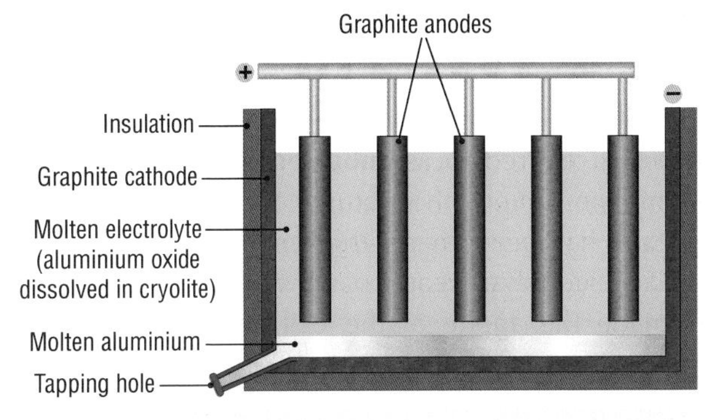

Fig. 28.11 This electrolysis cell is used to extract aluminium metal from aluminium oxide.

The positive electrode (anode) consists of a number of large blocks of graphite. The negative electrode (cathode) is the graphite lining of the cell itself. The aluminium oxide is dissolved in a molten substance called cryolite, Na_3AlF_6, as the presence of cryolite lowers the melting point of the pure aluminium oxide.

The following are the reactions that occur:

Negative electrode: $Al^{3+} + 3e^- \longrightarrow Al$

Positive electrode: $2O^{2-} \longrightarrow O_2 + 4e^-$

Overall reaction: $Al_2O_3 \longrightarrow 2Al + 1\frac{1}{2}O_2$

The electrolysis is carried out at a temperature of about 1000 °C. The aluminium is molten at this temperature and is tapped off periodically at the bottom of the cell. Note that oxygen is given off at the positive electrode. At the high temperature of the cell, the large graphite anodes react with this oxygen to form carbon dioxide, i.e. the anodes are burned away and have to be replaced from time to time. This is of benefit to the extraction process as the oxygen formed is thus removed from the system. Otherwise, the molten aluminium could possibly recombine with the oxygen to form aluminium oxide. In addition, the heat given out by the reaction between the graphite and the oxygen helps to keep the electrolyte molten.

You will observe that, in the reaction occurring at the negative electrode, three electrons are needed to produce one atom of aluminium. Scaling this up, aluminium smelters producing several tonnes of aluminium each week consume vast quantities of electricity. An aluminium smelter would have a large number of cells, each with a high consumption of electricity. For this reason, these smelters are usually built in countries that have cheap hydroelectric power. Hence, there are no aluminium smelters in Ireland. The nearest aluminium smelters to Ireland are located in Anglesea in Wales and Lynemouth (near Newcastle) in England.

We must place more emphasis on the recycling of aluminium. The cost of producing new aluminium by melting products such as drink cans is a small fraction of the cost of extracting aluminium from bauxite.

The aluminium that we see used in windows and doors is referred to as **anodised** aluminium. This is aluminium where the natural oxide coating on its surface has been made thicker. It is made thicker by an electrolysis reaction in which the aluminium is made the anode of the cell – hence the name anodised aluminium. The piece of aluminium to be anodised is connected to the positive electrode of the cell. Dilute sulfuric acid is used as the electrolyte of the cell. The cathode of the cell consists of a circular piece of aluminium (Fig. 28.12).

The following are the reactions that occur:

Positive electrode (anode):

$$2Al + 3H_2O \longrightarrow Al_2O_3 + 6H^+ + 6e^-$$

Negative electrode (cathode):

$$2H^+ + 2e^- \longrightarrow H_2$$

Anodised aluminium is more resistant to corrosion than ordinary aluminium. In addition, the oxide layer of anodised aluminium has a porous nature that allows it to be dyed, e.g. aluminium window frames may be dyed brown. Similarly, saucepan lids can be dyed a variety of colours.

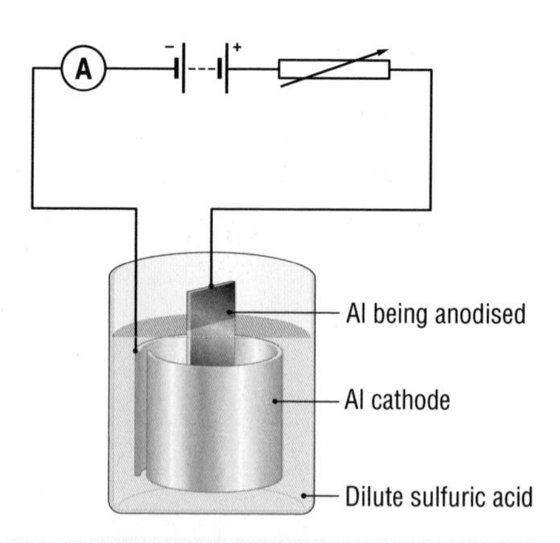

Fig. 28.12 The piece of aluminium to be anodised is made the anode of the cell, i.e. it is connected to the positive electrode of the battery.

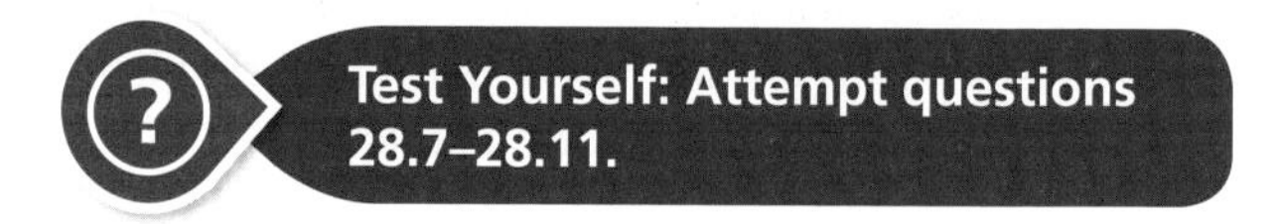

Test Yourself: Attempt questions 28.7–28.11.

28.6 Manufacture of Iron and Steel

We have already seen that highly electropositive elements such as sodium and aluminium are extracted from their ores using electrolysis. However, it is easier to extract the transition metal **iron**, since it is located lower down the electrochemical series. (In Chapter 5 in the textbook, we studied the typical properties of transition metals, i.e. formation of coloured compounds, variable valency and use as catalysts.) Iron is extracted using **chemical reduction**, i.e. by reacting the ore with a reducing agent. Carbon is the reducing agent usually used.

Without doubt, iron is the most important metal in our lives. It has been known to us for thousands of years. It has a wide variety of uses, e.g. construction of buildings, manufacture of machines, tools, railways, springs and car bodies.

We will first study how iron is extracted from iron ore using chemical reduction in a blast furnace. We will then study how the electric arc process was used to manufacture steel at Haulbowline, Co. Cork.

(I) The Blast Furnace

Haematite, Fe_2O_3, is the main ore of iron from which iron metal is commonly extracted. The extraction of iron metal is carried out in a tall furnace called a blast furnace (Fig. 28.13).

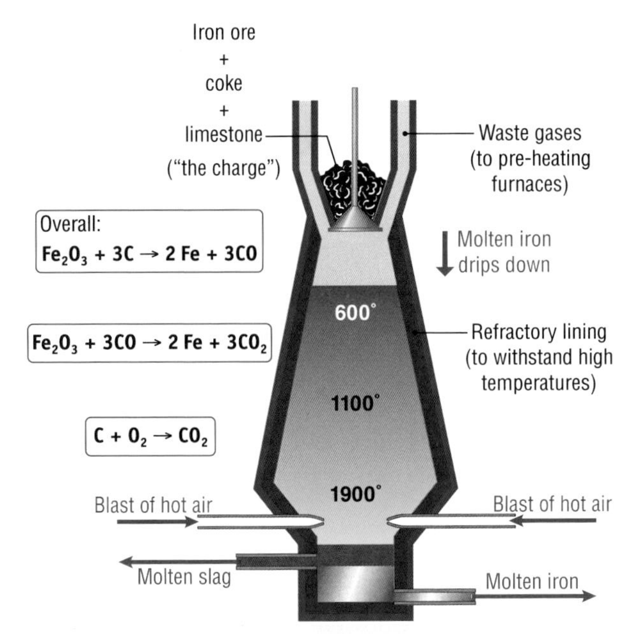

Fig. 28.13 A blast furnace is used to extract iron metal from iron ore by chemical reduction using carbon (in the form of coke). The furnace has a height of about 30 metres and a diameter of about 10 metres.

The operation of the blast furnace may be summarised in the following points:

1. A mixture of iron ore, coke and limestone is added through the top of the furnace.
2. Hot blasts of air are blown in at the bottom of the furnace. The overall reaction that takes place in the furnace may be summarised as follows:

$$Fe_2O_3 + 3C \longrightarrow 2Fe + 3CO$$

i.e. the carbon (coke) acts as the reducing agent and causes the iron ore to be reduced to iron metal. This is an endothermic reaction and therefore heat is required to enable it to take place.

3. The coke has two other functions. Firstly, it acts as a fuel to provide heat for the blast furnace. The coke burns in the hot air to form carbon dioxide:

$$C + O_2 \longrightarrow CO_2$$

This is an exothermic reaction and helps to maintain the temperature of the blast furnace. Secondly, the coke provides a physical support for the materials in the furnace. Coke is a porous material and it allows the hot gases to move upwards through the furnace, as well as allowing the hot molten iron to drip down to the bottom of the furnace.

4. The carbon monoxide formed in (2) above acts as the main reducing agent to convert the iron ore to iron metal:

$$Fe_2O_3 + 3CO \longrightarrow 2Fe + 3CO_2$$

Any carbon monoxide that remains unreacted is collected with the other waste gases and burned in special stoves to heat the blast of incoming air at the bottom of the furnace.

The ore is normally added in the form of pellets rather than in powdered form. One reason for this is that the pellets leave spaces to enable the carbon monoxide to move through the ore and bring about reduction. Another reason is that the gaps between the pellets allow the molten metal to fall down towards the bottom of the blast furnace. Thirdly, if the ore were in powdered form, it is possible that some of it would be carried away by the hot waste gases.

5. The purpose of adding the limestone is to remove impurities in the ore. When the limestone is added, it decomposes into lime and carbon dioxide:

$$CaCO_3 \longrightarrow CaO + CO_2$$

The main impurity in the haematite is sand, SiO_2. The lime reacts with the sand to form a substance commonly referred to as **slag**:

$$CaO + SiO_2 \longrightarrow \underset{\text{Calcium silicate 'slag'}}{CaSiO_3}$$

The slag runs down to the bottom of the furnace. Since the slag is less dense than the molten iron, it floats on top of the iron. The slag is removed at intervals and becomes a solid on cooling. Slag is usually used for road building and cement-making.

6. From time to time, the molten iron is 'tapped off' from the bottom of the furnace and is poured into large containers called 'pigs'. A modern blast furnace can produce 10,000 tonnes of molten iron each day. This impure iron is commonly called pig iron or cast iron. It is quite brittle and is used for making items such as manhole covers and car engine blocks. However, most of the iron is converted into **steel** since there is a far greater demand for steel than for pig iron.
7. Steel is manufactured in two stages. Firstly, pure oxygen is blown on to the surface of the molten iron. This removes various impurities such as carbon and sulfur by burning them off as the gases carbon dioxide and sulfur dioxide. Secondly, various amounts of different elements (e.g. manganese, chromium, tungsten.) are then added to the molten iron to give steel of a particular specification, e.g. hardness and resistance to corrosion.

There are many different types of steel. The steel used in the manufacture of a car body will have a different composition to the steel used in the manufacture of a paper clip or a razor blade. All steels contain iron and carbon, i.e. steel is an alloy of iron and carbon. In general, the percentage of carbon in steel is less than about 1.7%.

There are environmental considerations that need to be taken into account when producing iron and steel by the blast furnace method. Iron ore is commonly obtained by quarrying and this can cause severe devastation to the landscape. However, industries are now obliged to restore the landscape to an acceptable state. In addition, there is the potential for air pollution to be caused during the steel-making process when sulfur dioxide is produced by burning off the sulfur impurity. The sulfur dioxide is normally removed by a 'scrubbing' process in chimneys, i.e. the acidic gas is neutralised by passing it through limestone. Other possible sources of pollution are dust from the iron ore and slag. In modern blast furnaces, this dust is kept to a minimum and is removed electrostatically.

(II) Electric Arc Process

An alternative method of manufacturing steel involves using scrap iron and scrap steel as the raw materials. This was the method used to manufacture steel at Irish Ispat in Haulbowline, Co. Cork. A special type of furnace called an **Electric Arc Furnace** was used to melt the scrap. The Electric Arc Furnace is like a large steel kettle, lined with refractory bricks (Fig. 28.14).

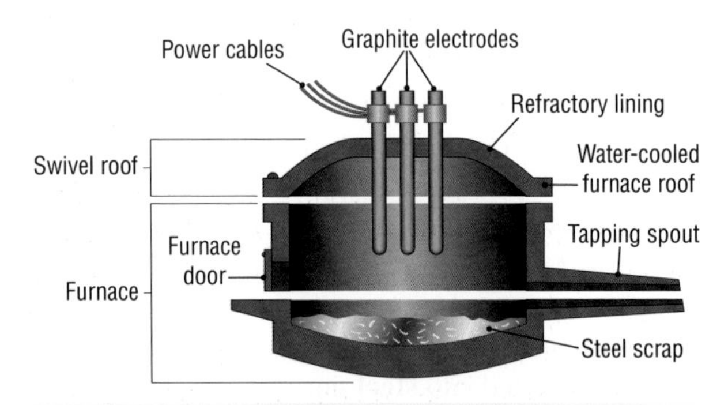

Fig. 28.14 Steel was manufactured at Irish Ispat in Haulbowline using an Electric Arc Furnace.

The steps involved in the manufacture of steel using the electric arc furnace may be summarised as follows:

1. **Charging**. The lid of the Electric Arc Furnace is swung back and the scrap steel is placed in the furnace using an overhead crane. The scrap metal is commonly called the '**charge**' and filling the furnace with the scrap metal is called 'charging' (Fig. 28.15). About 150 tonnes of scrap can be placed in the furnace.

Fig. 28.15 Charging the furnace with scrap iron and steel.

2. **Melting**. You will note in Fig. 28.14 that there are three large graphite electrodes inserted through the roof of the Electric Arc Furnace. These three electrodes are lowered down into the furnace close to the scrap. A huge electric current is passed through the electrodes producing an arc between the electrodes and the scrap. The high temperature produced by the arc (3500 °C) melts the scrap metal (Fig. 28.16).

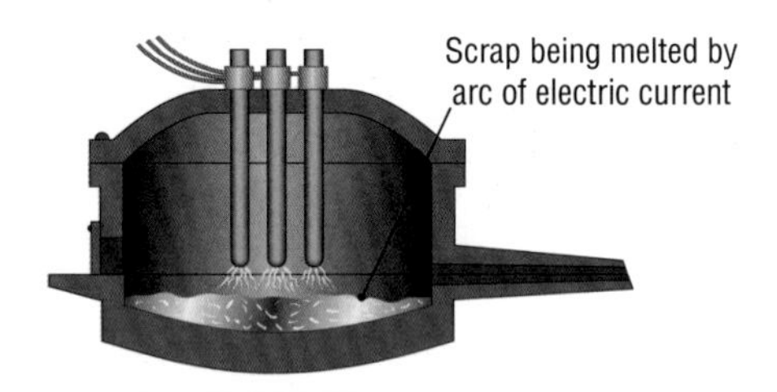

Fig. 28.16 Melting the scrap iron and steel with the arc from the carbon electrodes.

3. **Sampling and refining**. A sample of molten steel is taken from the furnace and sent to the laboratory (Fig. 28.17). The sample is analysed for the presence of various elements such as carbon, sulfur, manganese and copper. This is done by looking at the various emission line spectra of each element.

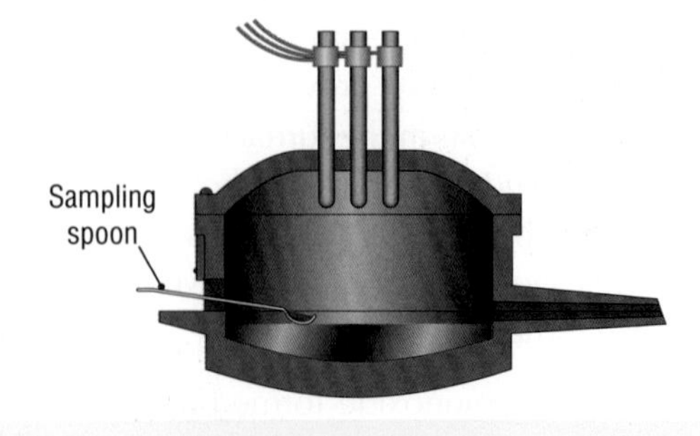

Fig. 28.17 A sample is taken from the molten steel and sent to the laboratory for analysis.

Oxygen is then blown into the molten steel using a long pipe called an **oxygen lance**. The main purpose of the oxygen is to remove excess carbon in the form of carbon dioxide. Other impurities such as silicon are oxidised to silicon dioxide.

$$C + O_2 \longrightarrow CO_2$$

$$Si + O_2 \longrightarrow SiO_2$$

Calcium oxide (lime) is then added to remove impurities such as silicon dioxide as a slag.

$$\underset{\text{calcium oxide}}{CaO} + \underset{\text{silicon dioxide}}{SiO_2} \longrightarrow \underset{\text{calcium silicate 'slag'}}{CaSiO_3}$$

The slag is less dense than the liquid steel and floats on top of the steel. The furnace is tilted backwards and the molten slag is poured off (Fig. 28.18). After cooling, the slag is used for land reclamation and road building.

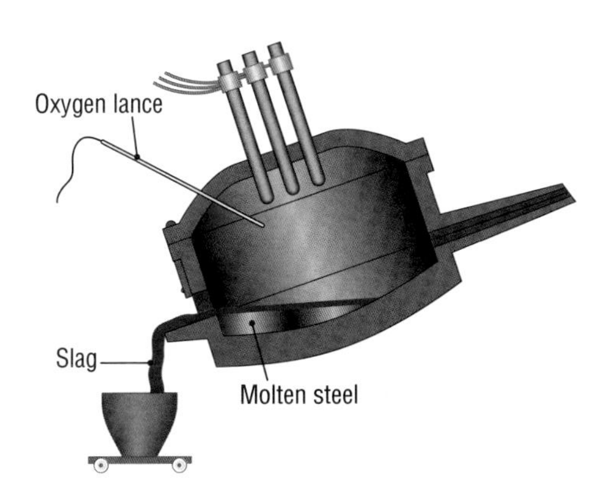

Fig. 28.18 The slag floats on top of the molten steel and is removed.

4. **Tapping**. The furnace is then tilted forward and the molten steel is transferred to a ladle (Fig. 28.19). Various other elements (manganese, chromium, vanadium) are now added to the molten steel in the ladle to alter the properties of the steel as required by the customer. The ladle full of molten steel is then brought by crane to a smaller furnace where the temperature of the steel can be altered and further treatment can take place. The cycle from scrap to finished steel takes about 90 minutes.

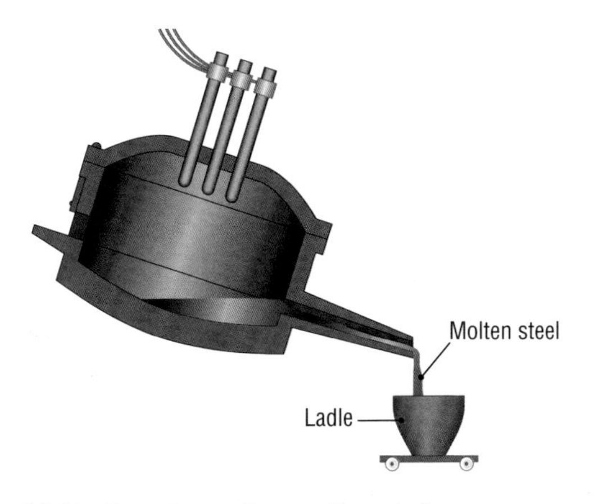

Fig. 28.19 The molten steel is poured into a ladle.

5. **Casting**. The molten steel is then poured into the top of a casting machine where the steel solidifies to produce a slab of red-hot steel (Fig. 28.20). This is then cut into various lengths to give steel products required by the construction industry, e.g. beams, columns and channels.

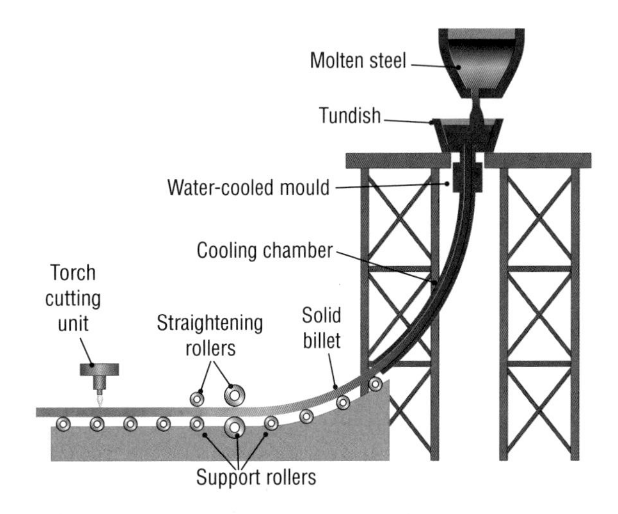

Fig. 28.20 The molten steel is converted into a red-hot slab of steel in the casting machine.

The Irish Ispat plant was the largest recycling plant in Ireland making 325,000 tonnes of steel from scrap steel each year. At the height of production, scrap metal that arrived at the plant in the morning left the same evening as finished steel!

The company paid great attention to protection of the environment inside and outside the plant. All emissions were strictly controlled to ensure that they met the statutory requirements. Fumes from the furnace were collected by ducts and fans and were filtered to remove particles of dust. The workers were supplied with protective clothing such as earmuffs, helmets and boots.

Strict control was also maintained on water quality used in the process. Large amounts of water were used for cooling items such as the Electric Arc Furnace and the continuous caster. This water was recirculated in a closed-loop system so that there was no discharge into the harbour.

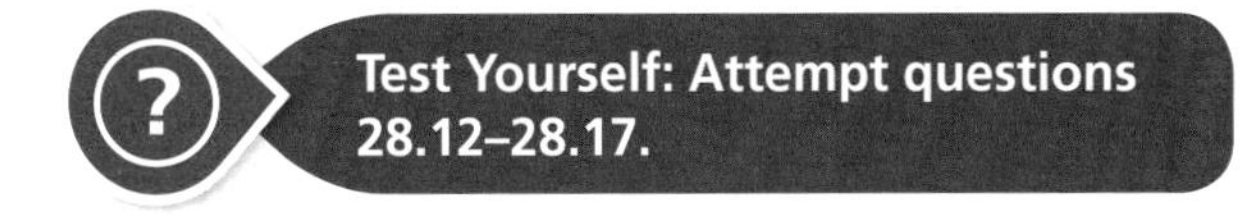

Summary

- Galvani showed that electricity is generated whenever two different metals are placed in a conducting solution.
- Volta was the first person to construct a battery.
- There are many ways of preventing corrosion: painting, greasing, galvanising, coating the surface of one metal with another metal, using sacrificial anodes and alloying.
- When lead bromide is electrolysed, lead is formed at the negative electrode and bromine is formed at the positive electrode.
- Sodium is extracted from molten sodium chloride in a Downs cell. Calcium chloride is added to lower the melting point of the sodium chloride. Sodium is formed at the negative electrode and chlorine is formed at the positive electrode.
- There are five stages involved in obtaining aluminium oxide (alumina) from bauxite. Aluminium metal is then extracted from aluminium oxide by electrolysis. Cryolite is used to lower the melting point of the pure aluminium oxide. Aluminium metal is formed at the negative electrode. Oxygen is formed at the positive electrode.
- Iron metal is extracted from iron ore in a blast furnace using carbon in the form of coke as the reducing agent. In addition, the coke acts as a fuel and as a physical support. Carbon monoxide also acts as a reducing agent. Limestone is added to remove impurities as slag. The pure iron is then converted into steel using oxygen to remove impurities and various metals are added.
- Steel is manufactured from scrap iron and scrap steel using an Electric Arc Furnace. The scrap is melted using an electric current, it is analysed, treated with oxygen, various metals are added, and lime is added to remove the impurities as slag. The molten steel is then solidified into a red-hot slab and cut into various shapes.

EXAM EDGE

Use Chapter 28 Exam Edge to study the sample answers to questions that have been asked on past Leaving Certificate Chemistry examinations on the topics covered in this chapter.

Questions

28.1 (a) Volta's pile consisted of layers of .... and .... plates.

(b) Elements at the top of the electrochemical series have a .... tendency to lose electrons.

(c) Why are potassium and sodium stored under oil? ....

(d) The compound $Fe_2O_3.xH_2O$ is commonly called ....

(e) Give two conditions under which corrosion takes place more quickly?

....

(f) Aluminium is quite high in the electrochemical series but it does not appear to corrode.
Explain ....

(g) What is galvanised iron? ....

(h) 'Tin' cans are made of .... coated with tin.

(i) What is meant by the term sacrificial anode? ....

....

(j) Stainless steel is an alloy. Explain the meaning of the term alloy.

....

(k) In oil refineries, magnesium alloys are often bolted on to the steel structures of the distillation and cracking units. What is the reason for this? ....

....

28.2 Write a brief note on the contribution of Galvani and Volta to the development of electrochemistry.

Explain the meaning of the term corrosion. Where in the electrochemical series would you expect to find metals that corrode easily?

'Corrosion is an electrochemical process'. Explain the meaning of this statement.
List three ways of preventing corrosion and explain how each method you have named helps to prevent corrosion.

Aluminium is an important metal that is widely used in the manufacture of aircraft. Give two reasons why aluminium is such a suitable metal.

28.3 Lead(II) dibromide may be used in the school laboratory to demonstrate the electrolysis of a molten electrolyte. What property of the compound makes it particularly suitable for this purpose?

Write equations for the reactions taking place at the anode and cathode in the electrolysis of molten lead(II) dibromide. [LCH]

28.4 Sodium is produced industrially by the electrolysis of molten sodium chloride to which some calcium chloride has been added. Draw a labelled diagram of the cell in which the electrolysis is carried out and write equations for the reactions taking place at the anode and the cathode. What is the reason for adding the calcium chloride? [LCH]

28.5 Sodium is a more electropositive metal than zinc. This is shown by the greater reactivity of the metal and also by the greater stability of its compounds.

(i) What is meant by saying that sodium is a more electropositive metal than zinc?

(ii) Metallic sodium is obtained by electrolysis in the cell shown in Fig. 28.21.

(a) The molten electrolyte usually consists of sodium chloride mixed with another substance. What is the other substance and why is it used?

(b) What material is used for the anode? Explain why iron is not used. [LCH]

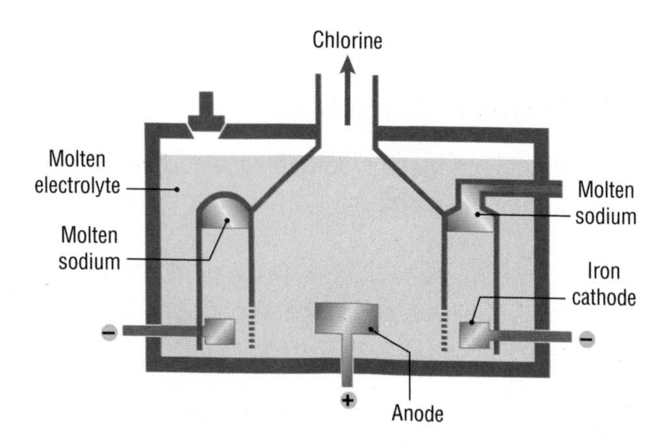

Fig. 28.21

28.6 (a) Which metals are commonly extracted by an electrolytic method? In the case of one of these metals give a brief description of the electrolytic process involved in its extraction. [LCH]

(b) In the electrolysis of sodium chloride in the Downs cell, write down the equations for the reactions taking place at the positive and negative electrodes.

Name one useful by-product formed in the Downs cell. Why is this product normally collected using a hood?

28.7 Aluminium is obtained from alumina (Al_2O_3) by the electrolytic process carried out in cells similar to the one shown in the diagram, Fig. 28.22.

(i) Name the ore from which the alumina for the electrolytic process is obtained. Write an equation for the reaction between alumina and sodium hydroxide.

(ii) The electrolyte used is a solution of alumina in another substance. Name the other substance and explain why this mixture is used. How is the molten aluminium removed from the cell?

(iii) The same material is used for the anode and cathode. What is this material? Assuming that the electrode reactions only involve ions from the alumina, write equations for the reactions taking place at the anode and the cathode, and also for the overall reaction taking place in the cell.

(iv) The anode material has to be replaced from time to time. What reaction is responsible for this? Explain why this reaction is of benefit to the extraction process.

(v) Alumina is produced in Ireland but it is shipped abroad for the electrolytic stage of the process. Suggest a reason for this. [LCH]

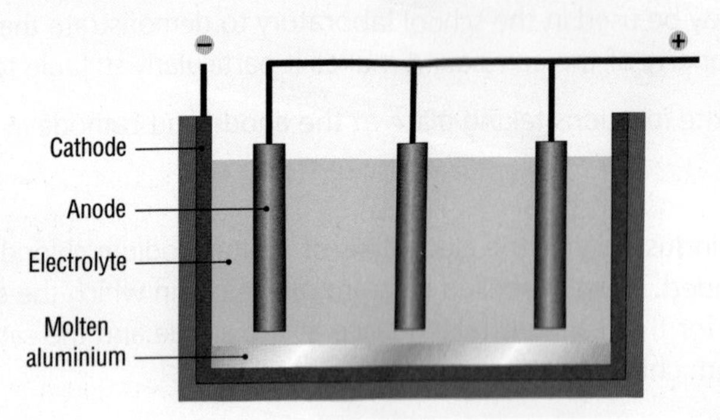

Fig. 28.22

28.8 Aluminium metal is obtained by the electrolysis of pure aluminium oxide dissolved in molten cryolite using carbon electrodes. The cell operates at a temperature of about 1150 K.

(i) Why is the electrolysis not carried out on molten aluminium oxide?

(ii) Write equations, showing the electron changes, for the reactions occurring (a) at the cathode, (b) at the anodes in the cell.

(iii) What important economic factor, other than the availability of raw materials, might influence the siting of an aluminium smelter? Give a reason for your answer.

(iv) Aluminium metal is sometimes anodised. Explain briefly how this is done. What is the purpose of the operation? [LCH]

28.9 There are normally two stages in the production of aluminium from its ore. In the first stage, pure alumina is obtained, and in the second stage aluminium is extracted from the alumina by electrolysis.

(i) Name the main ore of aluminium.

(ii) Outline the steps involved in the production of pure alumina from the ore named in (i).

(iii) What property of alumina makes the electrolysis of the pure compound very difficult? How is this difficulty overcome?

(iv) The anodes used in the electrolysis have to be replaced at intervals. What chemical reaction is responsible for this?

(v) Describe, with the aid of a diagram, how you would anodise a piece of aluminium. What change takes place in the aluminium and what is the benefit of the anodising process? [LCH]

28.10 In its bauxite ore, aluminium is present as the hydrated oxide ($Al_2O_3.3H_2O$). In the extraction process, this oxide is first converted to another aluminium compound (X) and, at a later stage, X is changed back to the hydrated oxide. The hydrated oxide is then converted to alumina (Al_2O_3), from which aluminium is obtained by electrolysis. The electrolyte consists of a solution of alumina in molten cryolite.

(i) Explain the term *hydrated*. Write down the equation for the reaction of alumina with sodium hydroxide.

(ii) Name X. Explain why the hydrated oxide is converted to X in the extraction process.

(iii) How is the hydrated oxide converted to alumina?

(iv) Show, by means of equations, the reactions taking place at the anode and cathode during the electrolytic stage of the extraction process. [LCH]

28.11 The following are some metals in order of decreasing reactivity in which they appear in the electrochemical series:

Sodium Magnesium Zinc Iron Copper

Answer the following questions with reference to these metals. Which one of the five metals corrodes most easily? What method is used, in the school laboratory, to protect this metal from corrosion?

The resistance to corrosion of a metal, not included, in the above list, is often improved by anodising. Identify this metal. State the electrolyte normally used in the anodising process and show the anode reaction by means of a balanced equation. [LCH]

28.12 Oxides of iron are reduced in the manufacture of iron in the blast furnace. What is the main reducing agent? Show by means of equations how this reducing agent is produced in the blast furnace and how it reduces the iron ore.

What substance is added as part of the charge of the blast furnace in order to remove impurities such as silica (SiO_2) and alumina (Al_2O_3) which are commonly found in iron ores? In the case of one of these impurities show, by means of equations, the reactions that lead to its removal. What name is usually given to the material obtained as the end-product of the removal process? [LCH]

28.13 Haematite, an ore of iron containing iron(III) oxide, Fe_2O_3, together with SiO_2, Al_2O_3 and other impurities, was reduced to iron in the blast furnace (Fig. 28.23). The ore was added to the furnace in the form of pellets. The main reducing agent was carbon monoxide but some reduction by carbon also took place. Waste gases (carbon monoxide, together with some carbon dioxide) were removed from the top of the furnace.

Fig. 28.23

(i) Why is it important to have the ore in the form of pellets and not in powder form?

(ii) What use is made of the waste gases?

(iii) In the case of one of the impurities mentioned above, indicate clearly how it is separated from the ore and removed from the furnace.

(iv) Write balanced equations for the reduction of the iron(III) oxide (a) by carbon monoxide, (b) by carbon.

(v) The pig iron from the blast furnace has a number of other elements present as impurities. Name two of these elements and describe how they are removed when iron is converted to steel. [LCH]

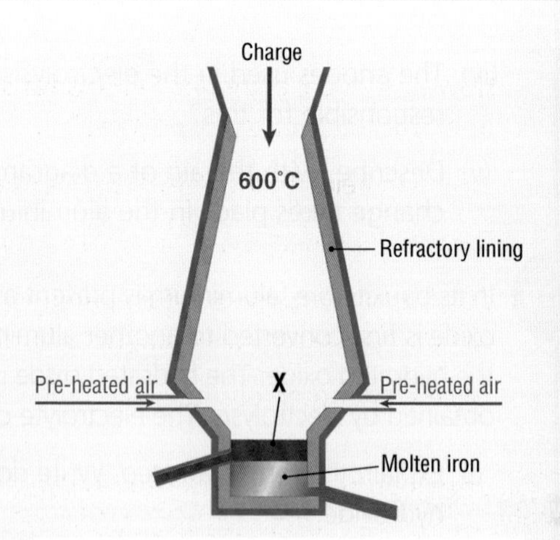

Fig. 28.24

28.14 A blast furnace, Fig. 28.24, is used to extract iron from iron ore.

(i) Iron ore and two other materials make up the charge which is fed into the top of the furnace. Name these materials and give one function of each.

(ii) Write a balanced equation showing the conversion of iron ore to iron.

(iii) Molten iron and another substance, X, are tapped off at the bottom of the furnace. Give the name of this other substance and state one of its uses. Also, give the common name for iron which has been obtained directly from the furnace.

(iv) Steel always contains a small amount of another element mixed with iron. Name this element and give the term commonly used to describe such a mixture.

(v) Suggest one method by which the properties of steel can be varied.

(vi) Given the position of aluminium relative to iron in the electrochemical series you would expect aluminium to corrode more easily. Explain (a) why aluminium is in fact far more resistant to corrosion than iron, (b) how this resistance to corrosion can be increased. [LCH]

28.15 What general method is used for the extraction from their ores of very electropositive metals such as sodium?

Name the main raw materials used in the blast furnace for the extraction of iron. The main reducing agent in the blast furnace is carbon monoxide. Show by equations how this gas is formed in the furnace.

Give an equation for the main reaction in which the iron ore is reduced to iron. How is the iron recovered from the furnace?

Iron ore contains impurities such as silicon dioxide. How are the impurities removed in the blast furnace?

What is the main chemical difference between the crude iron (pig iron) from the blast furnace and steel? Outline briefly the main steps in the conversion of pig iron to steel. [LCH]

28.16 Name the parts A, B and C in the diagram of the electric arc furnace, Fig. 28.25.

Give a brief description of how the electric arc furnace is used to manufacture steel. Your description should refer to the following processes: charging, melting, sampling and refining, tapping and casting.

A number of truckloads of lime arrived at the Irish Ispat steel-making plant in Haulbowline every day. Write a brief note on the use to which this lime was put.

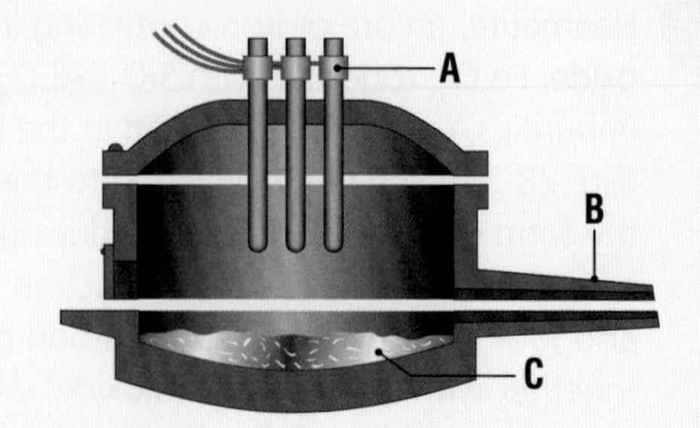

Fig. 28.25

28.17 How does the Electric Arc Process for steel manufacture differ from that used to convert pig iron from the blast furnace into steel?

Where in Ireland was steel manufactured by the Electric Arc Process?

Draw a simple diagram of an electric arc furnace and briefly describe how it is used to manufacture steel.

What is the purpose of adding lime to the molten metal in the electric arc furnace? What name is commonly given to the substance formed by the addition of lime? Give one use of this byproduct.

Write a brief note on the environmental aspects of iron and steel production.

REVISE CHEMISTRY LIVE

Chapter 28 in Revise Chemistry Live contains a summary of the key points in this chapter.

Answers to Numerical Questions

Chapter 4 The Periodic Table

W4.2	(b) 10.81		
W4.3	20.2		
W4.6	58.68		

Chapter 9 The Mole Concept

W9.1	(a) 7 g	(b) 23 g	(c) 40 g
	(d) 56 g	(e) 108 g	(f) 207 g
W9.2	(a) 355 g	(b) 20 g	(c) 4.5 g
	(d) 128 g	(e) 31.5 g	(f) 48 g
	(g) 1.6 g		
W9.3	(a) 160 g	(b) 55.5 g	(c) 142 g
	(d) 2 g	(e) 480 g	(f) 3 g
	(g) 60 g	(h) 17.55 g	(i) 72 g
	(j) 12.3 g	(k) 2.64 g	(l) 19.875 g
	(m) 8 g	(n) 35.75 g	(o) 288 g
	(p) 40 g	(q) 78.4 g	(r) 508 g
	(s) 0.017 g		
W9.4	(a) 5	(b) 4.5	(c) 0.0178
	(d) 4.5	(e) 0.125	(f) 0.1
W9.5	(a) 5	(b) 6	(c) 0.1
	(d) 0.25	(e) 0.1	
W9.6	(a) 1.5×10^{23}	(b) 4.32×10^{24}	(c) 4.8×10^{24}
	(d) 6×10^{20}	(e) 3×10^{21}	
W9.7	(a) 7.5×10^{21}	(b) 1.2×10^{24}	(c) 5.45×10^{23}
	(d) 1.875×10^{24}		
W9.8	(a) 900 g	(b) 0.12 g	(c) 2.07×10^{-10} g
	(d) 450 g	(e) 0.5867 g	
W9.9	(b) 6	(c) 1×10^{22}	
	(d) 9×10^{21}	(e) 4.8 g	(f) 8.33×10^{-3}
	(g) 3 g	(h) 0.3	(i) 1.6
	(j) 0.346, 1.704, 0.046		
	(k) 12 g	(l) 4	(m) 9 g

Chapter 10 Properties of Gases

W10.1	267.96 cm^3		
W10.2	7.5 L		
W10.3	1.22 m^3		
W10.5	(a) 7 L	(b) 6.11 L	(c) 10.54 L
	(d) 20 L	(e) 5.84 L	(f) 8.56 L
W10.6	7.94×10^{-3} moles		
W10.7	58		
W10.8	122		
W10.9	136		
W10.10	134		
W10.11	28		
W10.12	(iii) 87.3		
W10.13	(b) 750 cm^3	(c) 0.8 L	(e) 56
W10.14	(vi) 44.98		

Chapter 11 Stoichiometry I

W11.1	(a) 62.94%	(b) 51.22%	
W11.2	Magnetite (72.41%) > haematite (70%)		
W11.4	$C_2H_2O_4$		
W11.5	$C_4H_{10}O$		
W11.6	PbI_2		
W11.7	$CuSO_4.5H_2O$		
W11.8	7		
W11.9	45.83 g		
W11.10	21 g		
W11.11	1.96 g		
W11.12	1 g		
W11.13	1.91 g		
W11.14	2.55 g		
W11.15	(i) 0.2	(ii) 0.1	(iii) 2 : 1
	(iv) Cu_2S		
W11.16	224 L		
W11.17	(i) 0.05 moles	(ii) 1.12 L	
	(iii) 3×10^{22} molecules		
W11.18	(i) 6.4 g	(ii) 3.584 L	(iii) 9.6×10^{22}
W11.19	(a) CH_3O	(b) $C_2H_6O_2$	
W11.20	(i) 0.05	(ii) 0.2	(iii) 6.3 g
	(iv) 1.12 L	(v) 3×10^{22} molecules	

Chapter 13 Volumetric Analysis: Acid-Base

W13.1	13.19 g		
W13.2	(a) 540 ppm	(b) 180 ppm	(c) 770 ppm
	(d) 9 ppm		
W13.3	(a) 1.78 M	(b) 1.79 M	(c) 2.24 M
	(d) 0.125 M	(e) 0.59 M	
W13.4	0.0043 M		
W13.5	(a) 0.08 g	(b) 0.0158 g	(c) 1.53 g
	(d) 146 g	(e) 0.196 g	
W13.6	1.2 g		
W13.7	66.67 cm^3		
W13.8	2000 cm^3		
W13.9	250 cm^3		
W13.10	500 cm^3		
W13.12	(a) 0.0152 mol/L		
	(b) 1.12 g/L		
W13.13	(a) 0.08 mol/L	(b) 7.2 g/L	
W13.14	(a) 0.926 mol/L	(b) 55.56 g/L	(c) 5.56%
W13.15	(a) 0.972 mol/L	(b) 58.32 g/L	(c) 5.83%
W13.16	(a) 28.57%	(b) x = 2	
W13.17	x = 2. Yes.		

Chapter 15 Volumetric Analysis: Oxidation–Reduction

W15.1 (a) 0.0193 M (b) 3.05 g/L
W15.2 (a) 0.09 M (b) 35.28 g/L
W15.3 (a) 0.1175 M (b) 1.65 g, 89.19%
W15.4 (b) x = 5
W15.5 (ii) 0.12 M (v) 0.018 M
W15.6 (vi) (a) 0.09 M (b) 25.56 g/L, 27.55%, x = 6
W15.7 (iii) (a) 0.133 g (b) 0.049 g (c) 54.29%
W15.8 (iii) (a) 0.129 g (b) 0.048 g (c) 53.75%
W15.9 (a) 0.0532 M (b) 13.51 g/L
W15.10 (a) 0.1225 M (b) 30.38 g/L
W15.11 (vi) (a) 0.08 M (b) 19.84 g/L (vii) 99.2%
W15.12 (a) 0.489 M (b) 36.43 g/L (c) 3.64%

Chapter 16 Rates of Reactions

W16.1 (iv) 100 seconds
W16.2 (iii) Any answer between 27 and 28 seconds acceptable.
W16.4 (c) (i) 0.2 g, (ii) 0.33 g (d) 5 mins
(e) 0.4 g
W16.5 (iv) (a) Any value between 1.15 and 1.35 minutes acceptable.
(iv) (b) 0.012 mole
(iv) (c) Any value between 0.07 and 0.09 g/min acceptable.
(v) 0.015 mole oxygen produced, 0.03 mole H_2O_2 initially present.
W16.7 (iv) From graph, 51 cm^3 oxygen collected = 0.0023 moles
(v) 2×10^{-3} moles = 44.8 cm^3. Time = 1.2 mins
(vi) (a) Answers in the region 0.5 cm^3/sec - 0.7 cm^3/sec acceptable.
(iv) (b) 0 cm^3/sec.

Chapter 17 Chemical Equilibrium

W17.7 $[CH_3COOC_2H_5]$ = 0.93, $[H_2O]$ = 0.93
W17.8 (a) $[I_2]$ = 0.01 (b) [HI] = 0.08
W17.9 K_c = 4, moles ethanol = 1.6
W17.10 K_c = 1.5
W17.11 moles HI = 1.86, moles H_2 = 1.07, moles I_2 = 0.07
W17.12 $[N_2O_4]$ = 0.04, $[NO_2]$ = 0.12

Chapter 18 pH and Indicators

W18.2 (a) 5 (b) 2.08 (c) 0.65
(d) 11.36 (e) 8.41
W18.3 (a) 0.07 moles/L
(b) 3.09×10^{-7} moles/L
(c) 1×10^{-14} moles/L
(d) 0.62 moles/L
(e) 3.31×10^{-11} moles/L.
W18.4 (a) 0.70 (b) 0.70 (c) 1.30
(d) 10.40 (e) 2.30
W18.5 (a) 13.52 (b) 11 (c) 13.30
(d) 9.70 (e) 10.85
W18.6 10.98
W18.7 2.37
W18.8 7, 6.52
W18.9 2.51
W18.10 2.72
W18.11 1.25×10^{-3}, 3.82
W18.12 5.14
W18.13 1.225×10^{-4}
W18.14 (ii) 2.05
W18.17 (ii) 3.35
W18.20 0.002 moles/L; $K_a = 8 \times 10^{-6}$

Chapter 19 Enviromental Chemistry – Water

W19.2 (e) 360 ppm
W19.3 (c) (i) 230 ppm
(ii) 130 ppm
(iii) 100 ppm
W19.4 (iv) 300 ppm
W19.5 (iv) (a) 0.076 g/L (b) 190 ppm
W19.6 Suspended solids = 1960 ppm
Dissolved solids = 3650 ppm
W19.8 9.08 ppm, 1.92 p.p.m., BOD. = 71.6 ppm

Chapter 21 Fuels and Heats of Reaction

W21.12 ΔH = -55.216 kJ mol^{-1}
W21.13 ΔH = -54.6 kJ mol^{-1}
W21.14 ΔH = -433.3 kJ mol^{-1}
W21.15 ΔH = -716 kJ mol^{-1}
W21.16 ΔH = -278 kJ mol^{-1}
W21.17 ΔH = -74.7 kJ mol^{-1}
W21.18 ΔH = -106 kJ mol^{-1}
W21.19 ΔH = +225 kJ mol^{-1}
W21.20 ΔH = -111.7 kJ mol^{-1}
W21.21 ΔH = -713 kJ mol^{-1}
W21.22 ΔH = -153 kJ mol^{-1}
W21.23 ΔH = -814 kJ mol^{-1}

Chapter 24 Stoichiometry II

W24.1 51.1%
W24.2 6 g
W24.3 91%
W24.4 (ii) % yield ethanol = 52%, propanone = 74%
W24.5 (i) (a) 6 g (b) 0.15 moles (iii) 76.54%
W24.6 53.75%
W24.7 65%
W24.8 41%

Index

A

acid rain, 99–100, 104
acidic oxide, 94
addition polymers, 114–117
addition reactions, 114
air pollution, 99
allotrope, 111
alloy, 114
  protective, 124
aluminium, 123
  extraction of, 126–128
aluminium oxide, 127–128
ammonia, 78, 80–81, 86
ammonium carbamate, 81
amorphous, 109
anodes, sacrificial, 124
anodised aluminium, 128
atmospheric chemistry, 90–107
atmospheric pollution, 98–100
Atomium (Brussels), 113

B

batch process, 77–78, 86
bauxite, 126–127
blast furnace, 128 – 130
Bosch, Carl, 80
Bragg, Laurence, 108
Bragg, William, 108
buckminsterfullerene, 111–112
by-products, 79

C

calcium ammonium nitrate (CAN), 83
carbon allotrope, 111
carbon compounds, inorganic, 93–95
carbon cycle, 95–96, 104
carbon dioxide, 93, 104
carbon monoxide, 93–95
carbonate compounds, 93
cathodic protection, 124
catalyst, 80, 83
  iron (ammonia production), 80
  platinum-rhodium (nitric acid production), 83
CFCs (chlorofluorocarbons), 90, 96, 97–98, 101–103, 104
  uses of, 102
  CFC substitutes, 103, 104
chlorofluorocarbons, 90, 96, 97–98, 101–103, 104
co-products, 79
construction materials, industrial plant, 80
continuous process, 78, 86
corrosion, 122–124
costs, production, 79
covalent macromolecular crystals, 109, 110–112, 119
crystals, 108–113, 119
  crystal lattice, 109
  see also covalent macromolecular crystals; ionic crystals; metallic crystals; molecular crystals

D

Davy, Humphry, 123
denitrifying bacteria, 93
diamond, 110–111
dinitrogen oxide, 96
Downs cell, 125–126, 132

E

effluent control, 79
electric arc process, 130–132
electrochemical series, 122–124
electrolysis, molten salts, 124–125
enhanced greenhouse effect, 96–98, 104
  implications, 98

F

Faraday, Michael, 123, 125
feedstock, 79
fermentation, 94
fractional distillation, 91, 104
free radicals, 101
Fuller, Buckminster, 112
fullerenes, 112

G

Galvani, Luigi, 122, 132
galvanising, 124
global warming, 96–97, 104
graphite, 111–112
greenhouse effect, 96–98, 104
greenhouse factor, 96
greenhouse gases, 90

H

Haber, Fritz, 80
Haber Process, 81
high-density polythene, 115
Hodgkin, Dorothy, 109
hydrochlorofluorocarbons (HCFCs), 103–104
hydrofluorocarbons (HFCs), 103
hydrogencarbonate compounds, 93

I

IFI (Arklow, Co. Wicklow), 80, 82–84
IFI (Cobh, Co. Cork), 80–82
industrial chemistry, 77–80
industrial processes, general characteristics, 79–80, 86
inorganic carbon compounds, 96
ionic crystals, 109–110, 119
iron, catalyst in ammonia production, 80
iron, manufacture of, 128–132

L

lattice points, 109
lead(II) bromide, electrolysis of, 125
lime (quicklime), 85, 87
limestone, 85, 87
liquefaction, 91, 104
low-density polythene, 114

M

magnesium oxide, 84–86, 87
metallic crystals, 109, 112–113, 119
metals, 114
methane-steam reforming, 80–81, 86
Midgley, Thomas, 102
molecular crystals, 109, 110, 119
monomers, 114

N

natural fixation, nitrogen, 92–93
neutral oxide, 95
nitric acid, 82–84, 87
nitrifying bacteria, 93
nitrogen, 91–93, 104
  natural fixation, 92–93
  nitrogen cycle, 93
  nitrogen fixation, 92, 104
nitrogen dioxide, 99
nitrogen monoxide, 102, 104
nitrous acid, 99
nitrous oxide, 96

O

oxygen, 90–91, 104
ozone, layer, 100–101, 104

P

periclase, 85
photodissociation, 101
plasticiser, 115
plastics, recycling, 117–118, 119
Plunkett, Roy, 117
pollution, atmospheric, 98–100
poly(chloroethene), 114, 115–116, 119
poly(ethene), 114–115, 119
polymers, 119
  addition, 114–117
poly(phenylethene), 114, 116–117, 119
poly(propene), 114, 116, 119
polypropylene, 114, 116, 119
polystyrene, 114, 116–117, 119
poly(tetrafluoroethene), 114, 117, 119
polythene, 114–115, 119
Premier Periclase (Drogheda, Co. Louth), 80, 84–86
product yield, 79
PVC (polyvinyl chloride), 114, 115–116, 119

Q

quality control, 79
quartz, 110–111

R

rate, optimum process, 79
residence time, greenhouse gases, 97–98
rust, 123–124

S

sacrificial anodes, 124
safety, 79
secondary reforming, 81
semi-continuous process, 78
Shift Reaction, 80–81, 86
site location, 79
slag, 129
slaked lime, 85, 87
sodium, extraction of, 125–126
steel, 123
  manufacture of, 128–132

T

teflon, 114, 117, 119
thermoplastics, 118
thermosetting plastics, 118
thermosoftening plastics, 118

U

unit cell, 109
urea, 81–82, 86

V

Volta, Alessandro, 122, 132
Volta's pile, 122

W

waste disposal, 79

X

x-ray crystallography, 108–109, 119

Y

yeast, in fermentation, 94

Z

ziegler catalysts, 116